FROM BEAN TO BAR
IN BELGIUM SINCE

WITH CONTRIBUTIONS FROM
25 INTERNATIONAL CHOCOLATIERS

THE CHOCOLATIER'S SHOP

CALLEBAUT®
BELGIUM 1911

Lannoo

CONTENTS

"Signature Series" bonbons by Janice Wong, crafted with unique moulds designed by Janice herself

"Years ago, I had a conversation with my father. He said to me, 'when I die, son, don't shed a tear for me because I have led the life of 3 men'.

Building a chocolate business is a beautiful thing. At the start, I didn't realise it. But it truly is. It gives me pride when I tell people what I do. It has taken me on such a journey. I've met and hung out with a billionaire on his yacht. An ex-prime minister has been introduced to me (it should be the other way around, right?). I know of a number of Hollywood actors and famous sports stars who have eaten my chocolate. I've travelled to China, Japan, Malaysia, USA, Europe and Dubai. I've been on live TV, the Bake-Off Professionals, done other TV shows, radio and media demo events. All because of chocolate. And the adventure continues.

When I told my father I was starting a chocolate company, he asked me, 'who on earth is going to buy your chocolate son?' Well dad, I too have led the life of 3 men and it's all because of chocolate."

STEPHEN TRIGG – LAUDEN CHOCOLATE

PREFACE

Building a chocolate business is an incredible adventure. It can lead you into a roller-coaster-like journey (like what UK-based chocolatier, Stephen Trigg, experienced).

But let's face it: building a business takes time, bags of grit, and determination.

So how do you start a chocolate business? And once set up, how do you grow it according to your own ambitions?

During our courses and training at Chocolate Academy™ centres around the world, we met many chefs and artisans who dreamed about turning their entrepreneurial ambitions into a reality. They all had as many questions as dreams.

Questions such as:

» *Which financial resources do I need when I start – and where do I get them?*
» *How do I build a brand?*
» *How can I find customers?*
» *Should I sell online or at a physical shop?*
» *How do I know what will sell best?*
» *How can I minimise risk?*
» *Should I start alone or build a team?*

With this book, we wanted to offer you an as-complete-as-possible checklist to help you make informed decisions when starting and/or upscaling your business. And, as it goes with many things in life, there is no general right or wrong answer when making many decisions. It's all about choosing what works best for your business.

We asked chocolatiers from around the world what they struggled with most, which decisions they made and how those decisions worked out in the end. If there would be one general rule that applied to all chocolatier-entrepreneurs we interviewed, then it's probably this: some started with a roll-up-your-sleeves mentality; others seemed to have everything figured out. Yet, everyone learned, adapted, and improved along the way.

To say it in the words of one of the chefs, "keep chasing your dreams. And when something fails at a certain moment, which we all experienced, learn from it, get up and do better".

Wishing you loads of success in realising your dreams!

Minette Smith
Callebaut Lead Creative Chef

THE CONTRIBUTORS

This book wouldn't have been possible without the valuable contributions of all artisans and chefs we interviewed. A big shoutout to all of them! Here's a small recap of who they are to get acquainted. In alphabetical order:

1 **Lama Bassam Al-Ghrawi**

BASSAM GHRAWI CONFECTIONERY – BEIRUT, LEBANON

With a craftsmanship legacy that dates back to 1891, this family business has its roots in hand-made dried fruits, malban and nougat products. In its mission to inspire innovation in each piece of artisanal chocolate, the company managed to successfully introduce their products to the western world. In 1930, chocolate became part of their collection of sweets. With over a century of experience and continuous growth throughout family generations, the Al-Ghrawi legacy lives in its factories, retail outlets, and facilities. The Al-Ghrawi family enterprise aims to keep sharing their creations all over the world today, and in the years to come.

2 **Renata Arassiro**

RENATA ARASSIRO CHOCOLATES – SÃO PAULO, BRAZIL

Exploring her passion for chocolate and looking to create products with a unique personality — engineer-turned-Chef, Renata Arassiro, uses chocolate to bring her creative ideas to life. Combining Belgian chocolate of the highest quality with the vast ingredients Brazil has to offer, Renata has made the cover of renowned magazines and participated in international competitions. Since the very beginning, she's been designing the colourful bonbons that have won the hearts of her clients. Today, she is known not only for her chocolate skills, but as the first ambassador for Barry Callebaut in Brazil and a teacher for gastronomy professionals.

3 **Davide Comaschi**

DAVIDE COMASCHI / DA VITTORIO – MILAN, ITALY

Today, he is at the forefront of the future of chocolate. In the past, Davide Comaschi was a child who began his chocolate journey thanks to the flavours in his mother's kitchen and his father's passion for art. With both his parents being photographers, and having been born and raised in Milan, Davide grew up surrounded by the world of fashion and design, and a burning love for good food. In his quest to make chocolates *"that can break the routines we are all in, and provide you with a moment of pleasure for all your senses"*, Davide crafted his signature creation: triangular bonbons. These continue to be his business' iconic product up until this day.

4 **Fan Yu**

NIBBO – SHANGHAI, CHINA

A chocolate concept designed as a museum of flavours. Inspired by his work in Australia and driven to bring a new chocolate experience to China, Fan created Nibbo. With the purpose of imparting knowledge in a market where the concept of artisan chocolate is unknown, Fan built a brand that celebrates the possibilities chocolate bars have to offer. To match the careful consideration behind his brand, his packaging design brings the concept to life — inspired by a museum's archives room, each chocolate wrapper becomes a collectable item, and each flavour represents a new approach to chocolate in the Chinese market.

5 **Ryan L. Foote**

CHOCOLATES BY RYAN L FOOTE – HONG KONG

Known for a career driven by artistic imagination, Ryan has built a portfolio that ranges from art, design, and set design to food and beverage. His background and constant curiosity have led him to combine his passions into multi-sensory food art events/art installations. Evolving from these art events, Ryan incorporated chocolate into his artwork and then into a thriving chocolate business. Using chocolate as a bridge to bring people into an artistic world, Ryan merges state-of-the-art 3D printing with the timeless character of cacao. The results of his creative ideas are geometric and organic-shaped bonbons that look like miniature edible works of art.

6 Calum Haggerty

COCO CHOCOLATIER – EDINBURGH, UK

With a degree in finance, Calum wasn't made for a white-collar career. *"As a kid, I was already an entrepreneur, stocking up sweets in my locker and trying to sell them to other kids".* After a few years of working for the fire service in Edinburgh, he decided to purchase an existing chocolate business and transformed it into the blooming COCO Chocolatier enterprise. Calum approaches the business from quite an untraditional perspective: he had no chocolatier skills, yet found himself a wonderful team. He approaches the enterprise as a conceptual thinker and business coach, getting the best of the talent he surrounds himself with. Redirecting his business into a gift-related chocolate enterprise seemed the right choice for him, independent from traditional brick-and-mortar sales.

7 Jitsk Heyninck

JITSK CHOCOLATES – ANTWERP, BELGIUM

Jitsk gained experience as a R&D chef and expert at mould maker, Chocolate World, in Antwerp. But his true passion and dreams lied in creating and working with chocolate itself. So, he started his own beautiful shop-and-atelier in a refurbished Belgian brewery amidst a collective of artisans and crafters, such as butchers, brewers and cheese-affineurs. As a thoroughbred artisan, he quickly developed his unique signature which revolves around maximising home-made, seasonal products. With a love for natural produce, Jitsk sources top-class nuts, fruits and more from orchards and farms in Belgium, Italy, France and Spain, turning them into his unique pralines, pastes, fillings and marmalades. With an almost Nordic feel for purity, Jitsk is a rising star in the chocolate world.

8 Marco Infante

CASA INFANTE – NAPLES, ITALY

With the brand's idea of beautiful stories that are never born by chance, the Infante family shares their own legacy. Their goal is to carry the experience of three generations of artisans into their ice creams, pastries, and chocolates. After Leopoldo Infante opened his first pastry shop in the late 1800s, the business has been handed down from father to son with their original beliefs intact: high-quality ingredients and extraordinary goodness. Until this day, embodying the traits of Neapolitan tradition and the values that this family has built over time, Casa Infante lives on in the hands of the brothers Marco and Fabio Infante.

9 Jap Joy

FIDÉE – FOSHAN CITY, CHINA

To take chocolate lovers on a trip to nature, Jap Joy created FIDÉE with the sky, forest, flowers and land as the key elements of his chocolate concept. As an acclaimed package designer and lover of sweet treats, he ventured into the world of chocolate and began creating bonbons to offer along with his original package designs. The result was a western-inspired brand name for a very traditional Asian market. FIDÉE was born as a business that combines original recipes sold in packaging with unique designs. The brand became a pioneer by offering a new concept for the whole of China to experience.

10 Justine Lannoo

GOÛT FOU – ZELE, BELGIUM

Justine has been a passionate chef at the Callebaut Chocolate Academy in Belgium for quite some years, sharing skills and insights with many professionals in the industry. But her entrepreneurial mindset drove her to start her own business. With hard work, lots of joy and great social skills, Justine kicked off Goût Fou (that translates literally into "crazy flavours"), with a great variety of bonbons with expressive flavours, a touch of humour, and premium quality. The business immediately got noticed by Gault&Millau, which led to an award for "Best Chocolatier in Belgium". The adagio, "quality is doing good when no one is watching", explains her attention to detail and dedication to the craft.

11 David Maenhout

CHOCOLATIER M – KNOKKE, BELGIUM

David Maenhout was probably the very first chocolatier pioneer in Belgium, intrigued by translating culinary experiences into his rich palette of chocolates. Born and raised in a beer-brewing family, he chose another path and created Chocolatier M. Originally, David ran the business all on his own, developing a unique style which inspired many others. A fond traveller, David's fascination for local and exotic ingredients led him to incorporate them into his bonbons. He was also the first to collaborate with craftsmen around his hometown to offer products that would resonate amongst the locals. It wouldn't be an exaggeration to say that each of his bonbons is a flavour destination in itself. Over the years, he perfected his style, hired a team and expanded his business. Today, his creations have even reached Japanese department stores.

12 Håkan Mårtensson

HÅKAN CHOCOLATIER – BEACON, NY, USA

After enrolling in the Culinary Institute in Kristianstad (Sweden) at the age of 15 and discovering his passion for pastry and chocolate, Håkan began his journey as an artisan. Intending to use out-of-the-ordinary ingredients to excite the imagination, the chef left the comfort of his home country in 2008 and headed to the continental US, ready to take on the world. After a decade of dreams and obstacles, with his wife and young children by his side, he became a pioneer in the chocolate space — creating an offer with Nordic flavours and global influences, and a taste palette that is complex yet balanced.

13 Patrick Mertens & Inge Lijnen

CHOCOLADEHUIS BOON – HASSELT, BELGIUM

What happens when you put the talent of a master chocolatier and an advertisement creative together? You get BOON. Patrick Mertens and Inge Lijnen are each other's better halves in life. Together, they are the creative brain behind their blooming chocolate business in Hasselt. Their approach? Inge's career in the advertising industry was about creating compelling ideas for brands and bringing them to life. Together with Patrick, she now does the same – but in chocolate. Far more real, way more impressive. Their chocolate craziness attracts the attention of press and many fans to their shop. With a keen eye for design, they've created a unique signature chocolate style.

14 Pablo and Jacobo Moreno

MALLORCA – MADRID, SPAIN

In 1931, Bernardino Moreno and his wife, María García, opened their very first pastry shop. Not long after, their pastries and sweets became the talk of the neighbourhood. Fast forward a few decades and Mallorca has become a multi-branch business that celebrates traditional sweet and savoury Spanish pastry culture, along with chocolates and well-known *bocadillos*. With slow yet steady growth as part of their work philosophy, the family business now includes coffee shops and has extended its reach internationally, winning the hearts of customers in Mexico and Japan. With a heartfelt disposition to carry on their legacy, the Moreno family continues to innovate and welcome loyal and new clients, inviting them to be part of their story.

15 Mariane Oliveira

MARY'S BRIGADEIRO – TORONTO, CANADA

A proud black-woman-owned business with the mission to spread joy through chocolate. Now, also with the higher purpose of becoming a safe employment space for immigrant women in Canada. She was born in Brazil but moved to Canada for love. In Toronto, Mariane Oliveira (Mary) began her journey as a chocolatier and entrepreneur. She leveraged the city's multicultural influence by offering a traditional Brazilian sweet: the *brigadeiro*. What started as small batches being sold among her close friends and family circle, the uniqueness and newness the brigadeiros offered spread throughout the city. Today, Mary stands as the creative mind and business genius behind the colourful chocolate shop that brightens up the streets of East End Toronto.

16 Mirosław Pelczar

M. PELCZAR CHOCOLATIER – KORCZYNA, POLAND

Mirosław Pelczar was a genuine pioneer at the time he started his confectioner's shop in Korczyna. He was one of the first in Poland to make handcrafted chocolates. Without much knowledge from Polish peers, he self-taught and developed his own recipes. *"The choice of profession was simple and obvious. There were no dilemmas because, in fact, I knew from childhood what I wanted to do".* Mirosław acquired a passion for pastry and chocolate from his mother. Watching her make pastries awakened his vocation. The rest came with hard work, long days, and self-study. Mirosław participated in countless professional competitions and got accoladed numerous times, *"confectionery is my life. I have dedicated everything to it".*

17 Sebastian Pettersson

SEB PETTERSSON – STOCKHOLM, SWEDEN

A chef who turned his outspoken personality into a unique brand. Sebastian Pettersson always makes an unforgettable impression. Behind his inked body and tough appearance, you'll discover a humble, passionate, open-minded and friendly young man. Hardly 21, Sebastian made his smashing entry into the culinary world by participating and winning gold medals in the Culinary Olympics Jr. in 2016 and the World Culinary Cup in 2018. After working in pastry kitchens of Michelin-star restaurants, such as Oaxen Krog, Operakällaren and Ekstedt, Sebastian decided to start as a self-employed consultant; working part-time in coaching and competing in culinary competitions, and combining it with training, creative direction and food engineering of restaurants, pastry kitchens and pastry schools around the world.

18 Bernard Proot

DELREY – ANTWERP, BELGIUM

Being at the helm of DelRey since 1983, Bernard and his wife, Anne, have been transforming the Antwerp biscuits and chocolate scene into an international emblem for fine chocolatery and pastries. The couple injected a dose of exquisite artisanship and a sturdy growth model into their business – often based on their intuition and boldly balancing of different opportunities. In heart and soul, Bernard remains an artisan pastry chef and chocolatier, while Anne has an experienced nose for opportunities. Gifted with a sound business instinct and big dreams, they grew the brand into an internationally renowned icon with third-party outlets around Belgium, and 4 business outlets in Tokyo.

19 Julian Rose

JULIAN ROSE CONSULTING – OREGON, USA

If one would have to describe Julian Rose in a few words, the *enfant terrible* of the chocolate industry would probably come closest. With a curriculum that stretches from crazy product developments in chocolate and award-winning cannabis chocolate bars to teaching, Julian is ambivalent. Since his early childhood, pastry and chocolate flowed in his veins. From his involvement as head of the Chocolate Academy in Canada to his entrepreneurial stakes in different businesses, such as Moonstruck and Choc-Pro Chocolates, Julian has always been on the lookout for the next new opportunity.

20 Enric Rovira

ENRIC ROVIRA – BARCELONA, SPAIN

Raised and influenced by the world of a famous pastry shop owned by his parents, Enric Rovira took on the chocolate space in Barcelona. He imagined a new way to implement the job his father had taught him and became a trendsetter that combined chocolate with artistic design. Enric's tailor-made products have an edge that has defined his character since he opened his business with his cousin, Francesc Forrellat, in 1993. With three decades of experience in the chocolate world, and still faithful to his philosophy of elaborating high-quality products, Enric continues to fill Barcelona's chocolate scene with one-of-a-kind contemporary and customised designs.

21 Nikki Thakker

ÉNTISI – MUMBAI, INDIA

Her purpose was to introduce "fine chocolate" in the culture of her home country. Nikki has united her academic background in economics and her passion for chocolate to become an artisan chocolatier. She dedicates time to ideate and try each product herself, always aiming to seamlessly combine excellence and refined taste. At éntisi, Nikki ensures that each box of chocolates is a tribute to quality, creativity, and design. Every visit to their boutiques in Mumbai is a trip to discover something new. Sophistication, unique gift creations, handmade artistry, and exclusive style all come together in her products and stores.

22 Kirsten Tibballs

SAVOUR SCHOOL – MELBOURNE, AUSTRALIA

Probably, the "queen of chocolate" needs little to no introduction. After struggling through health issues during her youth, Kirsten fell in love with chocolate during many travels in Europe. So much she decided to acquire chocolate skills to pass them on to different people around the world. With her online video training in pastry and chocolate, Kirsten became probably the most frequented reference on the planet. At Savour School in Brunswick, Kirsten also meets up with chocolatiers-to-be and artisans to teach them both, basic and advanced chocolate skills. It's in her conversations with her many trainees where she developed a keen sense for failures and successes they may encounter on their entrepreneurial journey.

23 Stephen Trigg

LAUDEN CHOCOLATE – LEEDS, UK

A business born from chocolate lovers. Stephen Trigg and Sun, his wife, used to travel the world enjoying chocolates from all corners of the globe. Although enjoying great customer service and experience in their city's chocolateries, they were still missing that flavour punch they craved — Stephen and Sun began their journey as business owners and artisan chocolatiers following their motto: "It's all about the chocolate!". They turned their chocolate-making hobby into a successful business that managed to reach the skies — their chocolate creations have touched the taste buds of thousands of people in the UK, and travellers of British Airways, as they provided the airline with their on-flight chocolate assortment.

24 Olivier Willems

OLIVIER WILLEMS – OSTEND, BELGIUM

Ostend is called the "queen of the seaside" in Belgium. This vibrant fishermen's town is known for its headstrong character and rough edge. This is the attitude that characterises Olivier Willems too, reflecting his roots on his chocolate work: bonbons reminiscent of the sea with their wavy shapes, or their rich palette of colours. Just like the sea looks different every time, Olivier Willems' chocolates evolve. New herbs, new spices, new combinations. The influence of Ostend, the city by the sea, lets Olivier be constantly inspired by the environment in which he works. Top gastronomy ideas and daring dishes trigger him to push the boundaries, giving Willems the energy he needs to work hard every day.

25 Janice Wong

2AM DESSERT BAR / JANICE WONG PURE IMAGINATION / SOFTHAUS – SINGAPORE

Meet Asia's most renowned food curator. Janice considers herself rather a creator of food experiences, and thinks outside more than one box. Accoladed "Asia's Best Pastry Chef" by World's 50 Best in 2014, she is an entrepreneur in heart and soul. An economics graduate, Janice got intrigued with food after doing a few farm visits in Australia. Only a few years after, she found herself captivated by chocolate and pastry, and made her way into the then-still very new pastry scene in Singapore. She opened the 2am: dessertbar, started her chocolate factory, launched her ice cream brand, Softhaus, and curated edible art experiences around the world.

Enric Rovira works on one of his artistic chocolate installations, inspired by the iconic science-fiction movie Star Wars

Local and exotic ingredient pairings are one of the differentiating traits that make David Maenhout's Chocolatier M stand out

CHAPTER 1

LEAD WITH THE "WHY"

Patrick Mertens

FOR THIS BOOK, we interviewed many chocolatiers from around the world. When we asked them why they started their business and how they started it, the answers often led to similar experiences: "I discovered that chocolate is my passion. After acquiring the skills, I just started. First in a small garage. As I grew, I built my own production kitchen". Throughout their journey, many chocolatiers acquired better skills and better insights about their customers' needs and adapted their offerings accordingly.

If you're starting your chocolate journey today though, odds are that the marketplace is more crowded than 20 years ago. Starting today is quite different, so it will require a different approach. To lower your risks and increase your chances of success, you need to be well-armed and prepared to find your unique spot in the market.

As a starting chocolatier and entrepreneur, it's important to understand the "why" behind your business: your purpose. Why do you get up every morning? What is the driving force behind your hard work? Sure, making money is a pre-condition. But your "why" is way more relevant for customers to understand what they can find in your business or gain from your brand.

Knowing the reason behind the existence of your business will also guide you throughout the process of running this business. It will help you develop the right products that answer to your "why" and bring them to market in a unique way.

"If you're going to do this to get rich, do something else. The first 10 years, we would definitely have been better off with our previous jobs. If that's your motivation, maybe don't start. You have to put a lot into it and not expect big luxuries, certainly not the first few years."

PATRICK MERTENS & INGE LIJNEN –
CHOCOLADEHUIS BOON

Mary's Brigadeiros
by Mariane Oliveira

YOUR PURPOSE:
WHY WOULD YOUR BUSINESS BE RELEVANT TO PEOPLE?

Finding out the "why" can be a challenging starting point. But in today's world, where many others compete in the same industry, it helps you gain clarity as you start or grow your chocolate business. What's more, it helps you focus your plans and schedules, and develop the right products and experiences around this "why".

To give you an example, PHIL KHOURY is a chocolatier and pastry chef at Harrods. He doesn't just make chocolates or pastries. His products answer to "why" Harrods exists:

"Harrods is all about creating a world of wonder for its customers. Things you've never seen or tasted before. Understanding that 'why' is crucial for us as chefs. It's our guiding principle to create the products that already wow you from a first glimpse, and that overwhelm with taste and flavours you wouldn't expect at first. Our world of wonder is also about bringing the best of the best. In practice, it guides us as chefs to source and pick top-class ingredients that elevate the product into an amazing experience."

It often happens that a company's mission is mistaken with its purpose. To help you find your own, it's good to have the difference in mind:

PURPOSE
The reason your business exists.

MISSION
What your business is doing, and whom it's doing it for.

"My vision is to give India a chocolate brand it can be proud of and introduce Indian chocolates to the world."

NIKKI THAKKER – ÉNTISI

Take a look at how Ryan Foote, the entrepreneurial and creative brain behind Chocolates By Ryan L Foote, applied these concepts in real life.

Working as an artist on art installations at events, Ryan began exploring the combination of unexpected elements, such as food-centred artistic designs. These designs were the link between his passions: art, science and food.

Combined with his passions, Ryan's background as a sculptor and designer helped him define his mission: inviting people to be part of the artistic world through the one thing everyone has a relationship with — food.

Parallel to his mission, he found his "why", and was able to outline his purpose: creating unexpected experiences through beautiful designs that invite people to step into his creative world.

Like Ryan's, your purpose and mission will (and should) be connected. Once found, they will help you discover what sets you apart from the competition.

"At my core, I'm a creative person; chocolate is just how I manifest that creativity."

ENRIC ROVIRA – ENRIC ROVIRA

Questions you may ask yourself
TO FIND YOUR "WHY"

There are several models of questions that can help you find your purpose and the reason why your business exists. Here is a simple model of questions you can use:

1. **What are you passionate about?**
Think about the things that make you feel most fulfilled and energised. What activities or causes excite you?

2. **What are your skills and strengths?**
What do you do well? What unique skills do you have that others may not possess?

3. **What problems or needs do you see in the world that you could address with your business?**
What are the pain points of your potential customers or clients, and how could you help solve them?

4. **What principles guide your life and your decision-making?**
What do you stand for, and what is important to you?

5. **What would be your positive impact on the world?**
Examples could be: *"creating delights with a positive impact on the body and mind", "making people enjoy sweet treats while reducing my footprint on the planet", "bringing joy and happiness throughout my entire supply and production chain".*

By reflecting on these questions and taking the time to clarify your purpose and why your business exists, you can develop a strong foundation for your brand and business model, and set yourself up for success as an entrepreneur.

YOUR UNIQUENESS

HOW ARE YOU DIFFERENT?

Your uniqueness is what sets you apart from the competition. In the world of business, this means companies succeed when they offer a product that solves a need or fills an empty market space. Knowing what makes you different will help you market your brand's value in the eyes of those who are paying for your products.

Your differentiating element can go beyond your products themselves. It could be found in any part of your brand, from your business model to your customer experience. Once you've found this uniqueness, it should be the centre of your brand identity, and also dictate the range of products you offer. If you're still looking for your uniqueness, try answering a consumer's most important question:

Why should I pay (more) for this product?

The answer to this question will be your differentiating factor, your business' biggest strength. To see it put into practice, think back to Chocolates By Ryan L Foote.

Ryan saw that some 3D-printed chocolate show pieces had gained the status of small works of art. These pieces intrigued people yet were still far away from them because of their status. So, he took the concept of these big chocolate sculptures and replicated it at a smaller scale. Ryan created something unique: beautiful miniature chocolate shapes to give as gifts or share in special occasions.

Ryan found his uniqueness by redefining an existing concept, turning his passion for art and design into high-end chocolate gifts that people could actually buy, share and enjoy. Up until today, his bonbons retain their unique value and represent the differentiating element his clients are happy to pay for.

The "onliness" statement that helps you define your uniqueness

The "onliness" statement was first introduced by Marty Neumeier in his book The Brand Gap. It helps you to formulate your uniqueness in a concise way.

WHAT?	We are the only...	(describe what sets you apart)
HOW?	that...	(describe how you do business)
WHO?	for...	(describe your target group/s)
WHERE?	in...	(describe your geographic market)
WHY?	because...	(describe your purpose)
WHEN?	in times...	(describe your market environment and needs)

As mentioned earlier, a differentiating factor doesn't necessarily stem out of a business' products. Your uniqueness can be found in any part of your brand: your personal story and interests, your local environment, your way of working, how you deliver your product or even the customer experience you've created.

Wherever it may come from, remember your differentiating element is what makes you valuable in this world's competitive market. It will be the core of your entire business, the focus of your marketing efforts (Chapter 6), and what influences the products you create (Chapter 10).

The below example applies the onliness statement to MARY'S BRIGADEIRO and helps reconstruct the uniqueness of that business. To be closer to her partner, Mariane (Mary) Oliveira moved from Brazil to Canada. Here, the onliness statement shows Mary's brand extends beyond her skills to make great brigadeiros. It shows there is an underlying purpose behind that business, a purpose that undoubtedly relates to her current success.

As you might have already noticed, the unique aspect of Mary's Brigadeiro did more than define her product assortment and the message of joy she spreads through her chocolate. Her uniqueness has shaped her entire customer experience. From her website to her physical shop, bright colours, warmth and friendliness take over. And when it comes to her staff training, they are all coached to express this brand experience in the way they serve customers too.

Even before you produce your first batch of chocolates, your uniqueness and purpose will help you design your brand and what you want your customers to experience through it. So, start your quest to find your uniqueness and let it help you get your business started!

		The onliness statement to Mary's Brigadeiro
WHAT?	We are the only...	black-woman-owned artisan brigadeiro business in Toronto
HOW?	that...	delights with the colours and flavours of Brazil
WHO?	for...	people who look for something different, tasty, new and exciting
WHERE?	in...	Toronto and the Greater Toronto Area
WHY?	because...	everyone deserves the joy that comes with good chocolate
WHEN?	in times...	when generosity and empathy can be hard to find

"The brand stands for quality and freshness that evolve with trends — a culinary chocolate shop focused on progressive, culinary taste experiments. But we don't follow all trends because sometimes it's not feasible. And, anything we don't make ourselves; we don't offer. In the long run, I think that gives back more."

OLIVIER WILLEMS – OLIVIER WILLEMS

Olivier Willems offers big gift boxes of up to 48 signature pralines, featuring culinary taste combinations

YOUR OFFER

WHAT WILL YOU CREATE, PRODUCE, AND SELL?

Once you know why you're setting up your business and what makes it unique, it's time to approach your "what": your chocolate production as a piece of your brand puzzle.

This part of the process is about what you will be selling. Not only about the product or products themselves, but about what these stand for. Let's see what this looks like in reality.

Remember Ryan Foote? His chocolate designs are created either using modern sculpting techniques, 3D technology or custom-designed moulds. But "what" his brand offers is more than nice-looking chocolates, it's customised chocolate gifts with a *wowing* artistic appeal, completely tailored to his clients' needs. Chocolates By Ryan L Foote doesn't sell chocolates. It sells memorability.

By exploiting your differentiating element and building your product portfolio (Chapter 10) around it, you are not only impacting your chocolate creations, but giving a higher meaning to your business.

Below, you can find an overview* of the typical products in a chocolate shop portfolio and some of their pros and cons.

Although the products mentioned above are the most often found in artisan chocolate businesses, don't be afraid to use your creative brainpower. You might come up with your own chocolate formats or hybrid shapes to make your offer unique. Think about Martin Diez' volcano. Martin invented a new type of bonbon that was featured thousands of times on Instagram. The volcano inspired chocolatiers to make their own versions and find ways to produce it in an efficient way that worked for them. Now, take the time to think back to your purpose and uniqueness. Both can inspire you to create confectionery products that help you stand out from the crowd.

Besides confectionery creations, many chocolatiers also expand their offer with products that serve as bridges between seasons. Think of ice cream or gelato during hot seasons, periods when confectionery sales tend to drop. Or think of a menu of hot chocolates for take-out, to boost your sales during the colder seasons.

Product category	Pros	Cons
Truffles	Popularity, variety, versatility	Shelf life, higher cost, temperature sensitivity
Chocolate bars	Popularity, variety, convenience	Higher competition, standardisation, ingredient quality
Enrobed bonbons	Versatility, aesthetics, packaging, quality, production convenience	Less investment, skills needed, shelf life
Moulded bonbons	Versatility, aesthetics, packaging, quality	Complexity, cost, shelf life
Open bonbons	Visual appeal, variety, convenience, texture experience	Delicacy, complexity, shelf life
Chocolate mignardises	Visual appeal, variety, convenience, shelf life	Shelf space, storage
Chocolate dragées	Variety, shelf life, snackable	Investment, competition
Small seasonal pieces	Focus, value	Skill, cost

*You will find a detailed version of this table in Chapter 10 of this book, under the "Typical chocolate products" subtitle.

CHAPTER SUMMARY

Before starting or growing your chocolate business, think about the reason "why" you want to start or continue one. The "why" is your business' life purpose. As such, it should reveal why your company is relevant in this industry. You can take a look at how multinational brands express their purpose and find the inspiration you need.

As an example, think of Volvo, the car brand. Their purpose is to "make travel easier and safer for everyone". This is why their entire brand exists. And it determines *what* the company produces: cars that are safe for individuals and families, protecting them from hazards on the road.

Just like with any brand in any type of industry, finding your "why" will drive the development of your entire business.

Next to the "why", the "how" will be the way you decide to run this business. Next to your purpose and your uniqueness, the "how" will help you shape your customer experience: the way you want people to feel when in contact with your brand.

As a last element of this trifecta, you should also consider the "what". Your "what" is the mix or assortment of products and services you'll develop to be part of your offer. Your products should also embody your purpose and your uniqueness.

What does "leading with why" look like in real life? See how chocolatiers from around the world found their purpose and uniqueness and turned it into chocolate products.

Your purpose

It might be that your differentiating factor has been with you since the moment you thought about starting an artisan chocolate business. It might also be the case that you're struggling to find the purpose of your brand-new (or existing) company. Whichever the case, it might be of help seeing how other chocolatiers from across the globe worked to find their purpose — or bumped into it unexpectedly!

MARIANE, the owner of Mary's Brigadeiro, started small. She produced everything by hand and sold her first micro-scale batches of products among her partner's family and friends in Canada. Regardless of the scale at which she began her entrepreneurial journey; she knew the reason why she had started her business:

"I think of what exactly my business is leaving to the world, and what's the impact it's having right now. When you open something, you have a purpose in mind. Making chocolates, shipments of happiness, it's a purpose. But as time goes by, the purpose and mission can change. So now, one of the things I can see is how the business is impacting women's lives. Women who come here with nothing, to start, to grow back again their confidence."

Another impressive chocolatier and creative mind at the helm of her own business is JANICE WONG. Inspired by late-night food offers, she crafted a unique concept for Singapore's market. She created an experience where cocktails and drinks are not the only thing served long after dinner time, and opened the doors of 2am: dessertbar. Today, she is also the proud owner of Janice Wong Pure Imagination chocolates and her signature ice cream shop, Softhaus. As a chocolate entrepreneur who has brought to life chocolate businesses in different formats, she feels strongly about the importance of being consistent with the reason behind the existence of your business:

> **"We have grown, but even with much bigger sales of our products now, we still produce everything by hand. That is one of the most important aspects of our business. Our whole business is based on artisanal chocolate, and I want to be perceived as such."**
>
> MIROSLAW PELCZAR – M. PELCZAR CHOCOLATIER

"When you make a brand, it's always about the philosophy, the vital part. You need to make sure that you don't change every month, you know, stick to it. Stick to that one thing that you believe in."

Challenge yourself to find the reason your business exists. KIRSTEN TIBBALLS is the creator of Savour School in Australia. Known as the "queen of chocolate" and an international influencer, Kirsten reminds you to make your chocolate dream come true by following a practical step-one:

"The important thing at the start is to pick a style and a mission statement for your business, and to follow that through, from your product to your packaging. I think that everybody should have an open mind going into it and think of their mission statement and what they're wanting to sell as a full picture to their consumers."

As a chocolatier or entrepreneur, once you've uncovered what drives you to own your chocolate business, you will be a step closer to pinpointing that one thing that makes you stand out from the rest: your uniqueness.

“We made every effort to bring our uniqueness to life. Our goal was to create an important luxury brand that offered a product that was new and diverse. It started with the collection of Triangular Pralines. Today, the offering is larger and the packaging is more luxurious. That is our big differentiator.”

DAVIDE COMASCHI – DAVIDE COMASCHI

Your uniqueness

It might be that your uniqueness or differentiating factor is to be found in the products you create. This a more straightforward way of showcasing what makes you different, and it's the case of MARY'S BRIGADEIRO, where the one-of-a-kind shape and chocolate format made her business stand out in a big market:

"It's funny because, the brigadeiro gets all the attention itself. All the brigadeiros together also get attention. It makes people at least ask what it is. Besides that, we have a small card with an explanation about the brand which tells the story of the founder."

Mariane Oliveira is a special case; not all chocolatiers can offer a product range that's unique. It will be often that you will be competing with the same or similar products. Take the example of STEPHEN AND SUN TRIGG, the couple behind Lauden Chocolate in Leeds. Their offer is mainly comprised of bonbons, a typical chocolate product. But their creations are known to distinguish themselves from the competition in the UK. Although traditional in format, the punchy flavours of their bonbon fillings cannot easily be found anywhere else:

"It's something different you cannot find. British Airways told us, *'we chose you because you're underground, and we cannot find you on the high street'*. It's that kind of thing that they find interesting, when you're creating something different than other people."

Brazilian chocolatier and owner of RENATA ARASSIRO CHOCOLATES, RENATA ARASSIRO, understood the importance of offering something different as she built her brand. With decades of experience in the artisan chocolate space, she continues to offer traditional chocolate formats, but in a way that makes them unique:

"The products are almost always the same: bonbons, dragées, or tablets. The difference is how I create my products. When I started out, I was using very typical Brazilian products that nobody used at the time; exotic fruits, fruits that are spicy. I started with these kinds of different ingredients, and this started to spread. People would say, *'Renata is using cupuaçu, Renata is using some very different products'*. Instead of just copying European flavours like raspberries, pistachios or almonds, I was the first one to start choosing these regional ingredients. I think this is one of my characteristics."

Beyond flavours, making your offer visually appealing is also a concept used by chocolatiers around the world. But it doesn't stop at crafting products that look different — visually impacting consumers can be achieved in multiple ways.

HÅKAN MÅRTENSSON is a Swedish chocolatier, currently based in a small town in the United States. Some of his products are heavily influenced by Nordic flavours, which separates his offer from the rest. However, another prominent differentiating factor of his business (and how he gets people who don't know about the brand to walk into his shop) is the location and the aspect of his chocolate store:

"We're located in Beacon. It's a small place with 15.000 people. You have the sun shining on the glass of the store, you won't see what's inside. It's crazy mysterious. People who walk by, they're coming back to see what's in here. It's also higher end than all the other places here, it has a very New York vibe to it."

Influencer chocolatier and independent freelancer, Chef SEBASTIAN PETTERSSON, agrees with how the looks of your business can make or break the success of your endeavours as an artisan chocolate maker. Being visually appealing is a concept that he puts into practice not only in the pieces he creates, but in the way he has built his online persona through social media:

"My vision is that if it's attractive enough, people will come. If you don't stand out from the crowd, you're going to be one in a row. Then, people might not come to you because you're not close enough, you're not open, you don't have exactly what they're looking for, etc. There's always going to be something. But, it helps if you have that little extra something; and it doesn't have to be the product, it could be the personality of our front-of-house, for example."

In addition to direct consumer sales, Jitsk Heyninck has also established a strong presence in B2B commissions, such as the Duvel bonbon box, bespoke-made for and with the Belgian beer brand

Just like Sebastian said, "that little extra something" can be found in many places. And this was the case of Mallorca, a Spanish-based business ran by the Moreno family. Although brothers MARCO AND JACOBO MORENO believe multiple characteristics can attribute to your differentiating factor, they found their uniqueness in the way the company was handed down from older generations:

"It's really difficult to actually focus on one thing. For us it's about maintaining the legacy and tradition amidst constant change."

As you might have noticed, the element or elements that make you unique may be right under your nose, or might need a little digging. If you feel like you're stuck when looking for answers, let yourself be inspired by CALUM HAGGERTY, the creative thinker behind COCO Chocolatier. This chocolate business presents itself as a "canvas for artisans and artists alike". They present their company as a place "where creativity and cocoa collide". And although based in the UK, they have travelled great distances to find the influence they needed to craft their uniqueness:

"We found inspiration for the products and visual impact in the streets of Colombia, investing to find that differentiating factor. This was so completely different to anything that I'd seen in Europe or anywhere. It was the vibrancy what made it different, its personality. So, I decided to get out there talk about art and design a lot. Loads of people are going to tell you that's wrong and that's fine. I think you've just got to do something that makes you different and something that you like."

Understanding the unique character of their brand, the team at COCO Chocolatier is known for crafting more than chocolates that taste good. They collaborate with artists to create different packagings that stand as small pieces of art. For them, the uniqueness they found by travelling led to the creation of their offer: good chocolates wrapped in extraordinary creative designs.

“I was in South Korea and I thought, ‘there are so many chocolatiers, but what exactly is missing? Why is everyone always harking back to what’s already there? Why does everything always have to be easy?’. And from the thought, ‘people say it can’t be done, but I think it can’ grew Jitsk Chocolates.”

JITSK HEYNINCK – JITSK CHOCOLATES

The Jitsk Chocolates shop visually represents the brand's philosophy: an atelier of craftsmanship and love for chocolate

CHAPTER 2

NEW OR EXISTING BUSINESS?

Mallorca
Pablo Moreno

OWNING A BUSINESS **isn't a heat-of-the-moment decision. If you're looking to own your artisan chocolate shop, starting a business, taking over an existing one or even continuing a family legacy are options. Each of which will have a list of pros and cons to consider.**

Your vision for a chocolate shop can be achieved regardless of the road you decide to walk. However, there are different elements to take into account in these different scenarios.

These elements or deciding factors will be present throughout your entire journey as a chocolate shop owner. They will underlie your brand's identity, your business model and plan, as well as all your marketing strategies.

"We've been in a family business all our lives, and there's a lot more than just an idea to it. You may be able to manufacture the perfect product, but everything involved in a business is way bigger than only the products you sell."

JACOBO & PABLO MORENO – MALLORCA

Skillset

Are you a chocolatier, an entrepreneur, or both?

It can be that you're a passionate chocolatier who's decided to set up your own shop. Before you launch your new brand, assess your existing skills as a chef and, if necessary, spot if there are improvement areas. Taking courses and practising your craft is always a good investment.

Understanding your talents will help you to create an offer and a brand around it, just like HÅKAN MÅRTENSSON, a skilled pastry chef who decided to venture in the world of chocolate after unexpectedly discovering his talent for it:

"I started doing baking and pastry design, and the more I did it, the more fun it was. I did an internship at a place called NK Nordic Company in Stockholm, which is a very, very fancy department store, the breeding ground for good pastry chefs in Sweden. When I graduated, they called me and offered me a job in the pastry department, which I did for a year. But they also had a chocolate room, where I got a position in 2003. That year I saw my mentor sculpting with sugar and chocolate and asked him to show me how he did it. I started to sculpt myself before realising I had a talent for it."

From an early age, it was clear that Håkan's talents were to be found in the kitchen. But sometimes, successful chocolatiers come from the most unusual places. This is the case of NIKKI THAKKER, creator of éntisi, the first boutique artisan chocolate shop in India:

"I got my MBA in the London School of Economics and then came a big shift. My journey of learning about chocolate happened once I decided to get into it. So, 100% of what I've learned has been on the job and not in a school."

After picking up on chocolate-making as a hobby, Nikki's career path changed rather quickly as she discovered her passion laid with it. Although an economist, she started her business from scratch and acquired the skillset needed to become a chocolatier, and a successful one for that matter.

Sebastian Pettersson expresses his aesthetics and style through clean designs and simple pairings, often heroising one recognisable flavour

Nikki isn't the only surprising case when it comes to multi-talent artisan chocolatiers. In Brazil, RENATA ARASSIRO walked a similar path:

"I'm actually an engineer. I worked as an engineer for five years, and during that time I always made chocolate as a hobby. I stopped engineering and dedicated myself to chocolate. And it was hard in Brazil 20 years ago, we didn't have chocolate pastries like in Europe, we didn't even have colleges or places where we could study. I had to self-teach everything."

It can be you already possess chocolate-making skills, or that you come from an industry completely unrelated to chocolate. A beginner or a master, regardless of where you stand today, there is always room to learn new skills. PABLO AND JACOBO MORENO, the brothers who have taken over their family business, Mallorca, believe in constantly investing in acquiring new skills or practicing existing ones:

"For us, the most important thing is learning. Every year we go to as many courses as we can, even if they seem basic. There's a basic ganache course? We'll go. Sometimes it's not only learning from the teacher, but from the way you interact with the people in the course and talk to them, the networking you do inside the hospitality and restaurant world. It's really amazing."

There are many possible scenarios. But the concept remains the same: understanding your skillset is the first step towards choosing the best route to start your chocolate business or grow your existing one.

Opportunities and resources

In our first chapter, you've briefly seen how a market gap can be turned into an opportunity. A market gap or need is a space where impact can be made. Along with your "why" and your "how" (Chapter 1), spotting a market gap can also help you understand the products you can offer, and the kind of business proposal that would work best depending on your context.

It might be that your market expects to see an existing business modified or revamped, or it can be that an entire generation of consumers in your town is ready for a completely new chocolate concept to hit the streets. This was the case with the Mallorca family legacy. Once THE MORENO BROTHERS took over, they noticed how much the market that surrounded them had changed. To keep their legacy alive, they had to adapt to the times without losing their identity:

"Our business is 91 years old, so it's not that we came up with it. Our great-grandfather started it and then the business became big. Now, we're the fourth generation. And, one of the most important aspects of our company is its legacy. We had to maintain it. But at the same time, we realised a lot of things, chocolate especially, were the same as in the 80s. So, we had to change the way we sold and produced everything to make it more current."

Whether your market calls for a new concept or updating an existing one, you'll need to take a look at your finances (Chapter 7) before getting started. Along with your skills and market knowledge, your existing budget and ability to access funds will help you delimit your options. STEPHEN TRIGG from Lauden Chocolate experienced this first-hand as he left a high, stable income to pursue his chocolate vision along with his wife:

"The hardest thing was walking away from being paid really well. But I was walking into work and looking at the clock at nine o'clock, waiting for it turn five o'clock to leave. The difference now, which I tried to explain to people, is that I probably work harder than I ever have in my life, I'm not paid anywhere near as well, but I'm so much happier. I've tried to describe freedom, but a lot are like, '*you work for so many hours*'. But I'm not working, I'm just living."

Stephen's story proves that sometimes, all it takes to start your business is some personal savings and a lot of courage. And that it is important to understand the industry you'll be navigating to build realistic financial expectations.

Just like Stephen, KIRSTEN TIBBALLS understood the implications of venturing into the artisan chocolate world:

"I was still earning an income outside of the business, which gave me the ability to reinvest where I needed to. You need to take that into consideration: a lot of people in business are basically working for the same money they would if they were working for someone else, but they have a lot more responsibility."

Side by side, understanding your finances and market gaps will help you clear up the path to the realistic possibilities to own your business. Other factors such as local industry insights and competitors should also be taken into account before making any final decisions.

Risks

Starting a new business from the ground up or taking over one. Both involve risks that need to be considered, the main one being that there is never a guarantee that your first attempt at either will be a success. KIRSTEN TIBBALLS shared the story of one of her students, a woman in her mid-thirties who understood the risks implicated in owning her own business, and who decided to grow slowly during her spare time:

"I met a woman who was very high up in the corporate world and had worked for a credit card company for 20 years. But her passion was actually patisserie and chocolate. She didn't know a great deal about it, so she trained with us. At any opportunity she had, she would volunteer with me and travel wherever I went. She took leave for all of this, and learned as much as she physically could. Then she took a package from her former employer and opened a business. During COVID, she moved the business to 100% online. Within three months she had to source a factory five times the size of the shop she was working out of (she was also very good at social media and at marketing herself). But I would say one of the biggest traits that has benefited her is that she was creating products that people actually wanted to eat."

While starting your own business can take some time, taking over an existing one might save you steps compared to the process of putting together a new brand. You might even acquire the location and stick to the business' range of products. This also means you will most likely have access to ledgers and previous sales and marketing data. All of it, valuable information.

But taking over a business comes with challenges you might not encounter when you start your own. An existing business already has a determined identity that cannot be discarded or modified in the blink of an eye. When building COCO Chocolatier, owner CALUM HAGGERTY realised the pros and cons of taking over a business that wasn't performing, and of changing multiple aspects of it to create the vision he had in mind:

"The company was busted when I took over. What was very evident to me was the seasonality of a business that is just based in one region of Edinburgh. You were just standing there waiting for someone to walk by, and products didn't even have a label at the front which told you the flavour, so a third party couldn't sell it.
So I started changing a couple of things: the brand, the aesthetic and also the business model. Thanks to the latter, we've had this kind of success, due to us being B2B, not B2C. I spent a couple of years completely redesigning all of the products to focus on that market. Today, we are six or seven times bigger than we were then, and the vast majority of that is by going to B2B trade shows. That's how we did it. Staff changes came with this too. People explaining that what had been done wasn't financially viable.
I was basically scrapping everything but the name. And even the name got changed at the end."

Calum's experience is the perfect example to show that when you take over an existing business, you inherit more than the brand and its qualities. You also inherit its benefits and struggles. If you're torn between starting your business or taking over one, considering all risks involved is a crucial starting step.

Goals

"Without a vision you're not going anywhere. Technique can be learned, knowledge can be acquired, but the real secret is the ability to have a dream and strive to realize it."

Just like Marco Infante, who manages the Casa Infante family business in Naples, it's crucial to understand that besides the market and your own financial position, you should consider your goals as a chocolate shop owner too. Because a successful business will always need passion and drive to succeed.

Your vision and creativity will be fundamental to creating a unique and compelling story or continuing a legacy. Either way, you will need a genuine love for artisan chocolate to win your clients and keep them loyal.

"When you focus on what you do well and are consistent, you're sending a clear message to the market. You're making sure people remember you for it. This is what creates a long-term bond with your customers."

BERNARD PROOT – DELREY

This bonbon assortment by Fidée shows consistency in shape and a specific colour palette, reflecting the land, sky, flowers and trees

STARTING FROM SCRATCH

Going from zero to hero takes time. Starting a business means crafting something where there is nothing. And although exciting and freeing, the road to success will be met with many challenges along the way.

Although now a renowned chocolatier and entrepreneur, RENATA ARASSIRO's business needed time to flourish in the streets of São Paulo:

"I began by making chocolate truffles at home, I didn't have space. Then, I started to integrate teaching to save money. It was after I had saved some money that I looked for a space and hired two more people, only two. One with me for the production and someone to sell."

Just like Renata, many other artisan chocolatiers began their businesses at home. Now a multi-store coffee and chocolate shop in China, FIDÉE was born in its owner's apartment:

"I started making chocolates at home. But our chocolate-making process was making too much noise. Our neighbours were kind of annoyed at us about that and started complaining. So, we had to open the shop to make chocolates."

Just like Renata and Jap Joy, it might be that your business starts small and slowly scales as the market demands it. Understanding some of the most common challenges when starting your own shop will help you be better prepared to face and overcome them.

"We grew so much we were doing classes seven days a week. Once we outgrew the facility we were in, we moved to a new facility where we were able to have a shop that sold specialised equipment and ingredients."

KIRSTEN TIBBALLS – SAVOUR SCHOOL

Expect longer work hours

In contrast to already operational businesses, starting from scratch means not having a usual 9–5 workday. STEPHEN TRIGG and his wife didn't seem to get a lot of sleep when they decided to turn Lauden, their chocolate business, into their main income:

"The first two years, I was dragged like a child into the business. I didn't really want it. I had a career in IT where I was paid quite well. It was a nine-to-five job, and life was quite comfortable. Why would I want to work in the evening? Why would I want to work weekends? But my wife had owned a business previously, and she'd had success with it. Sun knew the kind of life and freedom it could give you, and I didn't."

Your work hours might start earlier, and will most likely extend significantly after opening hours. Your business will sometimes take over your weekends and spare time too. And if it's approached as a completely new or revamped brand; it will take a lot of time and effort to make it known.

Think of KIRSTEN TIBBALLS. Her business, Savour School, quickly became the go-to place for learning all there is to know about chocolate and pastry. And not only for people in Australia. As the owner of a business that boomed internationally, she understands the challenges regarding long work hours:

"We slowly grew the business. We worked not only seven days a week, but also at night. We would finish a class at three o'clock, and then we had to do a night class. We had people traveling from all around the world, from New York, California, Sweden, all to train with us."

Not everyone can jump on the entrepreneurial train overnight. Leaving a stable job to start your own venture isn't always possible. It often happens that chocolate shop owners start their business as a side hustle. If this is also your case, it's likely that for a period, you'll be working more than one job at the same time. KIRSTEN, the queen of chocolate herself, started her business while working another job:

"I started it in 2002 and I had a part-time job. It was just me at the start, I really did everything. When I opened the school, I just did hands-on classes. They were very successful, and then I started to expand very slowly. I then found that people wanted to purchase the equipment and ingredients we used in class... I started selling those too."

Financial stability fluctuations

Related to starting a business from scratch is the financial aspect of things. Starting a business means not having a steady income from that business itself. It sometimes means not being profitable at all for quite some time, and even being financially negative until the first profit is made. Although skilled in his craft, and with previous entrepreneurial experience, HÅKAN faced the struggles of investing all he could afford to open his chocolate business in the US:

"I had no salary for over a year, a pregnant wife, a kid and pets."

Income and expenses can see more ups and downs when you start and grow your business from scratch. Take into account that this will also influence the professional and personal decisions you make in the near future.

Multi-tasking

On your own, or as a team. Starting a new business often means you (and your teammates) wear many hats. You will take on more than one role, which will translate into longer work hours, investing time in learning new skills and dealing with tasks that go beyond your main job description.

RENATA ARASSIRO often remembers her experience at the beginning of her journey as a chocolatier before she began hiring staff to help grow RENATA ARASSIRO CHOCOLATES:

"I see myself as a chocolatier first. But when you do it by yourself, you have to do a lot of things at the same time. I started on my own, with only one more person in the production. Now, we have one more person in the front of the shop for sales."

"Inge would always say 'we should start a business together'. Inge's advertising qualities combined with my chocolate knowledge and expertise; it was obviously an ideal tandem."

PATRICK MERTENS – CHOCOLADEHUIS BOON

"I had started doing a lot of courses at Callebaut, which had actually inflicted more on me than what I had learned at the school. After that, I started making chocolates at home just for fun. My parents had a flower shop at that time, so I thought I could sell them in that shop, the garage could be converted into a workshop. It's the 'garage story' you often hear."

JITSK HEYNINCK – JITSK CHOCOLATES

Navigating uncharted waters

As no previous records exist, your portfolio, workspace and marketing strategies will be based on initial estimates. Once your business grows, you'll be able to start collecting real sales data.

Contrary to dealing with a business where there are records of sales and performance to help you adapt and improve, this will be a trial-and-error journey.

This was the case of business owners PATRICK MERTENS AND INGE LIJNEN, who experienced how the opening of a business affects your personal life:

"We were actually very naive. We had no hospitality experience and we started with a coffee section with 28 seats plus production. In 100 days, we gave birth to our second child, we had moved with a 2.5-year-old kid, and had opened a business. After a week we were both sitting at our kitchen table thinking, '*what have we done?*' All our money was in that business, and our private lives had become completely different. But we've grown systematically by always surrounding ourselves with people who can do different things."

As there are specific challenges to opening your shop, there are also positive aspects that only come from starting your own business from scratch.

Create with absolute freedom

Creating a business just the way you like it is one of the main reasons many chocolatiers go on this entrepreneurial journey. All decision-making processes are simplified as a limited number of people (or even just one person) call the shots. This is the story of DAVID MAENHOUT when he became the proud owner of his business, Chocolatier M:

"I didn't go directly to my parents to ask for financial help or anything like that. There was some opposition against my ideas, people didn't understand why I wanted to work with chocolate. I can really say that I went my own way and put my savings into it. I started things my way to see how they would turn out in the end."

Just like David, with a creative mind that expands beyond the walls of a kitchen, HÅKAN MÅRTENSSON never took for granted the ability to test the limits of what his imagination could fathom:

"I have a bunch of different ideas to build stuff. I'm building a place where I can be as creative as I want to be. I'm not in a capitalist mind on this place. My partners might be, they might get a good chunk of it, but for me it's about being able to do what I love to do. This is not a work for me. This is my passion. This is my life"

Work with flexibility

As an entrepreneur who's starting out, time is your biggest ally. When you start a business under your own terms, you can tailor your work and schedule to fit your life until your business becomes fully fledged. This is an advantage that shouldn't be overlooked. And just like it, opportunities that arise might only come once in a lifetime, which is why it's important to stay alert and take advantage of them.

STEPHEN AND SUN TRIGG underwent a unique experience when they began their chocolate adventure. Coming from completely different professional backgrounds, an opportunity seemed to appear before them overnight, as well as the decision to turn something they loved into a business opportunity:

"I was an IT consultant. My wife had a solid wooden furniture manufacturing company. And we both love chocolate. One day, we found a little shop in Leeds that sold chocolate bonbons. It was a great little experience... we must have spent nearly 60 pounds on chocolate there. Then, when we got home and we started eating it, we were just so disappointed. It was all sugar, no flavour. My niece was around and she said, *'oh, I make my own truffles'*. This triggered us. So our journey started with us making little bits and pieces at home just for fun.

After that, our wedding was approaching. We decided to make things for it ourselves. We made the wedding cake, the macarons, all of the bonbons. And the guests really wanted to know where they could buy the bonbons. My wife was like, *'great! We're gonna start a business'*."

Flexibility stretches beyond spotting opportunities and varied work hours. As you begin to build your business from scratch, where you work and how you structure your work is completely up to you (and the people who are by your side).

Managing oneself or a small team will always be easier than managing multiple staff members, as last-minute changes and communications will be handled in a simplified way. This ability to quickly adapt to the unexpected is yet another one of the perks of starting from zero.

Tell your story your way

Alongside your passion for chocolate, starting from zero is the ideal way to craft a brand identity that represents you and your message to the world. Chef JULIAN ROSE is a renowned independent consultant with almost four decades of experience in the world of chocolate. Raised amidst his family's bakery, he grew up and developed a particular love for chocolate.

Julian understood the importance of understanding a brand to communicate about it. When he sold his pastry business, he kept the chocolate part of it to care for himself:

"In 2004, this opportunity just fell upon us and we accepted. We sold the business, all of it. But I kept the chocolate part. It was interesting because the chocolate business was a big part of our business, but the new owner knew nothing about chocolate and didn't want to make any. So, he did not purchase the equipment for it. We pulled everything out and we resettled in a small commercial space just for manufacturing."

In a way, Julian started from scratch. And when you start a business without linking it to a previous identity, reputation, or expectations, you get to write the story of your brand. You hold complete power over how it is shared with the world.

TAKING OVER AN

EXISTING BUSINESS

If you have previous experience running a business or managing staff, taking over an existing chocolate shop might be a good fit. Your ideas and passion for chocolate-making will always benefit from an entrepreneurial mindset, whether a partner's or your own.

Regardless of the reasons that move you to acquire an existing business, there will be specific limitations you should bear in mind.

Expect higher prices

If you're buying an existing business or brand, you're not just paying for an acquisition. You're investing in the time and money that went into creating that company and growing it. Compared to starting a business from scratch, buying an existing one will require a significantly higher financial investment.

Before taking over a business that's already been consolidated, make sure you undergo a proper valuation process. In these cases, professional help is recommended — you'll want to verify that the price you're paying for the acquisition is fair and that you're aware of potential liabilities (and what they are).

Uphold a reputation

Because you're buying an established brand, you're also buying what this brand has built over time. Its products, its clients and their expectations, all leading to a reputation to uphold.

Before going his own way in the space of artisanal chocolate in Barcelona, ENRIC ROVIRA was faced with the challenges that come from being in charge of an existing company:

"My father started a pastry shop as a family business. I worked with him for a few years and eventually, there was a generational clash. I wanted to change the way to think about the products. He wanted to remain in a more classic space. I was lucky to have access to some family facilities to start my chocolate business. For me, starting the chocolate business was like looking for my creative freedom."

When it comes to creative freedom, KIRSTEN TIBBALLS suggests starting chocolatiers ask themselves important questions without letting their imagination run too wild. This will affect a brand, but also when it comes to selling and acquiring businesses because of their previous reputation, particularly if it's tied to a family name:

"What happens if you've built this whole business up around your personal name, and then you need to sell it? There's going to be someone trading with your name. How do you build another brand outside that if somebody else is trading under your name and everything you've built up?"

"What if we wanted to sell the business one day? We thought it was important to choose a name that wasn't personal. It would be much easier to market it and possibly sell it, or give it a reputation without having a person attached to it."

PATRICK MERTENS & INGE LIJNEN –
CHOCOLADEHUIS BOON

Although in time all brand elements can potentially undergo changes and improvements, these don't happen overnight. All upgrades and modifications have to be slowly introduced to avoid missed expectations and brand inconsistencies, whether you're the one buying into an existing business or selling your own.

Just as with any decision, along with challenges comes a series of positive aspects when taking over an already-established chocolate shop. These are some main ones to consider.

Anticipate being profitable sooner

When building a business from the ground up, it takes time to become profitable. Receiving the right permits and approvals, testing out the market and getting clients. It all takes time. Although it varies for each business, there's an initial period in which your shop won't be making money.

In contrast to this scenario, if you acquire an already successful chocolate business, the profits might come almost straight away.

Reduce start-up-specific risks

One of the greatest advantages of acquiring an existing business is that the brand has been market proofed. When you're starting from scratch, after you've done your research and created your brand, it will take time to see how buyers respond to the idea you've created (and to adapt to their response).

If you buy an existing chocolate shop, you'll lower this initial risk and be able to fast-forward to the improvement phase of your chocolate shop.

At Jitsk Chocolates, short shelf life creations take pole position in the counter, while longer life products are placed as serve-yourself, impulse products on shelves

CONTINUING AN EXISTING (FAMILY) BUSINESS

In the artisan chocolate world, legacy or family businesses are common. Although they have a personal brand name, it is also common to sell or acquire them while keeping the name and the main range of products they offer.

Acquiring or inheriting a family business can offer similar benefits and challenges as acquiring any other business. However, there are still particularities that you'll encounter only when it comes to family-owned brands.

Become part of a legacy

Family businesses can hold added value when compared to more generic brands or franchises. Brands that foster a family name usually have a story behind them, which strengthens the brand identity and creates a particular kind of loyalty among clients.

This is clearly seen in the Bassam Ghrawi Confectionery business. What started as a local shop of hand-made traditional sweets became an international company in the decades that followed:

"By the time the third generation of manufacturers stepped in, the Al-Ghrawi family has not only increased their consumer base, but has also managed to create over 500 different sweets, each with a distinctive taste. This served to establish the company as a leader in the industry. Improving our retail shops branding by word of mouth and social media led to strengthening our brand name too."

Meet Lama Bassam El-Ghrawi, general manager of the Al-Ghrawi international family business

When you buy or inherit a family business of any scale, you become part of its legacy. While getting the benefits from the existing business and client pool, you also become responsible for meeting their expectations and upholding the reputation the brand name carries with it.

The owners of the Mallorca family business were met with challenges that came from trying to uphold the reputation of the company while looking to adapt to the new needs and behaviours of their consumers today:

"For some things, we just had to look back and see what our family was doing 40 years ago. We'd take that as an inspiration and then come up with things to fit the current market."

Expect to be linked to a family name

Being the owner of these kinds of businesses implies being connected to the name of the business, which is usually a family name. Whether the family name is your own or a different one, you will be linked to this name and the reputation it has built as a brand.

MARCO INFANTE from Casa Infante thoroughly understands the implications of representing a brand that's connected to a family. But this doesn't stop him from innovating:

"Chocolate has always been part of my life, both in the pastry and ice cream sectors. It wasn't, therefore, something that I planned but a natural consequence of continuous evolution and research. I've always felt the urge to experiment and search for new products and combinations for my fillings."

It's important to note that decisions like these, regarding business changes, are also influenced by the identity of this existing brand: what will remain the same, what will be subject to change and how these decisions will be communicated to win new clients and keep current ones well-informed.

If you have a specific vision you wish to bring to life or a new concept to hit the market, starting a new business might be the most practical option. If you're looking for a profitable business with an already established clientele (and your budget allows it), you can take over an existing business and take things from there.

Regardless of the route you wish to follow, take into account that benefits and challenges will always be present, and that working on your chocolate and entrepreneurial skills will always be an asset to you as an artisan chocolate shop owner.

Remember that not all opportunities might be within reach, and not all opportunities that are accessible might be the best for you. The key is to find the balance between what can be done, what the market needs and what's within your time and budget capabilities. Considering these elements will help you outline realistic possibilities.

The following chapters in this book will guide you in your quest to set up your own business. They will also serve as a guide to make improvements and upgrades in case you have taken over an existing chocolate shop or are thinking of expanding your brand.

"The business used to be called Willems-Mettepenningen. Those were two surnames, mine and my first wife's. After we separated, the name still stuck with people. It took years to disappear."

OLIVIER WILLEMS – OLIVIER WILLEMS

A memorable Casa Infante shop showcasing the brand's traditional heritage through typical Italian signs and wooden displays

Sfogliatelle
Ricce & Frolle
CASA INFANTE
QUI... NUVOLE
ASA INFANTE
Caffè
CAFFE
LEOPOLDO
AL VOSTRO SERVIZIO
NAPOLI
Nuvole
BoBo
Sfogliatelle

A packaging by Fidée stands out in the local market for its transparent exterior with bonbon flavours engraved on the outside

CHAPTER 3

UNDER-STANDING YOUR MARKET (POTENTIAL)

Nibbo
Bean to bar chocolate

Understanding your market potential is **A CRUCIAL STEP** towards starting or growing a successful artisan chocolate business. But before jumping into the chocolate-making process, it's essential to analyse who your potential customers are, their needs, preferences and behaviours. This way, you can tailor your product and marketing strategies accordingly.

This chapter will guide you through the process of researching and studying your market, so you can identify its characteristics and discover what they value most. With a clear understanding of your market potential, you'll be able to create a unique and desirable brand, with products that resonate with your clients.

KIRSTEN TIBBALLS, known as the international queen of chocolate, discovered the potential of the Australian market when she compared its characteristics with what was happening in the space of artisan chocolate in Europe:

"When I first started in patisserie, over 35 years ago in Australia, probably 70% of what was being used was compound chocolate. It wasn't until I first went to Europe that I saw amazing creations made with a product known as 'couverture' chocolate. That blew my mind and inspired me to actually get as much learning, training, and education as I could in Europe. Then, when I came back to Australia, I found that it was hard for me to work for somebody else and be able to communicate what I had learned. I thought 'we are doing it all wrong, there's this amazing product out there that we should be using, and this is what we can do with it'. So, from there, I started Savour School."

Just like Kirsten, MARIANE OLIVEIRA focused on the potential that could be found in a new international market. When looking to sell traditional Brazilian chocolates in Canada, Mary realised there were two ways of looking at her situation:

"Toronto is the most multicultural place in the world. People here are always looking for something new and different, and I had a chance to introduce that — something they would love or hate. When I came here, this didn't exist, so the first thought could've been, 'there is no market'. But instead, I thought, 'nobody has done this before, there is a huge market for me, and I will be the first one to create the brigadeiro concept in North America'."

Even in his presentations, Fan from Nibbo uses a minimalistic style that demonstrates the brand's aesthetics

Kirsten Tibballs recommends to balance out confectionery assortments by combining classic flavours for traditional customers with flavour pairings for the explorers

"Pick your markets carefully based on climate and national events.

In the southern hemisphere, we're in the perfect climate for selling chocolate. In summer we have Christmas, Valentine's Day, Easter and then we have Mother's Day. In the winter months, people's consumption of chocolate increases.

Whereas, in the northern hemisphere you have a lot of sales around a similar period because it's cold. This also coincides with festive events where people celebrate with chocolate, and people are more likely to invest in gifts. The market continuously changes and evolves, you have to stay up to date to be successful."

KIRSTEN TIBBALLS – SAVOUR SCHOOL

RESEARCH YOUR MARKET

Before launching a business in any market, the first step is to delimit your market, understand how it works and how things are looking for this market in the upcoming years. Researching your market is always necessary, even if you have previous business experience. A good example of the importance of market research is ENRIC ROVIRA. As a pioneer in the artisan chocolate scene in Barcelona, he still acknowledges the importance of constant market research up until this day:

"Times have changed. The market we knew in the 90s doesn't exist today: bonbons were sold in pastry shops inside boxes wrapped in patterned papers with big bows, and 90% of these bonbons were not moulded ones. Back then, the bonbons I offered as a planetarium [a collection of bonbons that look like the planets in the solar system] were all moulded with the same mould. Up until this day, they have been the biggest product success of my company."

To compare the market in which he started to the market he currently works for, one of the elements Enric analysed was production techniques. So, like it was for him, researching the chocolate market that's specific to you is a key to succeed in it. And to get started, these are some of the elements you'll want to keep your eye on:

Jars with samples are placed next to the different flavours of chocolate bars at Nibbo

- Market size
- Location
- Demographics
- Segment
- Demand
- Consumer needs and behaviour
- Competition
- Sales

Despite the hard data you might find about your market, remember there are different ways to approach this information. Just like Kirsten and Mary did, JAP JOY, creator of FIDÉE chocolates, chose to see his context as a market gap, instead of as a lack of interest:

"Almost no people make artisan chocolates here. So, there's no competition in the whole of China besides a few shops who do these kinds of chocolates in the country. For consumers, this was a new thing, they were like *'wow, these are something I've never seen. I want to try them'*."

Just like his bonbons, the packagings created by Jap Joy are inspired by the colours found in nature

Note that these starting chocolatiers and chocolate experts focused on their regional market, but also understood the implications of artisan chocolate on a bigger scale, because when it comes to chocolate worldwide, it's estimated that the global artisan chocolate industry will continue to grow in the upcoming years.

Aware of all the bits and pieces that make up the chocolate world, international chocolate consultant, JULIAN ROSE, has been advising chocolatiers to keep an open mind when it comes to their businesses, from concept ideation to trying out different chocolate formats. Although he advised for the industry to evolve, he noted a lot of people remained conservative to innovation, so he put his advice into practice himself:

"In my travels, I had seen a gap. I kept telling some artisans, *'you should do chocolate dragées, it's not that difficult'*. But nobody really knew how to handle it. So, I started a panning business. I purchased a belt coater, but there were no machines for artisans' belt coaters. So, I had a mechanic build me a smaller one. And then I would customise the flavours to whatever people liked. My concept was that I would bring 12 different chocolates and say, pick a chocolate, pick your ingredients and then tell me if you want a special finish, a colour, a flavour. I was there to fill a gap, to give them customisable high-quality at a good price.

Soon, customers were asking me how they could make them. So, I started offering trainings. Although these could undermine my business, I was confident enough that they would probably not be able to do what I was doing. But slowly, some people started making cheaper versions of my products. Not long after, I sold that business and went into the market as a consultant."

Although being aware of the international chocolate market is fundamental, as you saw in the example, the market where you should focus your research is the one where you'll be launching your business.

NIKKI THAKKER, from éntisi, is yet another chocolatier who found inspiration in other cultures' approach to artisan chocolate, and introduced the concept in her own market space. Instead of conforming to the traditional sweets from India, Nikki fought to create a community around what she had learned about artisan chocolate during her experience abroad:

"I absolutely love the chocolate in Belgium, France, Switzerland, all around Europe. And one day, what struck me was, *'why do we only find these chocolates in Europe and not India?'* That's how the idea was born. Sheer lack of an organised chocolate market in India manufacturing, so I felt that was the huge gap which I wanted to cater to.

In India, I would say 90%–95% of the chocolates you get in the market are actually not chocolate, they're compound. India being an extremely hot country, compound is much more stable because it does not melt that easily and does not require that much know-how."

Hampers with bonbons and cookies are how éntisi creates gift options while upselling their entire assortment

Although inspiration can be found around the world, you don't have to cross borders to learn about your market. With the internet at your fingertips, and by paying attention to your surroundings, you can be well underway to understanding the role of chocolate in the market you've chosen.

This is the case of the birth of M. Pelczar Chocolatier. Born and raised in Poland, MIROSLAW PELCZAR had great awareness when it came to the artisan chocolate space, and he also understood the place it had in his home country. Although known to never follow trends but stay true to his own creative ideas, Mirosław noticed the importance that market awareness had for any business:

"When I started, chocolate was a luxury product in Poland. Not many traditional pastry chefs knew how many possibilities chocolate gave them to express themselves and wow the customers. It was a time in Poland when there weren't many artisan chocolate shops, so I believe we were also pioneering this type of business."

As a rule of thumb, with an overall notion of the role of artisan chocolate in the world, and with a deeper understanding of the position it holds in your own market, you can begin your journey of delimiting which group of people in your specific market is the one with the potential to become your target audience.

IDENTIFY YOUR TARGET AUDIENCE

Like it happens in every business, you can't create products for everyone. You should make clear choices and creations based on who you're trying to cater to. To do so, the elements you've identified at the beginning of your market research can be further refined to define your specific target audience.

Age, gender, neighbourhood and even a consumer's available income matter a lot. Compared to your overall market, specific traits like these will help you define your target audience: the specific group/groups of people that represent *your* ideal consumer.

Truth is, not all chocolatiers who came together to tell us their stories started their business with a specific target group. Some of them began their business without a defined audience, and started adapting their craft after they began to sell their products.

This was the case of FAN YU, the chocolatier and entrepreneur that created Nibbo, a one-of-a-kind artisan chocolate concept shop in Shanghai:

"Today, we have a very accurate target audience. But in the beginning, we had quite a rough estimated range. We would say, for example, females between 18 and 50 years who are family members or students. That was a very broad target group. And after one year or two years, it's been narrowed down. Because we know who exactly comes to our store, we get more accurate as time goes by."

The open display at David Maenhout's shop is designed to encourage customers to explore the details of each creation

As you can see, it may take you weeks, months, or years to narrow down your specific target audience. However, in today's market, where competition is fierce, setting up or growing a chocolate business with an already delimited target audience in mind will give you a head-start and get you closer to success.

Before thinking of officially launching her brand, or even thinking about how to market her products, MARIANE OLIVEIRA from Mary's Brigadeiro knew that narrowing down her target audience was a must. Without external help or a budget to invest in research, she took it upon herself to outline her target group of people:

"I was looking for a place to offer my brigadeiros, so I thought of a coffee shop, but one in a location that's a little bit upscale. If I offered the brigadeiro in a coffee shop where students go, they wouldn't pay $3 for one. If hungry, they would buy a brownie, because it's bigger and it's the same price. My product couldn't compete against a brownie. So, the students were not my market. I needed to put the chocolates in a place where people had a bigger budget.

Then, the way I started to look at this was thinking about how much a shop charged for an espresso. Some charged $2, so my brigadeiro would not be there. A person who paid $2 for an espresso would not pay $3 for a brigadeiro. It took us a while to understand this, so many trials and mistakes.

In the end, someone gave me advice that was very precise: 'If your product is for everybody, it's not for anybody'. You can't please everybody with your creations, so knowing your audience is definitely step one."

Just like it happened for Mary, market research can definitely help you to define your audience. This won't only help you build your marketing strategy (Chapter 6) when the time comes. It will also help you to prepare your business for future changes.

The welcoming attitude of Mary's Brigadeiro's staff attracts a lively audience of all ages

Understanding the shifts in your target audience is an asset that even the bigger and older artisan chocolate businesses value. Take a look at the Mallorca business. Although the MORENO FAMILY's legacy amounts to decades of experience, the business pays attention to constant changes in their audience, tailoring not only their marketing efforts, but their offer (Chapter 10) to adapt to our ever-changing world:

"In the past years, our customers' average age was around 60. We realised we needed to focus on trying to widen that customer focus. So, we started to show younger people what they wanted to see in our company, without having to change who we are and what we do: we communicated more and better, improving the way we explained things.

We learned that if you show people things they know, you will have a lot of competition. If you give them what they don't know, there's no competition. And this is what happened when we used Callebaut Ruby Chocolate. People could've said, *'oh, it's chocolate with strawberry'*.

"Although we remain accessible, we are on the higher end with our products and prices. We know our clientele is open to it since they consume more expensive coffee."

JITSK HEYNINCK – JITSK CHOCOLATES

So, this is where you tell them the background story and the real value it has. If you don't, then you're selling nothing. And, it gave us so much richness to discover how to make the client know these things, because people are very interested in where things come from nowadays."

You might be like Mallorca, a business of a bigger scale. Or you might be a one-shop chocolate business owner looking to create or optimise your offer according to your relevant market. Regardless of your size, there are different (paid and free) ways to deep-dive into your market by using different kinds of tools. For example, as Savour School became more successful, KIRSTEN TIBBALLS saw the need to learn more about her clients, and made a conscious choice to invest in it:

"I think it's essential for any business to understand their client base, so we do surveys. We try to do one every 18 months, and it's quite in-depth. We offer quite a good prize to encourage people to participate, and we do one for our general customer base and then one for our online subscribers. In our last survey, we had a 20% response, which gives us a really good grasp of what our customers look like: male or female, demographics, whether they're professional chefs or home cooks, etc."

As you can see from the previous examples, there is no need to survey thousands of people or set a huge budget to better understand your target audience; nor to outline target groups at the very beginning. You can get started simply by talking to family members and friends, by reaching out to people who you think would be your ideal customer and asking relevant questions.

You've got the theory in place, are you ready to put it into practice? Then here's how you can begin studying your local market today:

As founder and chef of her now multi-shop business, Mariane Oliveira still makes the time to meet and greet clients

1. Online and offline, **delimit the geographical reach** of your local market and start to look up information about it. Try to identify the needs and preferences of your potential customers by first looking into their characteristics (age, job, financial situation, places they frequent, how much they are willing to spend). Look to have one-on-one or small group discussions with people who represent that target audience, this may also help you to understand their expectations.

2. Make a list of which **other businesses** could be your competition and place these businesses on a map to see where they operate. Study your competitors' products or services, selling prices and marketing strategies. These elements can help you identify gaps in your market (and spot opportunities for your business), get an idea of how much similar companies charge for their products and differentiate your business from the rest.

3. **Create customer personas.** Based on your market research and target audience, create customer personas. To build a target persona, highlight demographic information such as age, gender, income, and education level, as well as psychographic information such as interests, values, and lifestyle. Many businesses have multiple personas within their target audience.

Mary's
HANDCRAFTED CHOCOLATE

TEST YOUR PRODUCTS AND IDEAS

To understand how your target audience responds to your products and ideas, testing them on a small "sample" audience is one way to get in-depth feedback on how they're perceived.

FAN, from Nibbo chocolate, makes of this notion an annual team building and research activity by travelling throughout different regions in China:

"We do a road trip with the team. We drive our van, travel to different places, talk to thousands of different people and share our chocolate with them too. We shoot videos and ask questions to get feedback. We want to know what fine chocolate means to real people. When we come back from our trip, we look at the feedback and the local ingredients we discovered, and we make flavour bars based on the cities we visited."

Just like Fan, when you get a clear idea of the products you want to offer and the story that makes you unique (Chapter 1), organising sample testing among different groups may give you a lot of information about how they like your concept and ideas, the price they're prepared to pay for your products, where these products would be a bigger hit and even the location to set up a shop.

If you're getting started, keep your focus on the few key products that you consider are your signature offer: products that highlight your uniqueness and style.

While designing packaging, Jap Joy chooses materials and textures that match the brand's aesthetic inspired by nature

And when you're fishing for feedback, remember there is no use in showing or discussing your entire assortment, only your core products. After testing his concept and sampling his products, JAP JOY was able to successfully deliver what his market was after:

"Based on my perspective, the customers in the Chinese market don't care about whether chocolates are made by hand or by machines. They just care about the flavours, whether they're good or not. And, whether the packaging looks good. They need to bring those chocolates as a gift to friends and family, so good looks are important. Another thing they also care about is whether those chocolates are coming from a good source, like Belgium or France."

Just like with FIDÉE and Nibbo, we showed you how the owner of MARY'S BRIGADEIRO did market research without allocating a budget to test her concept. What Mary and these two chocolatiers in China have in common is their ability to analyse their market without investing a lot of money:

"In the beginning, I didn't have the money to actually pay a company to research the market. So, I pretty much went to coffee shops, bought the cheapest thing and spent two, three, four hours there with a notebook just writing: how people react, what's their behaviour when they buy coffee, do they spend hours or just grab and go, what are people dressed like, how much a coffee costs, could they afford a brigadeiro. I needed to understand how they would buy my chocolates, so I needed to learn about the behaviour of a culture I had no clue about."

Just like Mary and the others, with a clear overview of where your potential customers stand, you are ready to position your brand and products in the eyes of your ideal audience.

DEVELOP YOUR ROUTE(S) TO MARKET

Your route to market encompasses the channels you use to deliver your products to your target audience, and it should be developed according to your business objectives. To avoid getting lost in the number of possibilities, a practical way to get started is to consider the following options:

B2C

Selling directly to consumers (Business to Consumer)

This option involves creating a customer-facing experience. Whether that means investing in e-commerce, a physical store, pop-ups, a selling stand in a mall, B2C network spaces or even a franchise. When you opt for a B2C route to market, the goal is to help consumers find their way to your products. For this, you will need to develop a marketing strategy (Chapter 6) to let people know your brand exists and to achieve sales that come directly from the end consumers.

B2B

Selling to businesses (Business to Business)

In a B2B route to market, you leave the selling and product sharing to the businesses that buy from you. This can be either third-party retailers as well as corporate clients who place big orders in the name of their companies. In this situation, your business is a production centre of confectionery products: customer-facing investments are now in the hands of your clients, and your marketing strategy will need to be adapted to reach businesses instead of individuals. The most common client base of chocolatiers who choose this route includes: corporate companies (corporate gifts), local businesses, hotels, restaurants, retailers, etc. In the B2B route to market, your business' investment efforts will be focused on production efficiency, R&D (Research and Development), and B2B marketing, while heavier investments such as retail space or sales staff will be cut. When you go B2B, it's important to calculate product margins in a way that not only you, but your clients, can profit from the products you offer.

B2C + B2B

Hybrid models

Many starting and experienced chocolate business owners choose a mix of these routes. By selling directly to consumers, they benefit from a higher product margin in each sale. And, by developing a range of products to offer to other businesses, they fill their production pipelines (and manage to stay profitable) when direct-to-consumer demand fluctuates or decreases. Choosing a hybrid model is also a way to distribute initial risk when starting your business.

BREAKING IT DOWN:

different routes to market for artisan chocolate around the world

Enric Rovira and STEPHEN TRIGG are located in different countries, but they have something in common: they pay attention to their surroundings. By thoroughly understanding the market around them, they began building roads to reach their ideal audiences.

Stephen knew that unlike other chocolate businesses, setting up a shop in a high street might be the way to go in some other markets, but that it wouldn't be the way he would successfully reach his audience:

"As much as I would still like to have a brick-and-mortar, a physical shop, it is just the times. I've looked at big competitors and I can't understand how they do it. My gut feeling is they only make their money at the end of the year when they cashflow the whole company, especially in the UK market. When I go to Paris, I just can't get the concept, there's a chocolate shop on every corner. And I love it, but it wouldn't work here, we have a different mentality in the UK."

In contrast to the success of online sales today, and located in the vibrant Barcelona, ENRIC started his chocolate business in the 90s. When thinking about how to sell artisan chocolates in the city, and although a different time, he was also faced with the challenge of how to reach his local market:

"When I started, people didn't go to pastry shops to buy chocolate. It was easier to sell chocolate next to a bottle of wine in a specialty shop instead of waiting for consumers to go look for a chocolate shop specifically."

As you might have noticed already, choosing one or multiple routes to market and its channels is directly connected to the target audience you've outlined, and to the market where you operate.

Chocolatier M presents around a dozen chocolate tablets, each with a distinct flavour profile — some are the result of collaborations with breweries, roasters, and other local businesses

Stephen Trigg, always ready to welcome all clients with a smile

B2C
Business to Consumer

As explained before, B2C businesses sell directly to consumers. But let's go in-depth with the implications you'll have to consider if you choose this route, and let's see it play out in a real-life example:

» In a B2C route to market, you have access to the full profit margin of the products you sell. This means that, compared to B2B, where you have to lower your margin so that your retailer or reseller can also make a profit, in B2C, the entire product margin becomes your profit.

» A B2C approach requires investment in a space where your customers can discover, experience and buy your products: this can be an online shop, a traditional 'brick-and-mortar' store, a pop-up, or even a kiosk. Depending on how you wish to position your brand and the experience around it, the investments will vary. So, when calculating your product margins in B2C, you will also need to consider these investments.

» A physical or online store also requires investing in people: it can be sales staff, delivery services or people who keep your online shop up to date. Take into account that employee costs are often higher in a B2C route to market than in a B2B one.

A great example of a B2C investment is how NIKKI THAKKER understood her end consumers and built strategies to reach them with her brand, éntisi:

"A majority of the business is gifting, because people see it as a very good gifting item. If they're going to someone's place for dinner, they want to carry chocolates rather than traditional Indian sweets. Artisan chocolates are a novelty factor; whether it's for a wedding, birth announcement or simply going to someone's house for dinner.

So, we had a PR and marketing campaign since I was new in this industry and the business was new in the city. This agency that did our PR, they called important influencers and food bloggers and invited them to our shop. We did a lot of chocolate tastings with them and even explained the origins of cacao."

As we mentioned earlier, businesses that cater directly to consumers usually focus on a very specific target audience. Their sales objectives and marketing efforts look to make their brand known by forming an emotional link with their potential clients. So that third-party retailers could sell her chocolates the way she would do it herself, MARIANE from Mary's Brigadeiro reached out to them in a more personalised way, almost making sure that third-party sales people became advocates for her brand:

"We always send extra samples, encouraging them to try them. Even if they are not our team members, they become like an extension of our own sales team."

“The idea was an open B2C concept. We found a store that was on a second level, so you had to climb up to enter the space. It’s an open concept for clients who want full transparency on what we do and how we make things. Open kitchen concepts were not done in Singapore at the time, there were only a few places doing that.”

JANICE WONG – JANICE WONG PURE IMAGINATION | 2AM: DESSERTBAR | SOFTHAUS

MARIANE is well aware of the changes in product profit when selling in her own shop compared to selling through retailers. However, she keeps her routes to market diverse:

"Some buy the products from us at a lower price, a price where we are able to make a profit. Then, they sell the products in their coffee shops or specialty stores. It's important to have this wholesale as part of the business because it also helps you increase production."

Strategies to get the attention and loyalty of your target audience will vary according to the characteristics of this audience.

Despite what your audience looks like and how your products reach it, the B2C concept remains the same: offering your products directly to the consumer. An interesting way to analyse the B2B market is doing it from a B2C approach, and this is a mindset KIRSTEN TIBBALLS openly talks about:

"Branding your product under another company's label is a common strategy. Whenever possible, aim for co-branding to ensure your own label is also promoted. There are also many opportunities to sell your product B2B, where another company will brand it as their own."

If, like Kirsten suggests, you're talking to consumers without intermediaries, your business will take one of the following formats: brick-and-mortar shop, online store or third-party retailer. These formats can be set up independently, but they work better when they are used simultaneously to leverage each other's strengths.

One of the important aspects to always look out for, particularly when working with third parties, is to ensure they follow certain procedures to care for your brand as much as you would.

A good example of this is ENRIC ROVIRA. When he started his chocolate business, Enric was forced to sell his chocolates in different retailers around Barcelona. As he sought for retailers, he learned to look out for specific traits these third-parties should have to properly represent his brand:

"I didn't have a shop of my own, so the only way to market my products was through third-party retailers. We started offering the product in historical buildings with tourist traffic and in what were known as gourmet shops. The negative part we had to take into account was that the old buildings didn't use to have air conditioning, so the environment wasn't always the right one for chocolate."

"When customers come to my shop, there are a lot of bonbon flavours. They come to the shelf and say *'oh, my God, this is so beautiful. What is that? What is that?'* And that's when we get to explain everything.

This is why I'm not gonna put my products all over the market. Because there will not be a person to explain all that we offer, the bonbons especially. I prefer to sell everything in the shop and in small-size markets that have the same concept that we have for ourselves: artisanal. We also do some corporate sales here and there, and I think these market routes are enough."

RENATA ARASSIRO – RENATA ARASSIRO CHOCOLATES

Renata Arassiro's bonbons often feature local Brazilian ingredients at their heart, brought to life in a colourful presentation

Storage conditions are one of the many factors you'll have to consider when selling your products through retailers. This is another way of saying that all B2C channels will have pros and cons. So, regardless of which shape your B2C route to market takes, make sure you take the following basic elements into consideration:

1 Customer journey

All your clients will go through a buying process, also known as the customer journey. Each of the phases of this process opens a door for a business to spark a consumer's interest or sell a product. To make sure you reach your B2C consumers at all times during this process, these are the customer journey phases you should know about:

» **AWARENESS**
This part is all about making your brand known in the eyes of your target audience. Letting people know about who you are, the products you offer and your unique story is the first step of the customer journey.

» **CONSIDERATION**
This phase comes right after the awareness stage. Once people know your business, they enter a decision phase — whether they buy from you or not.

» **DECISION**
After considering your brand, and most likely comparing it to other chocolate shops with similar offers, consumers will make a choice. This is where your marketing efforts (Chapter 6) will pay off.

2 Brand content

How you speak of your business and the channels you choose to share it should adapt to the route to market you've chosen. To keep your content consistent with your brand, and organised so that it meets your business goals, it's always a good practice to have a content strategy in place (Chapter 6).

3 Generate leads

A good mix of content planning and networking in the right places is what will bring potential clients into contact with your brand. As a B2C business, you will be relying more on digital content tailored for end consumers and personal connections.

A great example of these 3 basics put into practice can be seen with JAP JOY and his chocolate shop, FIDÉE. Now owner of two shops, Jap Joy created his business with a limited budget. His brand grew slowly as he found a way to use his products to generate brand awareness and attract consumers to his shop:

"For the first shop, I worked with a partner, a pastry chef who made patisserie, and he also had a lot of fans. I asked, '*hey, can I sell my chocolates in your shop?*' So, people who went to the pastry shops to buy pastries were also curious about chocolates, and they would buy them. That's basically how I started.
Another way to sell our products is under another retailer. When we do that, we have to consider the way of selling, if we can join their ideas, business models, if we can fit perfectly with their brand. In other words, both brands have to get along."

"We get a lot of requests from retailers who want to sell our chocolates, but we have to think if that's realistic. The product that we have here has to look the same over there; it has to be treated the same, with as much love and passion. So, for me it's difficult to believe that can happen. I also don't want our brand to disappear into other businesses if people think our pralines are made by that other brand. So, I've always thought that if we sell something, it has to be under my name. For example, now I work for the catering industry more than I used to. When chefs come for a collaboration, we are specified on the menu now: coffee with Olivier Willems' chocolates. That's also how you get those foodies to your shop."

—

OLIVIER WILLEMS – OLIVIER WILLEMS

Some of Jitsk Heyninck's secondary products include hazelnut and chocolate spreads and artisanal ice creams — often sold through third party retailers

"Actually, if you look at our business plan in the beginning, we were doing 70% for B2C and the rest wholesale. But today, B2B is ultimately our biggest part: currently 80% or 90%. It's simply what the business has become by working with partners like Cru [Belgian specialty store]. The B2C part though, I still believe in that enormously, but it's less of a driver, less of a self-fuelled thing."

JITSK HEYNINCK – JITSK CHOCOLATES

B2B
Business to Business

A B2B route to market focuses on a target audience a bit more complex and diverse than the B2C route. In the B2B route, other businesses will be your customers.

One of the main elements to remember in this route to market is the financial aspect of things. Opposed to a business-to-consumer approach, in a B2B setting, you often need to calculate your reseller margins, as they also need to profit from the sales: since your products will end up in retail outlets, restaurants, hotels or even distributors that sell the product for you.

Although challenging in some regards, Kirsten Tibballs believes this route is worth taking advantage of, particularly when your goal is selling larger quantities:

"There's lots of corporate companies that will gift chocolates to either clients, staff, real estate agents, etc. So, I think there's an opportunity here to sell more volume."

Remember that on your B2B journey, you will be addressing people with a different proposition, and the relationships you build will be different, so will have a different impact on your business. In a B2B route, winning a single new client can mean a significant positive impact when compared to winning one new client in the B2C route.

You'll also notice that when you're looking at a B2B route to market, the elements you should consider will be the same, but on a different scale or setting.

Because your target audience are other businesses, your content and products will also have to be customised — businesses as end consumers will have different objectives. For example, you could be selling artisan chocolates to an airline. In this case, your products would have to have a longer shelf life and adapt to the transportation setting and logistics that this entails.

Just like in B2C, in a B2B setting, generating leads will also be an offline/online effort. The kinds of platforms and events might even be the same, but you will be speaking to other businesses instead of individuals.

B2C + B2B
A hybrid model

As a shop owner, you may find there is more than one channel where your products can succeed. For example, MIROSLAW PELCZAR created M. Pelczar Chocolatier to open the Polish market to what he perceived as "real chocolate". However, he never turned a blind eye at the opportunities that came from combining different routes to market:

"We do not work with any big supermarkets or retail chains. We don't want to be everywhere, as that would, in our opinion, kill our identity. We work only with small local shops, but this is not a substantial part of our business. Hotels and restaurants stand for a bigger part of our business. Since our chocolates are considered as local souvenirs and there are a lot of them in this region of Poland."

NIKKI THAKKER is yet another chocolatier-entrepreneur who saw the potential of choosing more than one way to reach her market. Although she faced initial challenges to create a hybrid route model, her resilience and faith in what her brand had to offer eventually paid off:

"Other than selling through our own stores, we are selling in other retail stores. But they're all éntisi branded products. There are also certain hotels we work with; they stock our products in the mini bars in each room. The B2B customers are more or less on those lines.

Initially, it was a bit of a struggle because I reached out to everyone myself. I was a salesperson for the first two years, I had pitched to many retail shops and many hotels and restaurants to shop our products... I think 80% of them did not even consider it. It was quite disheartening, but we continued to try. Thanks to the presence of our physical shop and the marketing that we were doing in certain events, there was some brand awareness that was growing. So, that organic part only started happening I would say after three years."

"My revenue from the B2C store is only a certain percentage, not all of it. I mean, selling can happen offline as well as online, as well as to customers and restaurants. The profit is a balance of all these things."

DAVID MAENHOUT – CHOCOLATIER M

Unlike some chocolatiers, STEPHAN TRIGG and his wife initially launched their brand focusing solely on the B2B market, as they believed it translated into a steady income compared to only selling to consumers. But, when hotels and airlines were affected by the pandemic, they managed to survive through the help from the community and B2C sales. Today, they understand the value of a hybrid model:

"We built up the business around retail, direct to the public and to businesses in hospitality and retail. For us, it goes back to the early days, when the least risky option for us was to start as B2B, because we would have steady customers throughout the year.

The early days we were attending to trade show, standing in front of someone doing a tasting and they would say '*Yeah, we'd like to exchange business cards and follow up*'. Then, if that chef would move to a new restaurant, he'd take us, while the old restaurant would also keep us in their network. It grew slowly. But once the roots are down, it's quite a solid business as long as you keep delivering.

Today, about 20% of the turnover is B2C, and that's via the website. Sometimes, we'll do a direct retail show, and we do a click and collect type of sale. Some other times, people literally turn up, and knock on the door, '*can we come in, we didn't realise it was not a shop*'. But it doesn't matter how they find us, no one gets turned away."

"Now, we work B2B with hotels who are loyal customers. After working with us many times, they know us and know that we can react very quickly to any kind of demand they might have. That they trust us helps the positioning of our company in the B2B market."

ENRIC ROVIRA – ENRIC ROVIRA

If like any of these chocolatiers, you believe a hybrid model is what fits your business, be prepared to take the next steps. You will have to make your different routes to market and channels work together by adjusting your content and offer to your target audiences and route-specific goals.

Have you started to see overlaps in product demand in different channels? Don't take it as a bad sign! This isn't a conflict, but a chance to exploit the potential of your product range (Chapter 10) according to what your audience is looking for.

Known to craft the impossible with chocolate, Enric Rovira captures clients not only with flavour, but with daring designs

POSITION YOUR BRAND

Businesses that work on their brand positioning see up to a 20% increase in their revenue. This is because brand positioning isn't just business jargon. It's how you build your brand's reputation and create a space for it in the mind of your customers.

https://blog.hubspot.com/sales/brand-positioning-strategy

A good example of this is JANICE WONG. She isn't only acknowledged for her skills as a chocolatier, but for her status as an artist and well-known event planner. Both of these aspects have helped her create brand identity (Chapter 4) and position it in her market:

"We do about 40 culinary art exhibitions a year. I figured that because we were in such a unique and niche market that people hear about it, see it on Instagram and as soon as they see somebody taking chocolate off the wall they go like, *'where is this?'*"

Using chocolate as a tool to build a reputation for all her businesses, Janice understood the task at hand: brand positioning goes beyond the chocolates you make.

This is also the case of CALUM HAGGERTY, who chose COCO Chocolatier as the new name for the business he had acquired. After buying a company which wasn't performing well, he decided to make changes that would lead to his current success. Those changes impacted the way the company's market position and the way it was perceived by his target audience:

"The word 'chocolatier', to me, says that we're actually making the chocolates. So, that was the first change. After that name change, we did the full transition into working with artists and designers for everything: we introduced the strapline of 'The Art of Chocolate'. Sometimes, we'll refer to ourselves as 'COCO', but always depending on whom you're talking to. If you're not talking to another chocolate company, you might say chocolatier just so they know what it is that you do."

Both Janice and Calum took elements from their brand identity and leveraged them to shape the way the audience would look at their brand. RENATA ARASSIRO did the same with her chocolate shop, but she did it by positioning her business in opposition to what was commonly known:

"I've always loved cupuaçu, and I wanted more Brazilian people to know the ingredients we have and that they're different. I didn't want to use only classic European flavours in my chocolates because I'm Brazilian."

Renata knew artisan chocolate was often linked to the European approach to the craft, particularly when using the highest quality Belgian chocolate. So, she decided to place her business on the other side of this concept, by creating European chocolate formats filled with Brazilian flavours — exotic to some, regional to her community.

It's your turn to do as these successful chocolatiers did: look to position your brand in the early stages of your business initiative. To make it happen, you'll need a couple of the brand elements mentioned in the first chapters of the book: your differentiating element and your market research. You'll use what makes you different to stand out from the competition within your specific market space.

When building his brand in the United States, HÅKAN MÅRTENSSON put this into practice. Håkan knew he wanted his brand to be seen as a unique chocolate experience with roots in his Nordic origins. He did an exercise where he asked himself relevant questions to be aware of how his uniqueness would impact the way he should position the brand (and communicate about it):

"Why would people buy my stuff? They won't do it just because I have a sculpture in the back of my shop. This is why you have to, although it's really hard, pinpoint what you are doing that's different from anyone else. Because, a lot of people are using the same ingredients, same techniques and so on. So, ask yourself what is it that differentiates you?"

As your business grows, your positioning strategy will have to adapt to your new goals and needs, as well as to changes in the market. Research to position your brand should be recurrent, as markets and consumer behaviour constantly evolve. Eventually, you'll have to evaluate if your company also calls for a change in your positioning strategy.

Signature triangular bonbons by Davide Comaschi are presented in a box inspired by their particular shape

"Coming from Barry Callebaut, I had some experience and structure. But to get your brand positioning right, I would recommend making a small market research. It's not completely necessary for small artisans, but it is important to start thinking at the investment stage.

For me, the partnership with Da Vittorio had a really positive response: the idea of sharing chocolate culture starting in the world of luxury had a waterfall effect and created a big appeal to our consumers."

DAVIDE COMASCHI – DAVIDE COMASCHI

DRAFT YOUR **BUSINESS PLAN**

Let's bring this corporate term down to earth. A business plan is a document that explains the goals of your business and how you plan on achieving them.

A business plan isn't a requirement to start your own brand. But you'll need it when it's time to register your business, look for funds or investors or if someday you decide to sell or expand your company. Take Mariane's from MARY'S BRIGADEIRO word for it:

"Most of the opportunities I see online to get some money or funding ask for a business plan, for your projections for the next months. It doesn't necessarily have to be a plan for 5 years. You can start small, but create a business plan."

Although Mary suggests you should have a business plan in place regardless of how small you start, you'll find that chocolatiers' opinions differ when it comes to creating one.

Kirsten Tibballs' Savour School is Australian made, but with an international reach. When asked about the relevance of a business plan for her company, KIRSTEN didn't stutter:

"I think a business plan is really essential to have an understanding of the working capital and how many products a business needs. It gives you a full picture before you actually get started, so you avoid making many mistakes. It also allows you to tick things off, *'we haven't even considered packaging'*, *'we didn't think of counters'*, or *'what's the correct humidity and what's the cost of that?'*. Once you've thought of everything, the business planning enables you to put it all on paper and decide how much you need to charge for your product, because you know what your total costs will be."

"It has become more and more important to work with a business plan. When you go to the bank with a plan, they come up with money faster; because they see the growth margin, they see the figures. That is the main goal of a business plan, that these people know you are doing well. Without a business plan, you find that you have to grit your teeth and move on to another busy period in order to be able to bridge that gap. You'll need an accountant who knows how to support you. But a business plan is always, always in our heads."

OLIVIER WILLEMS – OLIVIER WILLEMS

"Before you try things out, dig deeper. You need to know what's going on in the industry. Try to learn from the best, see what they are using and what ideas they are doing."

FAN YU – NIBBO

The MORENO BROTHERS manage the Mallorca family company, and they share Kirsten's opinion about what a business plan can do for you as an entrepreneur:

"The business plan is super important because it's where you analyse what you are actually going to do and how you're going to do it. Everyone needs a good business plan, and they need good assistance for it. There are a lot of good chefs that are not businessmen, and they need to understand this. That there are rules they need to follow and that they need to make money out of the business."

On the opposing side of this opinion, you'll have success stories that started off without a business plan. DAVIDE COMASCHI, Italian chocolate pioneer and father of the brand that takes after his name, started with nothing more than passion for creating tasty and luxurious chocolates:

"Business plans have a high cost, so I didn't have a complex one initially. We did start with a basic table that included costs, investment, and where we aimed to go. It was something very pragmatic. Once we had that, I managed to follow it, but I saw how many expenses popped up that were not part of the chocolate world specifically. These things turned out to be the most expensive ones."

Davide's take is that business plans will not cover all unexpected situations and costs you might have as your business progresses. This is one of the reasons chef STEPHEN TRIGG started his business without following anything but his gut:

"In the early days, there was no plan. The plan was just to sell chocolate and to make sure that the company could survive. That went on for quite a few years, but it was okay because I had a background."

Just like some decide to draft detailed business plans before investing a dime, some others jump into the production process straight away. In between them, we have chocolatiers with a different approach. NIKKI THAKKER had her business plan in her head. She knew what she wanted to do and where she wanted to go. And, as a true entrepreneur, she learned by doing:

"I had a fairly decent idea of what I wanted to do, but the majority of the understanding started coming after I started the work. I did not know what numbers to expect, I started getting an idea after around six months. So, check your finances on a monthly basis to understand in which direction the business is moving. I think you need a certain amount of data for at least 10 months for you to understand what's going on. So honestly, there was no formal business plan that I had in mind, that only happened later."

A business plan can be as simple as a one-page document (that you can adjust as your business progresses) or a more elaborated multi-page presentation. The important part is that if you've made it this far, you already have the information you need to draft your own.

A simple business plan will consist of mainly 5 parts:

1. Summary
2. About the Company
3. Market Research
4. Products & Services
5. Marketing & Sales

If you're unsure of what kind of information belongs in each of them or how much you should write, you can use this guide:

Build your business plan

SUMMARY	
Product overview	A general description of the product/products you offer
Customers	Specify your target audience and why they would be interested in your offer
Vision for the future	The relevance of your business in the future of the artisan chocolate industry

ABOUT THE COMPANY	
Mission statement	State your purpose
Key roles and members	Name the members of the company and their roles (yes, even if it's just you!)
Legal information	State the type of company you are and your company's official location and address

MARKET RESEARCH	
Industry overview	The role of the artisan chocolate shop industry + current statistics about this industry + forecast of the industry according to a reliable source
Customers: target audience	Describe your target audience + describe the different personas that make up your target audience
The advantages of your business	Explain your advantages in comparison to similar businesses
Legal requirements	Mention the regulations your business would adhere to

PRODUCTS & SERVICES	
Products & services	List your product range: all the products that are part of your offer (Chapter 8)
Pricing	List how you'll price the products (unit/weight/batches) and what each product price will be
Product life cycle	Describe the life cycle of each product in your range (think shelf life)
Intellectual property & rights	Mention if your brand name is a trademark, if you have intellectual property over recipes/concepts
Research & development	List the research and development (R&D) activities you are conducting / plan to conduct

MARKETING & SALES	
Communication strategy	List all the ways you will communicate with your clients / potential clients
Sales	Explain your sales tactics and channels, and how these will change as your business grows
Growth strategy	List the tasks/steps you will follow to grow your business

> **"Intuition is very important, this and a good business plan should always be paired with a market research."**
>
> LAMA BASSAM AL-GHRAWI – BASSAM GHRAWI CONFECTIONERY

To get a better understanding of how this template would work in real life, take a look at how you could apply it to an existing business, like Mariane Oliveira's.

If you're looking to gain some confidence before writing a plan for your own business, a good way to practice your entrepreneurial skills is to find a similar business and break it down into the different parts contemplated in the template. Once you've done this exercise with different businesses, it'll be easier to tackle your own business plan!

Mary's Brigadeiro

SUMMARY	
Product overview	Brigadeiros (traditional Brazilian sweets with a twist)
Customers	» B2C: People looking for sweet treats, innovation and newness » B2B: Retailers that want a sweet treat to offer with coffee / Businesses looking for corporate gifts or sweets for events
Vision for the future	Bringing joy to people by offering a unique chocolate concept in Toronto

ABOUT THE COMPANY	
Mission statement	» Bringing joy and people together through chocolate. » Create a safe environment for immigrant women to work and thrive.
Key roles and members	» Mariane Oliveira: business owner and lead chocolatier » Production staff: 3 people » Sales staff: 2 people
Legal information	Privacy Compliance Officer at 2489 Bloor St. W Toronto Ontario CA M6S1R6

MARKET RESEARCH	
Industry overview	Artisan chocolate is a growing industry as consumer behaviour shifts towards artisan-made concepts. With the artisan chocolate space on the rise, Mary's Brigadeiro has the potential to bring uniqueness to this growing demand.
Customers: target audience	» B2C: People looking for a different chocolate gift and ready to spend a little more on a different concept » B2B: Upper scale coffee shops that can offer a higher-margin sweet treat with coffee / corporations looking for a one-of-a-kind sweet experience
The advantages of your business	Within the artisan chocolate space, the brigadeiro is a new concept where premium ingredients meet with Brazilian tradition, bringing a new way to enjoy chocolate to the streets of Toronto.
Legal requirements	We follow Canada's food regulation standards

PRODUCTS & SERVICES

Products & services	**Core products** » Brigadeiros (15 flavours) **Secondary products** » Chocolate bars » Cookies » Frozen cookies » Gelato Gift wraps - branded » Drinking chocolate » Spread » Brazilian coffee beans » DIY Brigadeiro kit » Gift cards **Seasonal offers** » New brigadeiro flavours » Seasonal chocolates
Pricing	**Core products** » Brigadeiro box (4 / 6 / 12 / 24 / 36 / 48 / 60) **Secondary products** » Chocolate bars (unit) » Cookies (unit) » Frozen cookies (12 pack) » Gelato (unit) » Gift wraps - branded (unit) » Drinking chocolate (unit) » Spread (unit) » Brazilian coffee beans (unit) » DIY Brigadeiro kit (unit) » Gift cards (unit)
Product life cycle	Room temperature: 7 days Fridge: 12 days Freezer: 3 months
Intellectual property & rights	Mary's Brigadeiro is a trademark
Research & development	Product innovation is led by owner Mariane Oliveira through in-house tastings and customer feedback. Market research and recurrent feedback rounds are used to tailor the seasonal offer to keep it relevant for the target market.

MARKETING & SALES

Growth strategy	After profit margins surpass 10%, we will invest in marketing efforts to grow our social media account, which is one of our key drivers of new clients.
Communication strategy	Besides in-store B2C/B2B client visits, we make sure to keep active social media profiles and email address, where we answer questions regarding the brand and take orders.
Sales	» B2C clients can purchase our products either in our brick-and-mortar shop or through out online store. » B2B consumers can reach out to us with their specific requirements through our website or social media profiles. We get in touch with them so they can place their order according to their needs and our offer.

LEARN AS YOU GO

With a well-crafted business foundation, your research done and your business plan in place, all that's left is putting all this theory into practice with a start-up mindset: building the plane as you fly it.

RYAN FOOTE is an exemplary display of learning from unexpected challenges that the artisan world has had to face in the last years. Ryan was able to adapt to the radical shifts in the market, sought out a way for his business to thrive and until today, remains a flexible and creative business owner:

"Before the pandemic, there were nine months of protests in Hong Kong. That pretty much just took out every single bit of tourism out of the city. Suddenly, all B2B business we had for hotels was gone. Our business was already in a challenging situation before COVID, and then obviously when COVID hit, that amplified everything. I've had to rework the business model several times and I think that has been one of the most important things: constantly looking at how we can adapt. For example, when the tourism that we were supplying dried up, we started creating new chocolate shapes, collaborating with brands like Hennessy and doing whiskey-based chocolates, offering them in bars and events with the local community that were still able to happen, because instead of being able to travel, people stayed in Hong Kong."

When a hard period of trials seemed to be passing, Ryan and his business were hit by unexpected circumstances yet again:

"As soon as we shifted our business model, from October to March, Hong Kong went into a lockdown and all bars were closed during that time. And for us, that was the busy season."

As you can see, a flexible business model and an open mind helped Ryan overcome a series of unfortunate events. After adjusting his offer, his way of innovating new recipes and making sure to adapt to a rapidly changing market, his business was able to overcome it all.

Although planning for things always helps a company, nothing can be completely contemplated, so there is one last element that is crucial as a chocolatier and business owner. As STEPHEN TRIGG would put it, his business wouldn't have succeeded without this crucial element for a chocolatier's journey:

"I had all of the skills, but I was missing a couple of particular skills that beat every other skill hands down: determination and drive. You can be intelligent, you can have creativity, you can have great risk management skills and a lot of things, but *'I'm gonna get up and do this'* — that, for me, was one of the biggest things I had to learn."

All these real-life experiences from all over the world prove that as much as having the right theory helps, the one way to make your business work in the real world is to get out there and start *doing*.

Your brand will encounter challenges that not all your planning will prepare you for. So remember that your ability to adapt to the changes ahead will define the future of your freshly baked brand.

Each chocolate by Ryan L. Foote is a small 3D-printed work of art, and the packaging's complex design reflects this idea

"We knew what we wanted pretty clearly. Do you then know what's going to happen? No; but a business plan in itself can help a bit. It's not something we regularly refer back to, nor something that we look at weekly at all, but it is important to do it. It can help you understand where the business pitfalls might be."

—

PATRICK MERTENS &
INGE LIJNEN – CHOCOLADEHUIS BOON

This secondary product by Chocoladehuis BOON uses cacao to create a traditional Belgian liquor

CHAPTER 4

CREATE YOUR BRAND

Sebastian Pettersson finds a fun way to sign his creations while staying true to his signature style: surprising and clean design, austere looks, and recognisable flavours

Your brand is not only THE FOUNDATION for your business' success. It's the red thread that keeps it together, from new product ideas and social media strategies, to opening a new store. Regardless of whether it operates in a B2B or B2C market, building a strong brand is crucial for any business.

A brand is more than just a logo or a catchy slogan; it encompasses the entire experience that customers have with your business. Just like a weak branding can bring down your success, a strong brand can help you differentiate your business from competitors, build trust with customers and ultimately drive sales.

IN A B2C CONTEXT, building a strong brand can be especially important, as consumers are often looking for products and services that they can identify with on a personal level. A strong brand can help you build an emotional connection with customers and create loyalty over time.

IN A B2B CONTEXT, a strong brand can be equally important, as businesses are often looking for partners they can trust, to consistently deliver high-quality products or services. A strong brand can help you establish the credibility and trust you need in the eyes of potential partners.

In both contexts or routes to market, a strong brand can also help you command higher prices for your products or services, as customers are often willing to pay more for products or services that they perceive as high-quality or prestigious. Overall, building a strong brand should be a top priority for any business, whether it operates in a B2B or B2C market.

To make sure your brand withstands the passing of time and the rapid and unexpected changes of our fast-paced world, the first step is to create a solid brand identity.

> **"We made the decision to go for a premium brand positioning. Premium meant not only the chocolates and assortment, but also the packaging, display settings and so on."**
>
> MIROSLAW PELCZAR – M. PELCZAR CHOCOLATIER

"Years after the 2AM bar opened, came the chocolate factory. The bar is called 2am: dessertbar, while the chocolates are under my name. You can't immediately start a business and just call it 'Janice Wong'. Like, people need to know who you are and what you do first.

So, branding needs time. I mean, it needs a lot of tender, loving care. It's like a little baby. You have to let it evolve; you have to take care of it.

Today, my brands really resonate with my personality. They're not just a name."

JANICE WONG – JANICE WONG PURE IMAGINATION | 2AM: DESSERTBAR | SOFTHAUS

If you want consumers to form a genuine connection with your brand, you have to know who you are. Shaping your brand identity will not help grow a steady customer base, but it will uncover what makes you relevant in today's competitive market.

This is the case of JANICE WONG. Proud owner of three brands, all tied to who she is as a professional chocolatier and artist. Just like you, Janice had to know herself in order to create a business around her persona:

"A curator of food experiences. That's how I saw myself. Based on that, I decided to create a business where chocolate and pastry are my medium."

Just like Janice, BERNARD PROOT understands he sells more than delicious products in the well-know chocolate business he and his wife have built over the years: DelRey. Together, Bernard and Anne offer a legacy and a concept:

"For many, 'Belgian' is a symbol of craftsmanship and great taste. We play our card of 'Belgian Artisan Chocolatier'."

Janice and Bernard created businesses that are intrinsically linked to who they are as individuals. An approach that was also taken by Sebastian Pettersson. But in this case, he became the brand himself.

SEB PETTERSSON is not only an acclaimed chocolatier; he is a brand that started getting traction thanks to social media:

"I've always been very strict to what my Instagram is supposed to look like and I stick to that. If I want crispy pictures, I don't post iPhone photos just because I'm out of content. I didn't sit down and make a brand book for this, but if you're not so sure about your own brand and what you want to do, I think that's a very smart way to start it. Stick to that at least for a while, even if you feel it's not working.
I've denied so many collaborations with other companies because it doesn't fit me, so it doesn't fit my brand. I'm selective with the sponsors and the partners that I work with too. It's not being cocky or anything, it's just that you need to respect your own brand."

A brand's identity is something that should be present at the beginning of your journey as a chocolate business owner. This identity will stay with you for a long time. Continuing with their family business, the MORENO BROTHERS understand the power of who you are as a brand and the importance of staying true to it over the years:

"Brands have an ego. So, you have to be able to manage that ego, not in the perspective of yourself but of the brand. So actually, what we did last year was kind of a brand architecture analysis to be able to study how the brand was positioned and was being used right now, how it had been used in the past and the changes that happened in the last 90 years. We tried to unify everything so that you have something that is really cohesive. When people look at the brand, it doesn't matter which way you look at it, everything has the same feeling."

The triangular bonbons by Davide Comaschi are considered a premium offer for their taste and their luxurious shape and colours

To start shaping your own brand's identity, you need to start with the basics. It's not necessary to come up with the following brand elements in a specific order, but they should all be present as you create your brand. Because, as DAVIDE COMASCHI reminds starting (and experienced) artisan chocolate business owners, brand elements are all interconnected:

"What gives strength to the brand is the transparency and genuine identity I want to transmit with it. Also, the world of chocolate is so connected to art and design, enhancing its perception as a high-end product. The elements that impact the identity also impact the shop, the website and the overall perception and communication of the brand. So, coherence is everything: you need to deliver on your promise and to exceed expectations."

Although the order of the elements doesn't alter the result, it is important to remember that they should work together. In the following real-life examples, you'll see how all brand pieces come together as one.

1 Name

Brainstorming name options is like navigating a labyrinth. We talked about it with NIKKI THAKKER, and she opened up about her journey and the challenges that came when choosing a name for her chocolate business, éntisi:

"Choosing a name was the most challenging and most time-consuming part. There were hundreds of names that I was thinking of and that a lot of other people were suggesting. My husband told me that in Europe there were a lot of chocolatiers who named their businesses after themselves. I said, '*I'm not sure Nikki Chocolates is going to sound good*'. But he encouraged me to keep it close to my name. At the same time, we were asking people what they thought about the options. There were a lot of mixed reviews. Suddenly, my husband and I thought, *'why don't we name it éntisi?'*. So, Nikki Thakker Chocolates is N-T-C. We took the letters and wrote them as éntisi. So, the name has no specific meaning really, it came from my name. After that, we ran it across people a lot of them thought it was related to enticing something, enticing your mind, your senses. So that came across as quite interesting."

Éntisi presents its chocolates in a carefully designed shop that emanates warmth and an Indo-European type of luxury

Just like Nikki experienced, brand names are not only powerful because they represent your business, but because people might find a meaning in them that you might not have thought of.

And although there is no wrong or right way to choose a name for your business, we suggest you first ask yourself:

Will my brand have a personal or a non-personal name?

The answer to this question will help you brainstorm name possibilities and stir them in the right direction. So go ahead and ask yourself this question. And to get you going, keep KIRSTEN TIBBALLS' advice close to home:

"I think when someone is starting a business, the last thing they think of is a succession plan. But I think that's important when you're starting a business, to have a look at your long-term goals. Do you want to work in this business for 50 years or do you want to build it up and sell it after 25 years? I think using your personal name can make it challenging in the long run. If the business revolves around your personality and your name, it can be more difficult to sell than if it has a name that best reflects the products that you are creating."

Personal brand name

A personal brand name means using your name (or a clear derivative of it) to represent your business. Using a personal name isn't negative or positive in itself. Nonetheless, considering the repercussions of doing it before making the final call is a must.

JULIAN ROSE is one of the many business owners who went down this road since he perceived it as the most logical choice at the time:

"I think that for me, my name was the logical choice, because I'm known in the industry. If I would put any brand name, I think then you have to explain what the brand is. Whereas I have the advantage of being in the space for long enough that I'm known. My name is my brand, but I think commercially, a non-personal brand name is probably better."

If a chocolatier is already known for their creations (or for another reason), starting a brand under a personal name can help with brand awareness and initial success rate. When starting his journey as a business owner, MIROSLAW PELCZAR followed the same path Julian did:

"I have used my own name for the company name because, when I was starting the business, I was Polish Pastry Champion and had some other titles. I had decided to make use of the fact that my name was a bit recognisable in the industry. Then we just added 'chocolatier' to define the type of business."

"When brainstorming for a name, the marketing agency said, 'just use JITSK'. At the beginning I didn't want that because it's too much ego, and because my team is very important to me. But, at some point you want to be unique and I have never come across anyone with the same name. That was good for the business. So now, I think the name is good."

JITSK HEYNINCK – JITSK CHOCOLATES

Like Miroslaw's, a chocolatier's following can come from many places. Whether it's an established family business, social media or international championships. This was also the case of DAVIDE COMASCHI, who chose the name knowing the weight the World Chocolate Master competition had on a global scale:

"I chose to use my name because it had become relevant in the world of chocolate thanks to the World Chocolate Master championship. People would link my name not only with the brand, but see it as a guarantee of the quality of the product, since I'm always working hard in terms of quality, chocolate culture and innovation. So, I was ready to put my reputation on the line."

"How you're perceived matters. Customers don't always know artisanship; they might think everything they see in a popular store is artisanal. And perception is sometimes hard to break, so it can be tricky. For our brand identity, the notion of artisanship is important because, over the years we've built up a large regular customer base.

The restaurants know that we provide craftsmanship and not standard products. This is passed onto all our B2B customers; they know that we can do personalised work on a small scale and that the quality is good. Even the regular customers in the store know what to expect, and they also know the difference in quality and taste. So usually, I don't have to explain the artisanal concept much. All the different customers can experience the difference."

DAVID MAENHOUT – CHOCOLATIER M

Davide also understood the implications that would come from tying his business to him as an individual: consumers would make a direct connection between the business and the person.

But being a celebrity chef or a renowned personality in the world of artisan chocolate isn't the only reason behind success stories with personal brand names. When creating HÅKAN Chocolatier, HÅKAN MÅRTENSSON didn't make the choice out of reason, but out of passion:

"For me, putting your name on something says you're proud of your stuff. It says this is me, this is the intention of what I'm doing and this is nothing that I'm building to sell afterwards. This brand is going to be me. I remember it was really hard to find a name to build a brand, but I feel like if you're building a brand with your name attached to it, it's something that you won't surrender or give up. I could one day start another company that has another name, but it would never be so personal to me as this one."

If you're not a chocolate celebrity (quite yet), and you decide to use a personal brand name, it will require a bit more effort for customers to form a connection between your brand and what you have to offer.

But even if the challenges seem bigger when starting a brand under your name without a previous following, it doesn't necessarily mean it will impact the success of your business. MARIANE OLIVEIRA thought long and hard before choosing a name for Mary's Brigadeiro, and her story might inspire you to follow in her footsteps:

"I was trying to brainstorm a name that wasn't something crazy, but that also reminded me of Brazil or something related to it... I couldn't find one. One day, people started to say they were buying Mary's brigadeiros. And that's a very complicated word for the non-Brazilian or Spanish speaker. But I thought I could even use that as a marketing strategy even, the idea of people trying to pronounce it. At the time, one of my first mentors said, *'are you sure you want to put 'brigadeiro' in your business? Because in English we can't pronounce it'*. I replied, *'in 20 years you guys will be able to pronounce it'*. I chose to defend the name, it had to be brigadeiro. It's not a fudge, it's not a Brazilian truffle, it's a brigadeiro. I really wanted, in the future, when someone thought about a brigadeiro, to immediately think it's Mary's brigadeiro. This was a conscious decision."

Chocolate celebrity or not, there is something all these name-brands have in common: the person behind the name has married their business. This doesn't mean that divorce isn't possible, it means the association between the brand and name will be a long-lasting one.

Håkan Mårtensson always relies on high-quality images from professional photographers to build his brand's identity on social media platforms, website and other marketing channels

If you're leaning towards a personal brand name, let yourself be inspired by these success stories, but also remember that there are opinions on the other side of the spectrum. This is the case of Savour School by KIRSTEN TIBBALLS:

"Naming your business after yourself can be highly effective if you have a strong profile or celebrity status, as it can attract customers who recognise and trust you. This approach leverages your personal brand to boost business visibility and credibility. However, if you lack such a profile, planning for succession or selling the business can become challenging. In these cases, it's important to consider alternative ways for your business to grow and gain publicity without relying solely on your name. Unless you already have a significant following, using a personal brand name may not be the best strategy. While personal brand names work well for well-known individuals, they are typically the exception rather than the rule."

It's important to think of decisions like these, that impact the near and not-so-near future of your business. Maybe your business will expand into a franchise or spark the interest of big industry buyers, or maybe you'll create your own family legacy. Simply remember that with a personal brand name, you will be connected to the brand despite partnerships or ownership changes.

"I would say that my brand name is Seb Pettersson, while my 'real' name is Sebastian. I always introduce myself as Sebastian, but I would never write anything other than Seb Pettersson on social media. And this is basically because I thought the way I pronounce Sebastian and the way they write it in Swedish is one version, while it's another version in French, probably another in Spanish too. So if you think about 'Seb'... everyone can pronounce that."

SEBASTIAN PETTERSSON – SEB PETTERSSON

Non-personal brand name

Starting a business without a personal brand name doesn't mean you are less connected to your creations; it is purely a practical decision. Although passionately involved with their business, STEPHEN and SUN TRIGG decided to approach the choosing of the name Lauden Chocolate in a careful way:

"We were starting the company and couldn't think of a name. I wanted the name to sound prestigious, but didn't want it to be our name or surname. Because in the future, if we ever did want to sell it, I didn't want it tied to us. I think if your name is on the door, people are buying that. Then my wife said, '*what about my previous company name?*'. I honestly didn't really like it. I said, '*what does it even mean?*'. She said, '*it comes from the Latin cum laude, which means with pride or with honours*'. So, I was okay with that. I've never truly loved the name, it's sort of grown on me with time. This doesn't mean we knew where we'd end up, but we wanted to leave the option of selling open."

There might be something outside the world of chocolate that inspired you to start your business, a word that holds a special meaning to you as a chocolatier or that you simply like. This was the case of FAN YU, where he chose a fun play of words while making sure the name matched the rest of his brand's elements. After some thought, he ended up creating Nibbo:

"If you write a long brand name and have a simple store environment, that's kind of a conflict. That's why we have Nibbo. And, it's a pretty similar pronunciation to 'nibble'. You bite chocolate or you bite something, and 'nibbo' is just a cute way to say it. Also, it's easy for the Chinese market to pronounce and easy to remember, those were the first requirements for our brand name. Otherwise, it would've been quite hard to spread the brand image. As a plus, we also use the name to remind people of what they're eating... you know, cacao nibs!"

Fan believes the key is not to get lost in intricate words, and to find the balance between what inspires your brand and market practicality. Just like him, when JAP JOY created FIDÉE, he thought about what the brand name would be representing and how it would impact the brand perception among his target market:

"For Chinese people, if you're not a very old brand, like 100 years old, people would not use their names for their brands. Besides this, I wanted to focus on the products and not myself as an individual, so I chose not to use my name. I wanted to name the shop using the idea of the logo and concept instead. But, 'flower, sky, tree, land' was too long. After thinking, I noticed that in Chinese 'fidee' sounds similar to the words for flower and land. That's basically how I named the brand.

We then decided to spell the name with a double 'E' because it looks prettier compared to a single one. I also used the accent, because chocolate is something that comes from western countries and I wanted to represent that."

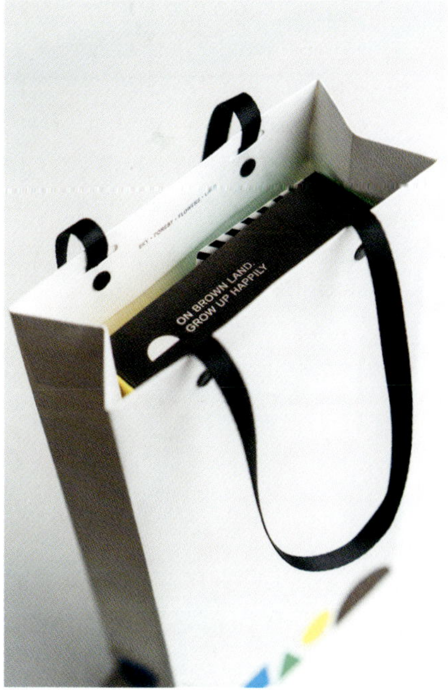

For a complete customer experience, Jap Joy offers branded bags that match all chocolate packagings

Personal or non-personal, the idea of simplicity when choosing a brand name seems to be present in most of these success stories. However, just like Mariane Oliveira did, don't forget to listen to your instincts!

2 Logo and visual elements

Visual elements are yet another piece of this brand puzzle we're putting together. Like the queen of chocolate said it herself, for a chocolate business to survive in today's world, it has to go beyond great artisan chocolate:

"When you build a brand, it's not just about the product. It's about the graphics, the name of your business, it's about what style of shop you have. I think people really need to take that into consideration, their packaging, the style, the fit, the branding. It's a full package. So, it's not just your ability to make chocolates anymore; that simply is not going to sell itself."

The Fidée packagings are created to fit each chocolate format

The first visual impression customers will have of your business will be your logo. As a distinctive mark that represents your brand (and separates it from others), the style and colours of your logo should evoke the identity of your business. When creating the aesthetics for his brand, this is how JAP JOY pieced together visual elements, along with the message he wanted his business to convey:

"This is our logo. It contains land, flower, trees and the sky. Those are our four elements. They represent our concept idea and the things that I hope people feel when they eat our chocolates: like they can go back to nature and feel there are elements from nature present in that bite."

Just like choosing a name for your business, a logo is a difficult choice and a decision that's long-lasting. Knowing that the logo would be a key component in positioning his brand in the Spanish market, ENRIC ROVIRA went all out and commissioned an expert to take care of it:

"My first big business investment was my logo, the identity of the business I was trying to create. I was in love with this minimalistic label of cava. So, I said, '*when I start my own business, I want the people who designed this to design my logo*'. And so it happened, even if this investment went against all the rules that I had learned from my family's business: don't spend money on packaging or image, what's important is the ingredients."

"The only way to do business with your own products is to have a strong brand and to be consistent with that brand."

JAP JOY – FIDÉE

"Our logo evolved. Every few years there was a little tweak. The choices had to do with our range and culinary path: we wanted to stand out!"

DAVID MAENHOUT – CHOCOLATIER M

Although a key component, you don't have to spend big to have a beautiful logo that represents your brand. As a matter of fact, many artisan chocolatiers started selling their products without having a brand name or an established visual identity. This was the case of the now-famous MARY'S BRIGADEIRO shop:

"In the beginning, it was really just white and brown, and I did feel like it was cold. As time went by, I thought I should create a logo, maybe draw a brigadeiro, but nothing came. I was feeling frustrated about it. I was completely lost, but sometimes you need to get lost to find yourself.
While searching for inspiration, I found two separate backgrounds online. Someone was selling these two digital designs. When I looked at them, they reminded me of a cocoa forest, and it brought me excitement and happiness. One is the mix of colours and the other is a drawing. After I saw them, I bought the rights to use them for my brand."

Whether you go for an image, a free template, or go the extra mile and create your logo yourself (or commission someone to do it), inspiration can come from the most unexpected of places.

This was the case of STEPHEN TRIGG and his wife as they discussed their visual identity:

"The logo is a giant oil painting that's in our living room, a painting that existed long before we had the company.
My wife did a series of paintings over the summer once. And this particular one, every day, I came home from work, and I looked at it like '*wow, that's really beautiful, darling*'. After about a month, I suddenly realised '*it's not getting nicer*'. The lady's profile was just changing every day, I thought it was never going to be finished. So, I took it and hung it on the wall.

When we were thinking about what to use for the logo, Sun said, '*what about the painting?*' And it did fit the brand on two aspects. Whenever she made a bonbon, someone would taste it and think it was nice. But the feeling of making that bonbon again the next day would be nicer. That was one thing. And the second was that we needed something visual. We're not Coca-Cola, so we needed a picture that would sink into someone consciousness, something people would remember.
It was all very strategic, from a personal and from a branding point of view."

"In a multifunctional world, being identified is important. Our brand lets us be identified as artisans in all the business divisions and product categories that we offer."

MARCO INFANTE – CASA INFANTE

"There is a bit of a disconnect sometimes with people, so I think you can't underestimate the power of branding, marketing, aesthetics and all of that stuff. That's why I put loads of effort into the packaging aspect, probably far more than a lot of businesses we knew when we started. And it's interesting, because fast forward five years, and now that's just a standard practice, in the sense that you wouldn't get any shelf space in any decent retailer without having good packaging."

CALUM HAGGERTY – COCO CHOCOLATIER

Wherever you get inspiration from, remember that simple designs aren't only easier to remember, they also have the power to give your brand the visual flexibility it needs: shop signs, business cards, packaging, social media profile pictures and even a giant billboard (if the time comes). Your logo should be future-proof, able to adapt to digital and printed formats in different sizes and spaces.

Because you will need to replicate your logo for multiple uses, consistency is also expected from the colours used in your visual elements. Choose a limited number of colours, write down their digital codes and stick to them throughout your journey as an entrepreneur.

FAN, from Nibbo, knew from day one that this kind of consistency was key when it came to creating a strong and memorable brand identity. So, he made sure that his visual elements were not only part of his logo and shop, but were also present in his packaging:

"We consider the name and the visual aspect as a whole thing, so we developed them together. We know what we want to express, and we know what we want customers to see. Something simple, nice and clean, with flavour-related and colourful packagings. At the beginning, our packaging was not like that though. It was quite 'the Aussie style': simple, light colour, some beautiful characters. But it turns out people here in China feel like it looks beautiful but not palatable. So, in situations like this, you definitely have to do something to illustrate the concept of bean-to-bar chocolate on the packaging to educate your local market."

3 Tone of voice

CALUM HAGGERTY believes in the selling power of stories regardless of the industry. And this is a concept he held close to him as he crafted the identity behind COCO Chocolatier:

"Being in business is telling stories, that's all it is. You need to have an interesting story, you need to have all these hooks that you can continuously talk about."

From Mary's Brigadeiro, MARIANE also believes that the ability to tell stories is the last element that will help you shape your brand identity and eventually be a driver for sales:

"If we think about it, it's not just the chocolate. It's the story behind it. The story behind the founder, the ingredients that they are buying from all the local businesses they're supporting. The artisanal chocolate in that sense, I feel is not even a concept — it's a lifestyle."

Just like your name and visual elements, what you say and the way you speak (and write) is also part of who you are as a brand. Customers expect a brand's tone of voice to match the essence of the brand. So, when talking to your customers, writing information on your website and even replying to emails or messages on social media, keep DAVIDE COMASCHI's professional advice in mind:

"The coherence in your speech is everything. If you communicate one thing but offer another, it becomes absolutely counter-productive. So, coherence when communicating things is the first thing."

PROTECT YOUR BRAND

Enric Rovira has consistently pioneered avant-garde aesthetics and flavour combinations in product design and packaging, reflecting his unique perspective on his Catalan homeland

RENATA ARASSIRO understands the implications of respecting you brand identity. After years of experience as the owner and chef in RENATA ARASSIRO CHOCOLATES and a renowned teacher for professional chefs, she has advice for all of those who are starting a business or continuing an existing one.

Advice that will help them protect the brand they've created as they progress as artisan chocolate entrepreneurs:

"You always want to grow, it's natural, you want to make money, but you have to grow naturally. Don't lose your essence. I've been here for 15 years because I didn't lose my essence. I always offered the clients the best product I can get. We just buy fresh products, we don't put anything that is artificial or synthetic. We only use fresh fruits and fresh ingredients. My identity, since I was a beginner until now, is that I always use very good quality products and I'm always innovating."

Work, time, and money flow into creating a brand, and protecting it starts long before you start selling. Protecting your brand is about staying true to who you are, but also taking all the legal steps to take care of what you've created.

Research to get the right kind of insurance over intellectual property (such as original recipes), name patents, and visual copyrights.

"It's really difficult to keep the brand identity super tight. We realised that it's super important to reanalyse your entire structure and reunite everything every few years. It's an investment that is going to make your positioning much stronger. This is one of the things that made us survive so many years, and actually kept us on top of the pastry world in Spain all this time: doing things in a way that's always identifiable."

JACOBO & PABLO MORENO – MALLORCA

“One way of taking care of your brand is making sure that the raw materials are always top quality, just like the team. There has to be close contact with the people I’m working with. We all have to share the work philosophy and the know-how of the brand.”

DAVIDE COMASCHI – DAVIDE COMASCHI

EXPAND YOUR BRAND IDENTITY TO **BRAND EXPERIENCE**

If you want to go from brand identity to brand experience too, it's important to ensure that all aspects of your business are aligned with your values and messaging. This includes every aspect of your business, from product development and customer service to marketing and sales.

COCO Chocolatier tablet wrappers are created by local or international designers and artists, elevating the bars into sought-after gifts

Brand identity and brand experience are closely related, but they are not the same thing. While we've seen the components of a brand's identity, and how it refers to the visual and verbal elements that make up that brand; brand experience refers to the feelings and thoughts that customers have when interacting with a brand, including the experience when discovering, choosing and ordering your story and products. A brand experience doesn't stop there, but it extends from customer service to the unboxing of your products.

One of the greatest examples of brand experience is Apple. From the minute you come across an Apple iPhone's publicity, to ordering it, receiving the product and unboxing it: they're all building up a customer journey meant to satisfy an experience that's unique to this brand.

Let's take this example and transport it to the food and beverage industry now: think of Starbucks. You're not just buying a cup of coffee, where you pay for the costs of sourcing, roasting, grinding beans and making the pour. You're tapping into the Starbucks environment experience, for which you're prepared to pay for a higher margin.

Can't wait to take your brand identity and turn it into your brand experience? In the next chapter, we will be deep-diving into how you can create your own brand experience as we break down the following steps:

1. **Define your brand values**
2. **Understand your audience**
3. **Create a customer journey map**
4. **Develop a brand strategy**
5. **Make use of your visual identity**
6. **Implement your brand strategy**
7. **Monitoring and improvement**

Now, since brand experience is such a crucial domain in the entrepreneurial world, we'll dedicate the following chapter solely to it. With the combined knowledge from this chapter and Chapter 5, you will not only have a solid brand identity. You will also be ensuring that it is aligned with your brand experience so that every customer interaction successfully reflects who your brand is and its reason for existing.

CHAPTER 5

IT'S ALL ABOUT THE EXPERIENCE

More than chocolate,
Nibbo by Fan Yu is a brand
that offers an aesthetic
experience for the senses

WONG
JANICE WONG
JANICE WONG

Consumers don't only buy products;

THEY BUY EXPERIENCES.

From discovering your unique story, to picking their heart's choice among your chocolate creations, to how you serve them — your business' success depends on how your customers experience your brand as a whole.

According to DAVIDE COMASCHI, one of the elements behind the success of artisan chocolate is its ability to offer not only a unique brand, but an experience that's different to the rest:

"Artisanal chocolate is about giving a unique experience to the consumer! Artisanship is in the work that goes behind the product. The thinking about the product, and the crafting it.

The idea of artisan chocolate is that of a fresh product. A product that is consumed in a short term is what creates this unforgettable experience. This also implies the importance of the ability to communicate this. Because, as you taste a fresh and artisanal product, there should be an important storytelling behind this."

Your offer, whether it's your core or secondary products, will become part of what Davide describes about the artisan chocolate experience. But there's more — besides the artisan character of your products, there will be other elements that are part of the experience you offer your clients.

This means that we can define brand experience as the complete sensory and emotional reaction people have when in contact with your brand. But said brand experience is not a natural consequence of the existence of the brand — it is something that's consciously crafted.

From the way people look at your brand to the things they feel when they encounter your products — as a business owner, you have to approach a brand experience as a buying process in which your brand has a desired effect on the clients at all times.

Janice Wong's signature bonbons and chocolate crayons are the expression of her purpose to elevate confectionery into edible art

Ryan L. Foote celebrates art holistically: exceptional bonbon shapes, elaborate flavour combinations, and unique ceramics designed for his hot chocolate and bonbon presentations

FROM PRODUCT TO

EXPERIENCE MARKETING

Experience marketing is a strategy that focuses on creating a memorable and engaging experience for customers, rather than simply promoting a product or service. By creating an experience that customers enjoy and want to share with others, companies can generate buzz, build loyalty and ultimately drive sales.

In the previous chapter, we introduced a brand known to sell more than just coffee. Let's retake that example for a bit: it's highly likely that you've consumed, or at least know, the coffee giant, Starbucks. Regardless of how you feel about their offer, there is one thing they are experts in: experience marketing.

The Starbucks marketing team understands brand experience is the key to consumers spending significantly more than the instrumental cost (sourcing coffee beans, roasting and making a pour) on their products. The reason is simple. The Starbucks experience makes the brand desirable beyond their offer — consumers are driven not only to have a drink, but to *be* there. And to be part of the Starbucks experience, they're ready to accept higher margins for each of the core products the brand has to offer.

So, what's the secret behind marketing this experience? Shaping the brand and its shops in such a way that clients create and grow an emotional connection with the business.

Ryan L. Foote's take on a hot chocolate cup: a ceramic mug that also serves as decorative art piece

For example, no matter where you are in the world, Starbucks shops will offer a cosy and welcoming atmosphere that feels *familiar*. It will have comfortable seats, friendly staff who call you by your first name and particular decor that makes you feel at home. This comfortable environment isn't an accident, it's been designed to represent each and every single Starbucks around the world.

The result of crafting this experience in each of all their shops results in customers having a sense of longing for the place. Clients start choosing it as the designated hangout spot, a space where they can sit by themselves to read or a reliable wi-fi location if they want to work or need a quick connection.

All these traits build up to customers staying long after their first coffee. Ultimately, this leads to them purchasing additional items such as pastries, sandwiches and different kinds of snacks. Yes, even if they don't necessarily plan for it in the first place!

Another way that experience marketing is known to drive sales is by offering unique or exclusive experiences that customers can't get anywhere else.

For example, a coffee shop might host a latte art competition or offer a special coffee blend that is only available for a limited time. The list of exclusive experiences is unlimited, yet the concept is always the same: creating a sense of excitement for what may soon be gone. The notion of exclusivity is almost always a trigger to increase clients' willingness to spend more on a product or service.

Additionally, experience marketing can be used to leverage your brand's digital presence and word-of-mouth awareness. Creating buzz around a brand is a strategy that even the biggest (and most successful) businesses in the world have been using to their advantage for a long time.

"Half of our first store was transparent because I did not want to lock myself away, I wanted to be in touch with the customers and the outside world even on the saddest winter days. This gave me a sense of connection with the world and also made it enjoyable to work. So, it was an experience for the customers but also for us. And, I remember well how our customers reacted to seeing how things were made, people are so fascinated by that! I don't really know how else to put it. It gives them confidence, seeing how the chocolates are made and how much love we have for what we do."

DAVID MAENHOUT – CHOCOLATIER M

Just like these businesses, you can encourage customers to share their experiences on social media or leave reviews. Companies leveraging the power of being online can create a sense of community among clients and drive potential new interest to their brand. Increasing the digital buzz around a business often results in increased online or foot traffic that translates into more sales, even if the prices are slightly higher than the competition.

A chocolatier that has used the power of social media and word of mouth to her advantage is NIKKI THAKKER, who turned her opening day into an exclusive event where people with a strong online standing could spread awareness about éntisi and what the brand stands for:

"We had about a two-day event where we had people visiting us. They were coming in every day to the boutique, and we would make them taste everything and gave them a little gift to take back home to share it with their family."

This is the moment of truth for your brand experience — the minute a customer encounters it. This interaction is part of the customer experience and the way it goes about should never be an accident. Customer experiences should be shaped with strategic goals in mind.

Because of the ever-changing behaviour of consumers, customer experience is subject to change, which means it's something to always keep an eye out for. The well-loved Spanish bakery, Mallorca, is a pastry shop that has been successful in the national and international market for decades. Despite years of success, the owners keep investing in learning and developing new ways to enhance their customer experience each year. JACOBO AND PABLO MORENO manage this family legacy, and they told us how one of their experience marketing efforts was all about packaging:

"80% of people buy chocolate as a gift. So, you have to offer an amazing experience from the moment they see the box, to the way they open it, and even to the explanations they find inside. This means you have to work around it a lot.

We've been investing a lot of money and research to actually engineer our own packaging with magnets. We want to create a package that opens smoothly, that you don't have to pull apart or struggle with. We usually work a lot in all parts of the customer experience journey, especially the part when the product is bought and leaves your control. Our goal is to make the packaging not complicated, but playful for people to enjoy."

Whether it's an event, the way you welcome consumers into your store or the shape of the boxes that carry your products, the customer experience you create is almost as important as the products you serve.

Now, regardless of where you focus your brand experience efforts, and whether you go for a traditional or ground-breaking one. The key is to craft an experience that carries the essence your business' identity.

But, customer experience is not only the foundation of your brand's reputation. Did you know it will impact your selling prices as well? Your product margins could be increased according to the type and quality of experiences you create for your target audience — are you ready to create one?

"Look at an artisan chocolatier and at the people who are going to invest in their product. They see it as a special treat. And it's either a treat for someone else, because it's a gift, or a special treat you buy for yourself that you want to indulge in. So, for me, an artisan has a responsibility to produce something that is a beautiful experience."

KIRSTEN TIBBALLS – SAVOUR SCHOOL

A UNIQUE BRAND EXPERIENCE

The success of the customer experience you create will depend on what your clients expect to encounter and what they end up encountering. If you're ready to design or revamp your customer experience, there's a golden rule to have in mind:

Create expectations. EXCEED THEM.

When thinking about how to impact his consumers with something different, HÅKAN MÅRTENSSON played around with his creations until he found a way to take them to the next level. Although the flavour of his chocolates would already offer his US clientele an experience of Nordic flavours, he wanted this experience to not only be tasted, but to be *felt*:

"The coolest thing I've done is to create something that I haven't seen before: a different way to eat a bonbon.

There's this one bonbon, you cannot bite it off. You have to put in your mouth, wait for two seconds and then you bite into it. It's called Passion Fruit Explosion, designed so that the caramel fills up your whole mouth once it bursts.

Another one is the Gucci Truffle, which has salt on top. To eat this bonbon, you turn it upside down to get the salt straight on the tongue. You wait for two seconds and then you bite into it. But it's not a shell, it's Norwegian brown cheese, very caramelised. When I explain all of this, I see clients standing and waiting for these experiences. Then, all of a sudden, they eat the bonbons and they're getting the full effect of the experience, because you told them how to eat them. Basically, they're coming in with an expectation and you surpassed that."

As he explains it, when consumers walk through the doors of HÅKAN Chocolatier, they expect, at least, to encounter good-tasting products. What they don't initially expect however, is the master chocolatier to welcome them and personally explain how they can get more than what they paid for.

This is one way you can exceed expectations too: through customer experience. Take the concept of what Håkan is doing here, which is using the surprise factor. The best part? You don't have to go out of your way or your budget to make it happen.

Håkan Mårtensson fills his creations with unexpected flavours inspired by his Scandinavian roots

Experiences are for all the senses

Before giving life to your brand's customer experience, you want to take into consideration that there are multiple brand elements that you can use to make it happen, and that there are many different ways of playing with the senses to create that experience.

Take the example of the AL-GHRAWI FAMILY in Lebanon. With over a century of experience in the industry, and having grown so much that their sweet assortment is in the hundreds, they know that the artisan chocolate experience is about more than chocolates that look and taste good:

"The sensory power of chocolate, in relation to its looks, is so great that it can communicate with the consumer. In the case of taste and smell, these are closely linked and add to the experience. We use chocolate to create an experience around other products, by coating all kinds of sweets that are totally unrelated to it. We also consider how colours and textures change with the seasons, so we use red during Christmas, green and yellow during Easter, pink and blue in spring, etc."

When entering their family business shops, customers can immerse all their senses in the world of chocolate. While the rich scent already gives them a pre-taste of what the products will taste like, the colours on display guide them through an assortment that offers them a product for each special occasion.

This is just one example of how a brand can be experienced. Besides being multi-sensory, remember that when you create your own brand experience, you can tailor it to any stage of the customer journey (Chapter 3).

We've mentioned that the customer journey encompasses all the steps a client goes through when in contact with your shop, from getting to know your brand to actually making a purchase. Inspired by Lama Bassam Al-Ghrawi's story, you might want to take the next elements into account when creating a bespoke customer journey in your brick-and-mortar chocolate shop.

Many Al-Ghrawi products highlight the Lebanese roots of the family business in their ingredients

1 Taste

Tasting chocolate is pretty straightforward. But what if you offered customers not only amazing-tasting artisan products, but an experience they had to undergo in order to taste it?

Think back to JANICE WONG. She is the link between her three brands — an artistic mind. This artistic essence lives in the chocolates she creates, and she makes sure she crafts experiences around how people can taste them:

"What we did in one event really blew everybody's mind: we covered the walls with chocolate ornaments. When the art unveiled, people were like, '*how did you do something like that?*'. The texture, the paint, it is all edible. It's an evolution of art concepts, where you kind of destroy the art. The art still remains art even though you're encouraged to destroy it. And then, then you also smell the wall, you get to experience it with all your senses."

Edible art as a concept has been around for a long time, but Janice made it her own when she asked people at her shows to actually *taste* the art they were asked to break apart.

Kirsten Tibballs showcases her skills by hand-crafting moulded bonbons in one of her workshops

2 Sight

Colours, decoration and even online assets (photos, videos, designs). Branded visual elements don't only make your brand identity, they are powerful tools that have the ability to transmit your purpose and showcase your offer in a way that fits your business.

RENATA ARASSIRO finds inspiration in the bright colours that are known to represent the joyful Brazilian culture. To differentiate her offer and let consumers know her bonbons were a special experience, she used colours and shapes to create an assortment that excites the vision and invites people in:

"People come and start buying with their eyes. There has to be shine, you have to have a different appeal. So, when they see our products, they see the value. Then, they eat them and get why the price is not the same price if they go to another shop."

Notice how Renata creates a visual experience for her clients at first, experience that helps justify higher price margins at the time of the purchase.

3 Hearing

From crafting an online environment to designing a unique atmosphere inside your shop, music and other sound elements can help you tailor your customer experience to immerse clients in your brand.

Well intertwined with the artistic scene, COCO Chocolatier's CALUM HAGGERTY made sure no form of art escaped the building of his brand experience:

"We're talking about 'The Art of Chocolate'. But if we talk about art, being artistic and creative, we've got the visual side and we've got the music side as well. I'm talking about videos that are about chocolate, art, design, culture and music. Most people probably wouldn't catch the music thing, but to me, this was quite important."

4 Smell

Have you ever walked into a shop and been surrounded by its scents? Being in the artisan chocolate business, you can play with your ingredients' aromas to transport your consumers into your offer the minute they set foot in your shop.

Believe it or not, the smell of chocolate as part of the customer experience is a strategy used by successful business owners, including JUSTINE LANNOO from Goût Fou:

"When people enter the shop, they have a complete experience. You step into the shop, and it smells like chocolate. You don't have that in every chocolate shop anymore. People are attracted by that, so when we are roasting nuts, we open the grids and that smell goes out and people come in spontaneously. There is a certain experience when you come to us, and I think that's important."

"We are in the shopping street in Zele and chose that building because it's 19 metres of glass front. Also, when you are in the shop, our counter runs through the glass wall, so you have a feeling that you are also suddenly brought into the studio. That's the concept I wanted to work towards, the 'I'm at home in this chocolatery' feeling."

JUSTINE LANNOO – GOÛT FOU

5 Touch

From furniture to packaging, you don't have to invest big to transmit the soul of your brand through all the elements your clients can touch.

When FAN planned on opening Nibbo, he noticed that the target audience in China wouldn't react the same way to the market in Australia. He had to impart knowledge about the added value of artisanal chocolate. So, he chose an interactive way to do so:

"No one had successfully done bean-to-bar chocolate in China. I noticed that the market in China did not value the same things as the Australian market. Maybe because the concept was new, or because there wasn't enough information to understand it. So, we had to adapt.

We found a Chinese designer who would redesign the whole packaging based on the image of the brand. We created a colourful and easy-to-remember packaging that would trigger curiosity when people saw it, '*is this a chocolate? Is this a gift shop?*' People wanted to enter the store to find out what was inside that packaging. So, the colours and the whole design became a tool.

Key information about the cacao and that specific chocolate is on the packaging. The origins, the flavours, all of it. The cards inside the packaging, where this information is, are also collectable. We wanted people to find an easy way into the artisan chocolate world and a way to get involved with it."

These are simply examples of how different chocolatiers from around the world have used different sensory triggers to create or enhance their brand experience.

"The central idea of having an open shop was, first of all, the smell of course. Chocolate smells nice, and I think that already entices most people to buy. But also, before, people could see me — it was an open studio, and they could see me through a glass wall in between. Now, we've renovated the shop without a glass wall so people can just walk through if they wish. We can make a visual partition with a telescopic sales block that sometimes has products on it too. Basically, we wanted to make everything movable. There are unique pieces in it that create a unique experience. This has only made us stronger."

OLIVIER WILLEMS – OLIVIER WILLEMS

However, brand experience goes beyond leveraging a stimulus, it's about where this stimulus can be found. Whether it's your packaging, your social media strategy, or the people you collaborate with, there are no limits to how you can express your brand to your clients.

Take a look at MIROSLAW PELCZAR. When he opened his shop, he didn't only want it to be a place where people bought chocolate and enjoyed a coffee. So, he transformed the entire shop in an experience on its own.

He created a sort of chocolate museum, where people could discover his brand by being immersed in his vision, the origins of his products and the timeless history behind chocolate:

"The idea was to create a space where something is happening all the time. I wanted a place with a lot of chocolate, machines, information about chocolate production, moving elements, chocolate sculptures and fountains, and so much more. This is why in the store, customers can find out all about chocolate production. It is a kind of chocolate museum and shop at the same time. We even host school trips here, and people travel from all over the country just to see it.
Our customers, after crossing the doors of our shops, are totally immersed in the chocolate world with all their senses! This is very important to me in everything that I do: trying to appeal to all the senses. For that, I use different colours, flavours and textures in my products too."

Mirosław Pelczar welcomes a school group to the museum-like atmosphere of his shop in Poland

As you've seen, expectations can be exceeded with unexpected unique packaging, the way you eat a product and even how you set up your shop. However, they can also be exceeded with intangible goods too.

INGE LIJNEN, one of the owners of Chocoladehuis BOON, opened up about how a little intervention in each purchase can make a huge difference:

"A handwritten card is always included, and I do it myself. I write a 'thank you' after checking who it's being sent to. And, no two cards are the same, right? Because all the little messages are personal. It might be that a person is sick, or that it's for a family member on a special occasion. Because of this, you get a tremendous number of responses, and I do it for our physical store as well as for the web shop."

Other ways to make customers feel special can be mentioning them on social media after an order has been placed or making your customer service very personalised. In the case of SEB PETTERSSON, he uses an intangible good to take his clients and potential clients by surprise. He leverages the contrast between the way he looks as an Instagram influencer and his soft personality once you meet him:

"Everyone gets super surprised, '*Sebastian has tattoos all over his body, he looks a little angry in every picture*'. But, if you meet me, I'm super humble and honest and really like to meet people. So, everyone is surprised when they walk into a class and I try to make them laugh, like a comedy show."

Just like Sebastian does, in a fast-moving world, making an effort to create genuine relations with your customers takes them by surprise in a positive way. And you don't need a separate budget to do so!

Now, it's time to look back at the brand identity you've built (Chapter 4), because this is where you'll get the right ideas to begin creating a brand experience that is completely unique.

"The store has to be a property with charm. That's something I've always said from the beginning. A customer comes into the chocolatery and that should be an experience, they should be able to look around and think, '*what happens here?*' With us, you have the workshop, but you also have questions about the property, '*what was this before?*' These were horse stables, so you can offer an explanation to customers, create another story with that. Basically, I don't want just a storefront that doesn't tell me anything."

JITSK HEYNINCK – JITSK CHOCOLATES

The Jitsk Chocolates shop also offers a coffee shop service with drinks and gelato options to be enjoyed in-store or to take away

CREATE YOUR OWN
BRAND EXPERIENCE

You have seen some of the most crucial elements that can be used to design a unique brand experience, and the importance of having this experience in place. You've also read about successful chocolatiers from around the world and how they have taken this theory and put it into practice.

Now, it is time for you to create a unique experience for your business.

As we've said, crafting a great brand experience requires a deliberate and thoughtful approach. This is why, you can follow practical steps to start building an experience that represents your brand. Here's how you can tackle the process yourself:

1 Define your brand values

Start by defining the core values that your brand represents. These values will guide all aspects of your brand experience, they should be reflected in every interaction with customers.

2 Understand your audience

You've done your market research, narrowed down your target audience, and if you've gone the extra mile, you've also worked on the different personas that make up this audience (Chapter 3). Use the insights you've collected to outline your audience's needs and preferences. Empathising with your audience will help you create a brand experience that resonates with them, creating a genuine connection.

3 Create a customer journey map

Map out each of the customer journey steps and identify their touchpoints. In other words, write down each of the stages where customers interact with your brand. This includes everything from your website and social media channels to your physical store or office. For example, if you want to have an online and offline business, include your customers' in-person contact with your shop, as well as the online one. Go into as much detail as possible — if your online presence is made up of a website and different social media channels, you can separate them into different touchpoints and set specific goals for each one.

4 Develop a brand strategy

Based on your previous research and your customer journey map, develop an experience strategy. Remember that at all times, your strategy should align with your brand value, general goals and purpose. To create said strategy, begin by outlining the objective of the overall brand experience, and add action points or tasks on how you will create a consistent brand experience across all touchpoints.

5 Make use of your visual identity

Developing a visual identity was one of the steps you followed to create a strong and consistent brand (Chapter 4). This is the perfect time to revise your visual elements and make sure they are coherent, that they reflect your brand values and resonate with your target audience too. Elements such as your logo, colour scheme, typography and imagery will be partially what defines the engagement between your business and your consumers.

6 Implement your brand strategy

You've used all your brand identity elements to create a strategy that brings your brand experience to life. Now it's time to start implementing it across all the touchpoints you've identified. Remember to keep track of the type and date of the actions you use to implement this strategy, this will help you track your performance: if something is really successful, or something needs improvement, write it down! So you can build a consistent messaging and brand experience that's always on the rise.

7 Monitoring and improvement

Regularly monitor customer feedback and engagement metrics (such as social media statistics, number of phone calls, number of satisfied clients, positive-negative feedback ratio) to identify areas for improvement and ensure that your brand experience is always evolving, as your consumers' preferences and buying behaviours will most likely will.

With the work you've done so far, and by following this methodology, you are ready to create a brand experience that truly represents your business, that resonates with your target audience and that is able to reflect your values and uniqueness. The results? Real customer engagement that has the power to turn occasional clients into loyal consumers over time.

"For setting up the whole brand, other than the logo, I wanted to design a shop that feels very natural. We have a lot of plants, bricks and specific shapes to give customers an environment that corresponds with our logo and ideas. So, we work a lot on conceptual graphic design, like how we display our chocolates and their colours in the shop and in the brochure. For example, the blue chocolates correspond with the concept of the sky, for the land we have brown and something strong, like red or yellow, for the flowers."

JAP JOY – FIDÉE

Mary's Brigadeiro
HANDCRAFTED CHOCOLATE
24pcs

CHAPTER 6

MARKETING STRATEGY

Mary's Brigadeiro's see-through packaging makes the product irresistible: seeing them makes you want to try them

JANICE WONG

MARKETING STRATEGIES AND GOALS

differ from business to business, and getting started is no easy task. That's why we asked social media and pastry celebrity Kirsten Tibballs her thoughts on the matter. Always balanced with her mindset and actions when it comes to chocolate entrepreneurship, she offers you her advice as you approach your marketing strategy:

"I think that everybody should have an open mind going into the marketing part. Think of your mission statement and what you want to sell as a full picture for your consumers. I think there's so much opportunity to sell not just a product, but your story as well, or what you want your business to be. Don't be restricted or necessarily follow what your predecessors have done, because you can write a new amazing story. And, I think the more different this story is, the higher the value to your consumers."

As Kirsten puts it, the way you approach the art of chocolate crafting is unique to you. You've worked for this uniqueness (Chapter 1) to be represented in your brand identity (Chapter 4) — this is *your* chocolate story. In this chapter, you'll discover the elements needed to share it with the world.

Remember JAP JOY created FIDÉE as a new chocolate concept in the Chinese market? As a pioneer when it comes to products and concept design, we asked about the role of marketing in a business like his:

"From my perspective, the reason why other similar businesses close down so quickly is because they only do a small part of the whole system. They only work the production, for example, but don't work on the marketing. They don't take the time to invest in good photography and show these photos to customers... I guess that's why they close down very quickly. That's what happens when you only focus on selling the products, but don't make every part of this system collaborate for it to work."

When Jap Joy talks about a system, he refers to your business as a whole that's made up of smaller pieces. While having high standards for your production and your brand are crucial to build a solid business, these efforts have to be tackled holistically. This system, your business, will only work when all its smaller elements are running smoothly and in tune with each other. One of these elements is your marketing department.

An original creation by Janice Wong: chocolate crayons you can draw with and enjoy as a treat after

In today's competitive market, wanting to share your purpose with your potential clients is one of the first challenges to tackle. Creating a brand and its products was only part number one of this equation. Now, to succeed as an artisan chocolatier and make your business known, strategic decisions regarding your communication and marketing goals need to be made.

This is the space where your marketing strategy plays its role — but what is it? Like its name suggests, a marketing strategy is the description of the action, channels and tools you'll be using to accomplish your marketing goals.

Whether you're just starting out or looking to refine your existing marketing approach, this chapter will provide you with some basic marketing knowledge and guidance so you can create a successful marketing strategy.

You will ultimately have to decide between creating an overall marketing strategy for your entire brand or create smaller strategies for different campaigns or channels. But regardless of the model you choose, some elements are fundamental in marketing strategies of all types and scales.

"We had just gotten started, so we just hung a simple paper on the door announcing the chocolate shop. That quickly created enough buzz, because even before we opened there were people waiting. Then we quickly started spreading our brand by working with the municipality of the city. And immediately, they started promoting that in the press as well. Then, local products also came into the picture, but we did that deliberately, to show local commitment in different directions."

DAVID MAENHOUT – CHOCOLATIER M

THE 6 PS OF MARKETING

Independent small businesses or multinational enterprises — companies of all scales allocate part of their budget towards marketing. But if you're just getting started, your budget might be limited or even zero. This isn't the end of the world, because allocating time to work on your marketing strategy is a good enough (and very important) starting point.

If marketing seems to be a salad of different alien concepts, a practical way to jump on this train is to understand the 6 Ps of marketing. This is a framework where 6 elements come together to form the foundation of a strategy and to guide you in executing it.

1 Products

Your products are more than the soul of your business. They are (and should always be) the focus of your communication with existing and potential customers. A good product description is the first step towards successful marketing.

Within this framework, products are defined as the tangible or intangible offer that your business provides to consumers. An example of a tangible offer is the chocolates you produce, while an intangible one may be the way you welcome customers into your shop. Never forget that even if you are in the artisan chocolate business, your products go beyond your chocolates. They are also the add-ons and services that are offered along with them.

If you're beginning to draft a marketing strategy, you've probably studied your market's potential (Chapter 3) and have an initial idea of the type of product that will become part of your offer (Chapter 1). So, take your pencil and start brainstorming about how you will communicate what these products (and services) are and the value they bring into consumers' lives.

Creations by different chefs with individual traits and distinct brand characteristics

Ryan L. Foote

Jitsk Heyninck

Sebastian Pettersson

Davide Comaschi

Olivier Willems

Once you've pinned down a product, try to pinpoint these aspects about it. This will eventually be the steppingstone to create a marketing strategy around your entire offer:

Attributes

Look past the obvious to tell consumers what your product does. More than being tasty, what do your chocolates make them feel or think? Party treats or special gifts — what are the uses clients can give them?

Mariane Oliveira is a chocolatier who understands the power of selling more than chocolate. When it comes to her marketing, she advertises more than her unique product proposition (the brigadeiro):

"My advertising is pretty much not the chocolate, but *'share the moment of happiness'*. It actually focuses on bringing people together through the story that's behind the chocolate."

Uniqueness

Think back to your differentiating factor (Chapter 1). Out of all your attributes, your differentiating factor is what makes each product (or your entire brand/offer) unique. This factor is a constant within your brand, it's what your entire marketing strategy should rely on and communicate. If you ever feel lost in your marketing efforts, look back to your uniqueness and make sure it's present throughout all your communication channels.

JUSTINE LANNOO from Goût Fou puts this into practice seamlessly, as she uses chocolate as a tool to express her uniqueness as a part of all her brand (and marketing) strategy:

"I just wanted to be able to express my creativity more and do it for me, to push myself and my limits much more. From there came the decision to start a chocolate shop, because chocolate is my great passion."

Benefits

You've told your customers what your products are like and what makes you stand out in the market. Now it's time to tell them what they have to gain from your brand. When it comes to sharing each product's benefits, look beyond the immediate satisfaction of chocolate.

Remember that the 6 Ps of marketing should work together.

A real-life example of how this can happen is NIKKI THAKKER's éntisi. Once she knew she had created a one-of-a-kind product, she actively communicated its benefits and differentiating element, although the product didn't make it in the long run. Let's take a look at why:

"We have a product called Honey Toasted Oatmeal. It's a raisin coated with milk chocolate, and it has toasted oatmeal and honey too. I think it tastes fabulous, and when we had done a blind tasting for that product, everyone had loved it. But somehow, on the packaging, because it says 'honey' and 'oatmeal', nobody wants to pick it up. I realised sometimes the name just doesn't strike, even if the product tastes really good. So we've had products we've discontinued or we are going to discontinue because of this reason."

Like Nikki learned, you'll find that even good products risk dropping out of your shelves because of how they're marketed. With this in mind, let's consider the next element with the power to influence buying decisions.

"You can put the most insane things in chocolate. However, I noticed that those are often trends. While they are fun and very interesting from a marketing perspective, that is not the course we want to follow. We want to do things that are accessible to a wide audience, something that's always happy and appealing."

PATRICK MERTENS – CHOCOLADEHUIS BOON

2 Prices

Talking about price is more than about how much money you can get based on how much it costs to produce something. Prices represent the worth that customers perceive in a product. They're a critical element of the marketing mix because they impact a business' revenue, profitability and no less than customer perception.

So, how is it that you coordinate your pricing strategy with your marketing one? First, you understand your customer base thoroughly: their willingness/ability to pay, your competitor's pricing ranges and your business objectives.

You've crafted a unique brand and took the time to define your target audience. Regardless of the price margin you decide upon, your job is to use your marketing strategy to explain to your target audience why your price points are *fair*.

Clients will accept a price tag as fair if they can identify the value of the product in the price point. If you want to make sure you're not asking too much (or too little) for your creations, think of combining the following elements:

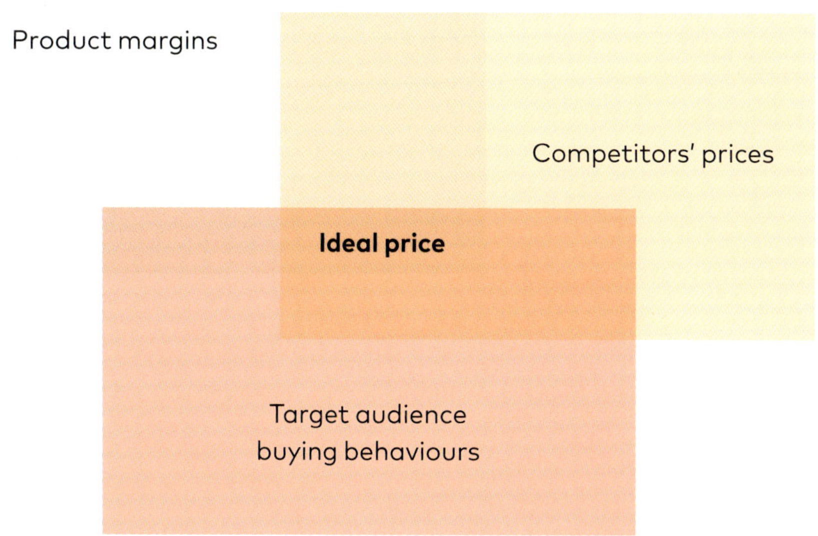

Find the sweet spot between how much you want to charge for your products, what your main competitor/s are charging and the amount your audience can afford (based on your market research).

PRO TIP! Be aware of how prices are influenced by your location, changes in the economy, product bundles, special occasions and seasons. Offering bundles of products at different prices or creating product packages that adapt to these aspects of your context is a good way to keep consumers engaged and on the lookout for more.

A good example of a good communication strategy that justifies your price points without even mentioning money was offered by the queen of chocolate, KIRSTEN TIBBALLS:

"I think that consumers want to have an understanding of the values of the company they're purchasing from. When we consider climate change, for example, we pay attention to the different ingredients that are being used. Today, this is important, naming ingredients is also of value. So, for example, if I use Callebaut chocolate, I would be promoting the fact that I'm using chocolate made from 100% sustainable beans, and this will resonate with a lot of consumers."

As you can see, in this example Kirsten isn't just offering a reason why a product would be placed on the pricier side. It is also conveying a message about the brand's identity, its purpose and way of working. This is how pricing as an element works on behalf of your strategy.

DelRey shop is in a strategic central location in the heart of Antwerp, Belgium

3 Places

Where can clients access your products? It might be a brick-and-mortar shop, an online store or both. Online or offline (Chapter 11), "place" refers to the distribution channels and methods used to make products or services available.

Also known as "distribution space", the place focuses on how your products are delivered to your customers, and it encompasses factors like retail locations, online platforms, logistics and transportation.

To get an idea of how to include places in your marketing strategy, here's a list of spaces that should be present in your chocolate business marketing strategy:

Brick-and-mortar shop

Where is your shop located? It might be that you're in a high-traffic area, or that you've chosen a less crowded space because there will be less competition. Despite your choice of location, the attributes of the neighbourhood where you are will influence your marketing decisions.

HÅKAN MÅRTENSSON is one of the chocolatiers who used his store as a marketing strategy itself. He worked on the place's decoration and structure to highlight his chocolates, and to bring to life the essence of his entire brand proposition:

"We have this custom-made display that was blowing people's minds. When people came in and saw this jewellery case for chocolates, everything else disappeared for them. And we realised, *'okay, so this is our model, this is how we're going to sell the space'*. Besides this, you can't really see our shop from the outside. With all of this, we ended up creating some sort of a speak-easy chocolate bar with a rock-and-roll vibe."

Online store

How are you making sure your online store accurately represents your brand? By using the brand elements you've taken the time to craft with the help of Chapter 4: these should be present in your online store. From visual aspects to the type of text your consumers find on your website, it will all be accounted for as part of your marketing efforts.

As a type of in-person experience, Ryan L. Foote does pop-up shops during festive seasons and art/design festivals for clients to be part of a sculptural chocolate moment

"We didn't invest much in marketing, especially in the very beginning. We didn't have a budget to do advertisements, or social media ads. We believed our chocolate was good enough and people believed so too. We only told some good friends when we started, and then we went to trade shows or professional expos. Those were also good places for other people to get to know us. In the beginning we went to the big ones, but then we started going to the small ones for smaller independent businesses too."

FAN YU – NIBBO

Markets and events

Local markets, food festivals or B2B/B2C events are often great places to network, create meaningful connections and make your brand known. During these events, you should focus on brand awareness (making your brand known) and upselling. Communicating key elements will be crucial, and what and how you communicate will also have a place in your marketing strategy.

"We used to join pop-up shops, like flea markets and carnivals, to sell our products. We would set up a little shop there, and that was one of the ways we promoted our products. You could say our key marketing strategy is basically selling good things in our offline shop, and then when people come to our physical shops, they take pictures and they send us the photos on social media or tag us there."

JAP JOY – FIDÉE

Retailers

If you choose to collaborate with third-party retailers or resellers, you want to make sure they can represent your brand faithfully, as you won't be there to oversee how they communicate about your products and your identity. Preparing materials and guides for retailers is always useful to guarantee that your brand is well-represented when you're not around.

Place is also about how you position your products: how and where they're located so that they look good and accessible. If you're looking to improve sales, whether it is online or offline, the placement of your range will also place a significant role. This is what NIKKI THAKKER noticed when she looked at what part of her product range was selling more:

"In our boutique there are certain products that always sell more, and we realise that they sell more because they're more visible to the eye. The bonbons that are kept in the display counter, they're visible and they're appealing. Wherever products are very visible initially, we also have to have very nice and attractive packaging."

4 Promotion

Communicating the benefits and uniqueness of your brand will be at the core of your marketing strategy. Successful promotion of these attributes will nudge people to go from being aware of your brand to buy from it.

Promotion channels range from more traditional ones (like pamphlets and small billboards) to digital ones (online advertisements and digital platforms). All the types of marketing promotion channels you choose should be monitored for brand consistency and alignment with your identity and tone of voice.

If you're unsure of what could make up good content for your marketing messages, you can follow the reverse-engineering technique often used by the team at the MALLORCA FAMILY business:

"You just have to do reverse engineering: really try to be and think like the client. That's one of the most important things, what you think the client would need to know in order to be interested in a product or to drive there and buy it. Sometimes clients are interested in the exclusivity of the ingredients you're using. Sometimes, it is about truly understanding what it is they are looking to buy and from what type of business. It might have something to do with the way some ingredient has been harvested or whatever. So, don't just give out all of the available information because nobody needs that much. Just find the key things they could be looking for."

"We do newsletters, social media advertising, sometimes we also appear in national TV. This we do especially around Christmas time, which generates a lot of traffic."

MIROSLAW PELCZAR
— M. PELCZAR CHOCOLATIER

At Chocolatier M, the care for customers is one of the multiple elements that shape the brand's identity around attention to detail

5 People

People are at the heart of marketing. From working in the kitchen to servicing customers, all people who work for your business are representing it somehow. Because this is the case, they are considered as part of your marketing strategy.

MIROSLAW PELCZAR's business in Poland thrives not only because his chocolates taste amazing, but because his brand offers more than just great flavours. Since people are part of his business' purpose, Mirosław makes sure his staff understands the role they play beyond their designated tasks:

"I try to motivate my team all the time, and to create a friendly atmosphere so they like their tasks. A happy team has a very strict correlation with happy customers! Our place offers smiles, great taste, happiness and awe. My floor staff is a very important part of that experience."

From the way they dress to the way they address customers — first impressions are often made by the people who work with you, and they're upheld by them too. Bear in mind that your team members have the power to attract or repel clients, so make sure you pay attention to your hiring efforts (Chapter 9), these are part of the foundation for a solid marketing strategy in the end.

6 Presentation

As you've seen in the first P of marketing (product), your assortment will have a certain list of benefits and attributes. Your marketing efforts are responsible for sharing these benefits. And, the way you present your products is one of the most important ways of creating expectations around your business, and delivering on them (Chapter 7).

Janice Wong is known for her large-scale artistic installations, including completely edible chocolate walls

Elements and concepts that are part of the presentation aspect of your brand include packaging (Chapter 9), messaging (Chapter 1) and overall branding (Chapter 4). As CALUM HAGGERTY would say, don't underestimate the power of this element:

"You can have a great product, but I see a lot of people underestimate the presentation. They think they've created the best chocolate in the world, but it's in this little plastic packet and they're standing at a trade show. It doesn't matter if it's the best chocolate in the world, no one's going to buy it."

The presentation of your products may start with your packaging, but it is actually the result of all the components your customers see around it too. LAMA BASSAM AL-GHRAWI spoke to us about how her family's business pays special attention to the detail of how the chocolates are packed as a part of everything that meets consumers' eyes:

"We design our showrooms based on occurring events to create beautiful visualisation in general. In this way, the customer can enjoy the entire journey, from the very beginning until the end."

Did you notice yet? All elements that give life to a marketing strategy work in function of each other, and they also overlap with the elements that have helped you build a strong brand. This is because taking the time to build a unique and genuine brand identity and to create a meaningful product range is the only way to design a strong marketing strategy.

NETWORK IN THE RIGHT SPACES

A good way to start spreading the word about your business (known as "brand awareness") is networking. In-person or online, network spaces are still one of the most powerful ways to build brand awareness and attract new clients.

The CASA INFANTE family business found a way to offer their products by talking to people beyond the world of chocolate. This is a great example of how being active in relevant network spaces can take your business to unexpected heights:

"We have actually promoted our brand in the HORECA sector by offering products that are suitable for restaurants and pizzerias. Once we entered the HORECA sector, we found a larger audience: after discovering us, people there looked for us online and became clients too."

As a result of seizing network opportunities, the products crafted by Casa Infante made it to restaurants, which served as a way to market their creations to new customers. People who enjoyed what they made became new clients, and third-party retailers became silent advocates of their family brand.

This isn't the only case where chocolate makers use their relations with other businesses in the same industry to expand their client base. HÅKAN was once approached by the chef of a high-end restaurant. Impressed by his chocolates, the chef asked if HÅKAN Chocolatier could spare a selection of chocolates for his upcoming restaurant, these would be included in the restaurant's little stand of high-end products. Håkan jumped at the opportunity of being associated with that kind of premium business:

"This was basically a rent-free concept for us. It enabled us to have a little hub in the city with another high-end brand and without extra costs."

"Word of mouth is very powerful. It allowed us to gain brand awareness in a very exclusive market segment."

DAVIDE COMASCHI – DAVIDE COMASCHI

Networking efforts can also lead to deeper insights into what other artisanal shops are doing. And they can actually have a direct impact on your portfolio and your sales. This is what happened with MALLORCA BAKERY, as its owners ventured into the world of collaborating and sharing through social media:

"The world is opening up a lot right now. There's a lot of cooperation between different chefs, and ideas being shared too. We've been to round tables with different chefs, talking about the different seasons and what we're going to do for them. Some of the best products we've had, we actually created by collaborating with others. Instead of trying to steal recipes, which is what some chefs have been doing a lot in the past, why don't we try to put recipes together and actually make better things?"

You may have picked it up already — regardless of your route to market (Chapter 3), fairs and expositions are great places to meet people in your industry and adjacent ones. However, they are also the perfect spot to test out your production and your concepts.

"We did a bit of marketing collaborations where we tried to work with other artisan brands who share a similar experience, but not in chocolate, maybe handcrafts and other things. We did it just to put a word out on social media for brand awareness."

NIKKI THAKKER – ÉNTISI

This was the experience of STEPHEN and SUN TRIGG, who found they had a gift for chocolate making after their (hesitant) first time at a local fair:

"We started in a local farmer's market. I remember this market was on a Sunday. So, we got up at nine o'clock on Saturday morning and started making our chocolates. We finished at 3am. We got up at six the next day, and my wife looked at me and was like, *'the chocolates are just not good enough'*. I was like, *'no, no, we've worked all day and all night, we're going whether you like it or not'*. But inside, I thought to myself, *'who's gonna buy any chocolate offers?'*, *'What are we doing?'*. We went anyway. We were sold out in two hours. That was the start of our journey."

Stephen and his wife found their chocolate calling in a local event. And if you're looking to spread awareness, you can also look at these fairs and beyond. This is what MARIANE OLIVEIRA did, when she started growing her brand awareness in the most unusual of places:

"My partner's family, they just talked to their friends about the brigadeiros. And then, my partner's mum went to the hairdresser one day and asked, *'can Mary put chocolates here so people who come here can buy them?'*. I didn't know anyone other than my partner's family here. They were my first customers, and they were the ones who helped me spread the word."

The limits of the food industry are not set. Maybe your shop offers that one product that works well with other kinds of products. Maybe your friends and family know of a place where a sample of your products could reach more people than you could on your own.

Don't be afraid to talk to the people you know, to approach other business owners and brainstorm about how you can leverage each other's strengths. Networking in all circles leads to identifying spaces for exposure, opportunities and unexpected ideas.

David Maenhout's advertising choices focus on high-quality and consistent imagery that represents the style of his brand

TRADITIONAL **ADVERTISING**

Would you say traditional advertising is dead? Here's a short story of how old-school word of mouth let everyone in HÅKAN's new home in the United States know about his new chocolate concept, and convinced them that his shop was worth the visit:

"We never put up a sign or anything. It all started with the rumours in the town. So, the first day, the first Saturday we opened, we sold more than our rent! Just that first day.

We knew that we were doing something good when we saw everybody coming in. In a place like this, in a community, things work like this: everybody talks to everyone, and everybody wants to be the first one on the store. People will go, *'have you seen the new place? Have you been in? Oh, it's so good. You have to try this'*. They want to be *that* person. We grew from there and today, we have people coming to us in big numbers, like 7000 tourists coming every week."

We live in digital times. This does not mean traditional advertising is dead. On the contrary, many traditional ways of promoting a business are being perceived as more human and personalised compared to digital ads. This was the experience of RENATA ARASSIRO, who also witnessed how being part of a neighbourhood community was an asset, and that traditional promotion methods still have a significant impact on sales:

"When I decided to open my business, I started to spread the news that I was going to open a chocolate shop here, a small campaign in the neighbourhood. We made some pamphlets that basically said, *'here I am, I'm a chef, and I'm the owner of this new chocolate shop'*. The pamphlets were spread all over the neighbourhood. I also sent some products to the press and they made some reports about the opening of the chocolate store. It all started like that. Then, the people who came to buy the chocolates ended up spreading the word. Buyers were bringing more buyers in the end."

This doesn't mean that you should not be relying on digital ways of advertising. It means that with online ads everywhere and social media saturated, you can leverage traditional advertising strategies as a way to connect with your clients and potential customers in a more personal way.

Don't expect offline advertising to be a giant billboard on a highway. Traditional can also range from personally taking a box of samples to potential customers to introducing yourself and your new business to let them know you're taking orders. Although known for her event planning and artistic background, JANICE WONG took the time to do these things herself every time she had a new concept to offer as a business — and it worked, even in a city as big as Singapore:

"There was a soft launch for the brand, but I think generally the success was thanks to meeting customers in person and asking them questions, talking to them, really being open about their opinions and feedback. We had people who really love what we do, and they kept coming back. It was the true word of mouth."

"Well, we have never placed an ad in those 16 years. We haven't spent a euro to sponsor the logo, or whatever. It's really always been word of mouth. It certainly makes sense to work with social media experts though. They can help you set up special promotions and reach the right audiences. Although you understand how social media works yourself, it is advisable to seek advice from people with more experience. They can guide you in planning actions and strategies to boost sales, especially during holidays or when you notice that the web shop is less active. It is important to make use of their knowledge and expertise to improve your online presence and execute effective marketing campaigns."

PATRICK MERTENS & INGE LIJNEN – CHOCOLADEHUIS BOON

DIGITAL PRESENCE

In a crowded digital space, working on your digital presence won't look the same for businesses of all scales and shapes. But there is one rule to drill down on: to stay consistent and true to your brand identity and your digital presence, even for the most traditional businesses like MALLORCA, will be a part of building genuine connections with your consumers:

"Once you have a brand and people care about that brand in any way, people really follow you on Instagram and we have a connection with our clients."

For KIRSTEN, crafting a strong digital presence gave her the space and the chance to expand her business, a space that an offline setting could only offer to a limited extent:

"We'd saturated how many classes we could do physically, and it wasn't going to be cost-effective to move again, or to open another classroom. So that's when I decided to do online classes. That was what I saw as the future of the business, because it had the ability to reach thousands of people from all around the world."

Although your chocolates might not be delivered to the other side of the world, it's important to note the power that your online identity can have, even for a local business. For example, HÅKAN didn't sell his chocolates across the country when he was starting out, but he did use his digital presence to strike an international deal:

"We got in touch with a company in Turkey that does polycarbonate moulds and they said, *'if you want to promote us, we'll promote you and we'll offer you all these moulds if you do stuff with them'*. New moulds meant new online content and new material without overthinking. So, I accepted and started to post. It was slow times because of COVID, but online, we looked like a very busy and successful business, while we were really trying to figure out how to get to the next step."

Håkan didn't only get a collaboration out of his digital efforts. He worked on the reputation of his brand, making sure that people kept an eye out for them while, on the low, he worked to keep the brand afloat in a time of crisis.

We also talked about this subject to ENRIC ROVIRA in Barcelona, about the role of a digital presence in times like today's. We valued his opinion since his chocolate business had started offline. He gave us a short yet powerful statement on the relevance of your digital presence as an artisan chocolatier today:

"For the current generations, if you're not on the internet, you don't exist."

So how can you make sure you exist for all generations? Don't close the door to the opportunities that building an online presence can do for you, and think about the topics we'll briefly introduce next: having your own website, social media and online advertising.

Do I need my own website?

Having your own website is not a prerequisite to start selling. However, setting one up is an investment that may have a big return, including more control over your product placement. But is this investment worth it? We asked KIRSTEN to give us her opinion on the matter:

"I would've started the online platform earlier, to be honest. I was very, very fortunate that I made the decision in October 2013."

The family behind MALLORCA agrees with Kirsten. Although it is an investment, digital assets are almost always worth making:

"The advice we'd give to any chef that really wants to start in the business is to invest enough money in technology. Get yourself a good website, make yourself known in the delivery platforms. Because, that's going to be the business of the future. The pandemic sped it up, but it was already coming, and it's going to keep growing at this speed. We know this because every year, we've been experiencing increases of over 100% in sales on our online stores."

Don't forget that your digital efforts should be combined with the rest of the marketing and brand elements we've covered. Investing in a good website should be met with the same attention as the rest of your branding. Because, like MIROSLAW will remind you, there are certain tangible brand elements that cannot be reproduced online:

"It is very hard to transmit your essence digitally, this is an aspect of online stores. My brick-and-mortar stores are based on full immersion with all the senses, and I am still looking for ways of, at least partially, copying this experience in our online stores."

Although still on his journey to discover how to represent his immersive chocolate experience on his website, Mirosław understands the importance of a website's function for a brand in today's world. And, undeniably attached to your business website, comes the matter of social media platforms and the role they play.

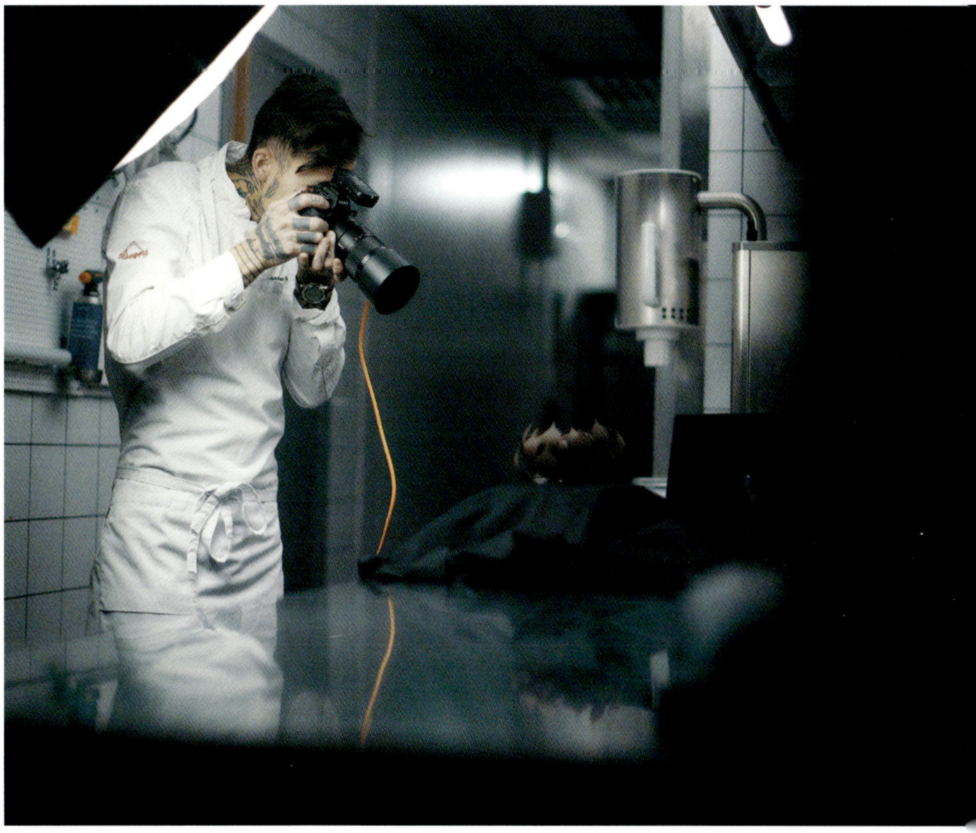

Sebastian Pettersson is also handy with professional cameras, making sure he's the creative director and decision-maker about the online aesthetics of his creations and personal brand

Social media

Social media will be partly responsible for making your brand known, and for redirecting traffic to where online sales happen (your social media business profile, your own website, a third-party platform or your brick-and-mortar shop).

If you thought the role of social media was relegated to a secondary one, think again. Marco Infante told us how CASA INFANTE's marketing strategy fundamentally revolves around the subject:

"Clearly, social media has been a game changer. Even though I've always been a maniac about the importance of the location, today, social media accounts for over 80% of our overall marketing mix."

Adhering to Marco's statement, TIBBALLS explained why she believes the advances of social media and technology can be used to your advantage, once you identify the power that exists within their reach:

"The world has changed. To be successful, you can no longer just be an artisan or a pastry chef. You need to have an understanding of social media, you need to be able to take photos of your products too. So... just do it! The cameras on the phones now are amazing. They give you the ability to do what you need. So, make the time to promote what you're doing, yourself along with your business too. And you don't necessarily need to use PR companies or marketing companies to do this. If you've got the budget for that, fantastic, if not, you can do little things yourself."

Without having heard this advice from Kirsten's lips, BERNARD PROOT has been implementing this approach since the very beginning of DelRey chocolates:

"From day 1, I believed we had to use the Internet to generate sales. Social media is indispensable. It takes a lot of time, but it keeps our presence alive. It offered us massive opportunities to build an international clientele; and even catapulted our diamond bonbon into a global bestseller."

When researching your market potential (Chapter 3), you've probably encountered other artisan chocolate shops like Bernard and Anne's DelRey store on social media. And just like them, most chocolatiers agreed upon one good piece of advice — find inspiration in others, but follow no one. Your social media profile should be built in a way that suits your brand identity and differentiating factor.

Bottom line, when working on your social media presence, stay true to your identity and, at the same time, try to stay informed about relevant trends and what they can offer a business like your own.

> **"I don't sell online actually, I only take orders by WhatsApp. Online, people can check out the products, but we don't have a web shop. So, they choose from our online products and pay in advance. Once the deposit is in our account, we can deliver it or they can pick it up."**
>
> RENATA ARASSIRO – RENATA ARASSIRO CHOCOLATES

Social media trends

You don't have to jump on every trend train. However, knowing which trends are taking over the world is a must. Because being able to tailor your marketing efforts around what's popular is one way to resonate with existing consumers and get the attention of potential new ones.

For example, one of the trends that blew up the past year (and that is here to stay) is that of advertising not only the final product, but how it was produced in the first place. RENATA ARASSIRO joined in on this trend when she noticed it was a social media success. Based on her personal experience with it, she encourages chocolatiers to try to discover what social media platforms have to offer:

"Production is something that always has a lot of views on our social media. I also see that content that is popular is carousel posts, this means a lot of pictures posted together.

Now, on the other hand, when I'm doing videos, I always try to speak while performing tasks. This shows people that I'm the chef. I know this kind of content helps, because I see how the views increase. And, this last bit might be funny, but I see that a very good song also helps too! When you make reels on Instagram, a nice song can help you a lot. Like these, there are so many details you have to analyse."

Another example is the DIY (Do It Yourself) global trend. You can take a look at how Mariane Oliveira made it work, and maybe be inspired by her approach:

Although not born from the chocolate space, this trend was implemented by Mary without ever having to give her recipe away. Just like her, if you think outside the box, you might be able to find more than one viral movement and use it in your marketing strategy and product development.

"I feel that sometimes I'm getting more involved with the projects in the city, maybe because of the recognition received. You come across as more credible and are sometimes even called upon for certain things to promote the city. I don't appear on television or anything for that matter, but those are certain things that are good to get your business going.

For all of this, social media is especially important. Everyone walks around with their phones. We used to make an effort to get extra customers to the shop. But once thanks to a city cooking event, we were able to achieve much more than sitting here in the shop waiting for a customer. So, you do need that advertising, you do need that support from tourism. And that evolved quickly among foodies: people find us faster."

OLIVIER WILLEMS – OLIVIER WILLEMS

Olivier Willems knows that eye-catching images of his creations boost sales on his digital platforms and in-store

Keeping track of your digital data

Followers, likes, views and link clicks — all these insights are available for free when you create a social media business account. Use them to study your content performance and compare it to your sales during specific periods.

But why? Tracking your social media content performance helps you keep track of how your audience reacts to what you share online. Did they like a specific trend? Did a certain post outperform the rest? Do people like photos or videos the most?

Look at the numbers, find out what kind of content your clients prefer, what gets you new followers and which posts are the ones that create sales or direct your followers to your website or in-person shop.

Remember to stay social on social media! Don't be afraid to engage with your audience online as you would offline. Ask them how they got to know you and what they'd like to see in the future. Polls, surveys, open questions, comment spaces and even direct messages — there are multiple tools social media platforms offer to create this kind of engagement.

Once your social platforms are ready for you to start posting, you can use them to update your marketing goals and upgrade your strategy, as the elements you discover through your online presence can become topics or goals that feed into your digital strategy in the future.

"I started with social media and it went well. One sponsor led me to another, and to great contacts around the world. Sooner or later, they get you into some kind of business. That's pretty much how I scaled from standing in a small pastry shop every morning. Nowadays I'm a full-time employee at a large company with hotels and everything, but I'm at that point where I can ask for some kind of freedom.

Now, what many people forget is that you might have a beautiful website, but we still need people to get there. And the investment linked to getting people on your online shop, finding you, making the order, paying and so on, that's the difficult part. It's as difficult as opening up a shop in the street and getting people in. Odds are that, in a busy street, you might have more people dropping in out of curiosity compared to an online shop."

SEBASTIAN PETTERSSON – SEB PETTERSSON

Online advertising

Savour School welcomes its visitors showing international collaborators in a creative way

Online advertising has become an essential component of today's marketing strategies. So far, we've been over the importance of your digital presence through a website and social media channels. Online advertising is yet another way to further reach and engage with your audience.

In simple terms, online ads are a tool designed for digital platforms (such as search engines like Google, social media, websites and other online channels) to promote products, services, or brands.

But, how does it really work? Online advertising works a lot like offline advertising. In different platforms and websites from different industries, there will be spaces meant solely for advertising purposes. For different fees, you can have your business advertised in one of them, usually on one that shares a similar target audience.

Creating online ads and selecting where to place them plays a key role in your marketing strategy. It is how you capture the attention of potential customers and drive actions such as clicks, website visits, online sales or brand awareness. And the good thing about online ads is that they're versatile — they might take more shapes than you would initially think.

SEARCH ENGINE ADVERTISING (SEA): These are ads that show up on search engine results, like Google's, and they are based on keyword use. For example, imagine you are based in Sydney and looking to promote your new business. So, you will invest in SEA and decide on keywords that represent your brand, such as: "artisan chocolate", "chocolate Sydney", etc. Any user who looks for these terms (or their combination: "artisan chocolate Sydney") on Google will get a list of different results. When paying for SEA, you pay for a space at the top of that result page, and your brand will show up there as sponsored content.

SOCIAL MEDIA ADS: This involves creating and placing ads on different social media platforms, where you will be able to target specific demographics, interests and buying behaviours. Unlike SEA, social media ads usually require a striking visual element. Some places where you might invest in social media advertising include: Facebook Ads, Instagram Ads, Twitter Ads, LinkedIn Ads.

Although social media ads are not a necessity when you get started (and when the budget is tight), it's a good investment as soon as your business allows you to allocate some money to start tapping into the online ads world. This is how MIROSLAW worked his way around advertising online — investing as he went:

"At the very beginning we did not invest much in marketing, only in some regional websites with some banners and adverts. As time passed and e-commerce started to really make a difference in our sales, we invested in advertising, social media and our own online shop."

With éntisi, NIKKI THAKKER also saw the way social media could impact her sales, and not only her online ones:

"We are doing promotions on Facebook and Instagram. I think that has done very well for us because you're able to reach out to a larger audience without being physically present everywhere. And, a lot of people that come to our store say, 'oh yeah, we've seen your brand on Instagram'. So, there are people who actually end up buying products because of the ads that they've seen online."

DISPLAY ADVERTISING: This focuses on visual assets like banners or images. And these ads are placed on websites or apps to reach a wider (or specific) audience. Examples: Google Display Network, Programmatic Advertising platforms.

VIDEO ADVERTISING: The name gives it away, doesn't it? This is about creating short-form videos that will show up as advertisement on platforms like YouTube, Vimeo, or other video-sharing websites, to engage users with multimedia content.

COLLABORATIONS: This is about partnering with brands who share a common vision, or people with a strong online presence who promote your products or services on their platforms in exchange for a commission, samples, or their promotion on your end.

"One of the ways to learn new things was to actually bring guest chefs into the school. When you bring a guest chef, you get to see someone else's considerations, concepts, ideas, way of doing things. This opens your mind to potential things you could do."

KIRSTEN TIBBALLS – SAVOUR SCHOOL

"People in Austria actually found us because of a book. They had bought a book from Gault&Millau and we were in it. It was a picture of our golden praline and the person needed it for an exhibition in Austria. So, that's how we got talking, and it turned out these people are Belgian chocolate resellers in Austria."

JUSTINE LANNOO – GOÛT FOU

CONTENT MARKETING: All content in the form of blogs or articles will fall under this category. Whether you're sharing this content on your own website or collaborating with digital magazines and blog sites, an article about your business should fall under (and budgeted as) content marketing plans.

INFLUENCER MARKETING: Influencer marketing also falls under the category of collaborations. However, people with the status of influencers usually have steeper prices to talk about your products, particularly when their following is high. There are different ways to engage with influencers, inviting them to your shops' events or sending them a bundle of your assortment for online reviews is often (depending on your business) a very profitable investment.

An interesting example of how influencing marketing can be tailored to your business' needs is that of MALLORCA, a family business that you wouldn't usually picture being connected to influencer marketing:

"So, one thing we did is we invited the press and some popular people to see the inside of the factories. We went to influencers and all that kind of stuff, and let them inside our factory, just to show a little bit of what was happening behind closed doors. This helped us give the brand the value it deserves; because it showed the way we work."

EMAIL MARKETING: If you have managed to build an email client base, this is about sending targeted emails to your list of subscribers or existing clients. The content of email marketing is usually about new products and services, or special offers and events.

Today, with the availability of free marketing software, setting up email campaigns is easy and often free (to get started). Your software of choice will guide you in creating engaging email content, and it will automate the process of sending out emails and gathering data about each campaign's performance. Some of the most used software include platforms like Mailchimp or Campaign Monitor.

Although some may say email campaigns are no longer relevant, successful chocolatiers like NIKKI use them to be connected to her clients, and to let them know of what's new in her shop:

"So, email subscriptions, we are doing that. We have a list of people who have subscribed to our email. We send them emails about any new product launches and any offers that we are running."

For some people like KIRSTEN TIBBALLS, email campaigns are not only effective to share information, but they have had a direct financial impact on her business:

"I self-published a book called Chocolate to Savour. I started our campaign, which was just purely through newsletters from our database saying, *'I've created a book, you can pre-order it here'*. It sold incredibly well! We actually generated an income before we launched the book. I sold 2000 copies before it was even printed."

Justine Lannoo captures small details and turns them into premium advertising material

YOUR MARKETING PLAN

A marketing plan is a map or guide that organises tasks based on your marketing strategy. This plan also helps you keep track of the results of said marketing tasks along the way.

Marketing plans are used by businesses of all sizes, and they're meant to show you what works, what doesn't, and the areas where the promotion of your brand can be improved.

While a marketing strategy outlines your goals and how to get there, a marketing plan can be home to one or more marketing strategies. If you have an offline and online marketing strategy, for example, they can both be part of the same marketing plan.

Create your first marketing plan

You don't need a marketing department to draft your first marketing plan, or to start putting it into practice. By following these steps, you'll have a basic marketing plan that's ready to be implemented.

1 Recycle your mission and set your goals

As mentioned at the beginning of the book, starting with the "why" will serve as a guide in the many stages of setting up and growing your business. If you've made it this far, it's because you've already outlined the mission of your brand (Chapter 1).

To create your marketing plan, the first step will be to restate your mission. This time, you'll do it from a marketing perspective. It doesn't mean going back to square one. Simply take your business mission and use it to set your first marketing goals.

For example, if your chocolate shop exists to offer exotic flavours in a conservative chocolate market, your marketing mission could be teaching your clients about the origins of these ingredients.

SEBASTIAN PETTERSSON is known as an Instagram chocolate celebrity. And after having created a brand out of his online persona, his business and personal goals are always a decision marker when investing in his next marketing tactic, whether it is accepting a collaboration or opening up a new social media account:

"I don't have TikTok. I could have reached a million more sponsorships and whatever, or gained thousands of followers with it, but I'm not striving only for money. And, I also respect my personal time, and my time away from a mobile phone."

How does your mission affect *your* marketing strategy? And how is it that you tailor your strategy around your identity as a brand? These are some of the questions that you should be able to answer when writing down your marketing mission. You'll need them because, like we've mentioned earlier, a single business can have one or more marketing strategies in place.

The reason it's possible to have more than one strategy isn't because your brand goals will change all the time — your brand purpose, uniqueness, and goals will remain the same. However, it is possible to create strategies for an offline audience and an online one. It's also possible that you've decided to create one marketing strategy for each of your different communication channels.

Olivier Willems brings his love for the seaside city of Ostend to life through the packaging of his chocolate bars

Whichever road you're taking, make sure you define an objective for each marketing strategy, this will guarantee you can measure your goals separately. Although separate marketing strategies means a bit more work, it can simplify your marketing management once you incorporate the different marketing strategies (and their performance) under your overall marketing plan.

A good example of a strategy that was incorporated into a marketing plan was that of MALLORCA. They created a specific mission for their social media strategy, and that was only one of the strategies that fell under the brand's entire marketing plan:

"For the last decades, people knew that we were a good pastry business and bakery, but there wasn't real knowledge behind the why. They didn't know how we did things. Today, one of the things people value the most are the things done by manual labour in our factories.

What we are doing through social media and advertisements is one of the key things that helps us share this knowledge, and that will also let us increase our prices compared to industrial labels. Because now, people will be paying for something they understand. Because we invest in talking to customers and making them know what the product is worth and why. In the very end, you cannot justify higher prices without correctly explaining it."

2 Determine your standards

Setting individual standards for your marketing strategies is the only way to track your progress and make improvements as you go. These standards, known as KPIs (Key Performance Indicators) tell you which actions or tasks have helped achieve a specific goal in your marketing strategy.

Just like your mission or goals, it's important to make standards measurable at the end of each action. In other words, make sure your KPIs are not abstract like "gain followers", but something concrete, such as "increase my Instagram followers by 5%".

To know if you've met your objectives, you will have to set a deadline or time frame around your marketing strategy goals. It's at the end of that cycle that you'll analyse your KPIs and check which of the tasks have helped you meet your goals (and which haven't). You will be able to make necessary changes to your strategy as you analyse the results.

3 Categorise your target audience in target personas

Think back to your market and the target audience you've outlined. The information you collected to do so will be valuable when you set out to create marketing strategies and incorporate them into a marketing plan.

It's highly likely your target audience is a big group of people where you'll find a mix of different ages and genders. These will make up smaller groups within your overall audience, and each of these small groups is called "persona". You'll make use of these personas to create a more detailed marketing strategy and plan.

For example, by separating younger from older personas, you can create a marketing strategy in different channels according to each persona.

Imagine you've created a specific product that costs less to make, meant to reach a Gen Z audience. To make your brand known to them, your marketing strategy might be focused on platforms like TikTok or Instagram.

If older generations are also part of your artisan chocolate target audience, more traditional marketing actions will be part of your marketing strategy for this persona.

It's important to consider that as your audience grows, target personas will help you refine your marketing efforts. However, if your business is brand new, it's best to keep your target personas to a minimum, or even postpone this categorisation until your sales start to pick up.

4 Describe your content strategy or strategies

Describing your marketing strategy in terms of the content you create shouldn't be a lengthy process. It should be short and concrete, summarising where you want to go and how you want to get there.

When we talked to HÅKAN MÅRTENSSON about his strategy, he told us that starting is as simple as setting objectives and actions and putting in the work:

"Becoming big on social media is about knowing exactly the work you do and putting down the time to show it. Give it three weeks, create 10 different posts and then lay them out as needed. And remember to plan all of this because it's a lot of work — a one-minute clip maybe takes weeks and weeks of planning and execution to get there."

To make the most of your time, a simple description table can help you organise each of the goals of your marketing strategies and the actions required to reach those goals:

Type of content	Post
Volume	One every 3 days
Goals	Make my brand known on social media
KPIs (standards)	5% engagement (at least 5 likes for every 100 followers)
Channels	Instagram
Budget	50 USD

Mariane Oliveira believes that an online presence on social media is a must, even if you do it yourself or only with a small budget

5 Define omissions

Answering questions, engaging with your followers, reposting — it's easy to find yourself doing things you hadn't planned for. This doesn't mean that tasks shouldn't be completed. They should, however, be scheduled and accounted for under a specific strategy, or belong to a different one.

To make the most of your time when working on your marketing plan, and to keep to your deadlines, it's important to mention omissions. Omissions will be presented as a list of tasks that a marketing plan (or a specific strategy within your marketing plan) will *not* be taking care of.

For example, if you notice that engaging with consumers is a personalised task and that it's part of your brand identity, you can always create an engagement strategy for one, or multiple, channels solely for direct contact with consumers.

6 Define a budget

If you've taken over an existing business, take a look at its past marketing expenses, and whether you want (and financially can) to keep them or modify them.

If your brand is new and it's your first time setting in motion a marketing plan, you don't need a big budget to get started. In fact, you can start with no budget at all. In this case, time will be your currency.

It's normal to feel stuck, especially when your initial budget doesn't allow for big marketing expenses. Let STEPHEN TRIGG be a source of inspiration if you're looking to move forward. He deals with his email marketing himself, and after doing it for long, he's learned about what works best for *his* business and how to make the most of the time he invests in it:

"The biggest thing for us is the marketing emails we send out. And we see customers come in because we've told them what's new. Now, strategically, I'll send the emails on a Friday. Here's my theory: I send them around lunchtime on this day. Most people are in the office, and they're having their lunch, already switching off for the weekend. So, they get distracted. And, you can see it work almost immediately — our sales spike on a Friday."

Type of content	Direct messages
Volume	Once a day
Goals	Engage with potential/existing customers on a personal level
KPIs (standards)	Answer all existing customers' questions. Answer at least 2 potential customer direct messages.
Channels	Facebook
Budget	0

7 Look at the competition

There are two main reasons you should keep an eye out on what's going on in your market space. One of them is inspiration. The other? Competition.

What others are doing might not work for you, and you won't be looking at the competition to copy what they do. But reading about how other businesses started, looking at what worked and why can inspire the content and communication methods of your marketing strategies.

Knowing and understanding other artisan chocolate shops of similar size will also shine a light on how they position themselves from a marketing perspective: keywords they use, their audience, core and secondary offer, etc.

Like we've mentioned, understanding the competition isn't meant to guide your decisions. But it will help you see who are the shops that have a similar offer. This way, you can strengthen your marketing efforts, focusing on what separates you from this competition (Chapter 1) and communicating it efficiently.

8 Distribute the tasks

You've created one or multiple content strategies according to your specific business needs. To finalise your marketing plan, it's important to assign tasks to specific people and, like we've learned already, give them a time frame.

In the early stages of a business, you'll see the need to adjust and correct time frames more often. This is fine, as you'll be learning as you go and implementing those learnings into your planning.

Type of content	Direct messages
Volume	Once a day
Goals	Engage with potential/existing customers on a personal level
KPIs (standards)	Answer all existing customers' questions. Answer at least 2 potential customer direct messages
Channels	Facebook
Budget	0
Person	You
Time frame	March 1st – April 1st

Even if you'll be the one in charge of your content at the early stages of your shop. Make sure the "PERSON" cell is always filled in. As time goes by, looking back at the results of your marketing efforts during specific periods of time and under certain contributors will help you make decisions in the future.

Update an existing marketing plan

For some family businesses like the AL-GHRAWI legacy, marketing has become a cornerstone of their international success:

"When it comes to marketing, we can say it's the core of our business really. Without the brand positioning and awareness that keeps people recommending us, we would be considered a brand with no actual purpose."

Small start-up or international family brand, your business should always have an adequate marketing plan at the core. Because, as times change, so will people, their behaviours and preferences. Respecting their business' time to expand, the Al-Ghrawi generations were able to turn a small shop that sold traditional sweets into a larger-scale company that continues to thrive in an ever-evolving and complex international market:

"When we opened our first factory in Beirut, our marketing structure was based on word of mouth. This is how our brand started to evolve among our local customers. After many years of progressive work and global expenditure, and with the expansion of the internet, we started to create pages on social media platforms such as Facebook, Instagram, Twitter and Pinterest. This is where we started our social media engagement. After we could build a large audience around the world, we decided to enter the e-commerce field and start offering consumers the chance to shop on our website.

Since our audience is satisfied with the aesthetics of our brand, we make sure to update our social media presence daily on every page. We participate in tradeshows from time to time as well. One of the biggest tradeshows we were involved in was the Salon du Chocolat here in Lebanon. And even if it's considered nowadays a traditional way of marketing, we still heavily rely on the word of mouth and customers recommendations. To update our future marketing plans, we are studying the enhancement of our SEO and SEM campaigns."

Meet part of the Bassam Ghrawi Confectionery team and family members

Longer-standing businesses tend to keep a record of their activities to update their marketing strategies. If you have access to the marketing input of the business you've taken over, study those records before creating a completely new strategy.

You can identify which strategies have worked in the past to keep them on your current marketing plan. And the strategies that didn't perform as well? You can tweak or replace with new ones.

Past records are also often used to point new strategies in the right direction. But, having taken over a family business or an existing chocolate shop doesn't always mean you'll have a record of past marketing endeavours.

If you have no previous input from the business you've taken over, or just like many other chocolatiers, you are starting from scratch, there is no marketing strategy or plan to begin with. But you can still get started. Even though there may not have been a plan, there is an incredible amount of open source and free marketing online tools you can learn from and be inspired by.

The following are some of the triggers that tell you it's time to take a second look at your marketing plan and strategies, and maybe update them to better adjust to your business' needs today:

CHANGES IN BUSINESS GOALS: If your business goals or objectives have shifted, such as expanding into new markets, launching new products, changing your target audience or undergoing a rebranding, this will most likely require updates to your marketing plan, so that it aligns with these changes.

A good way to align business goals with marketing ones is going back to the basics (Chapter 1), taking a new look at your brand as a whole (Chapter 4) and analysing your current marketing plan with these elements outlined. The elements you use to study your current marketing plan should also be the ones that you use to upgrade it or create a new one.

MARKET OR INDUSTRY SHIFTS: Have there been significant changes in the space of artisan chocolate? These can be emerging trends that are here to stay, new competitors, changes in consumer behaviour and taste. All shifts that have become permanent in your industry may be asking for you to adjust your marketing plan, to stay relevant for your consumers and to be able to compete with similar businesses.

UNMET PERFORMANCE GOALS: You might already have a marketing strategy in place. However, if you're keeping track of your performance and your marketing strategies are not helping you meet your goals — it's time for change.

Unmet performance goals can look like declining sales, low website traffic, low social media engagement or recurrent negative feedback about communication. Putting out the urgent fires will be your first step, and then it will be time to address the shortcomings on a strategic level: redesigning goals, the actions to meet them and setting strict deadlines to monitor and improve your marketing efforts.

“From the moment I did TV, I’ve gone on to do a lot more stuff in the kitchen. And I put myself forward for World Chocolate Masters, which was just an incredible journey. These amazing things are great for marketing, and they’re great for public relations and cementing who we are in the industry. But the biggest reward I get from owning my business is a customer giving me 20 pounds because he likes my chocolate.”

STEPHEN TRIGG – LAUDEN CHOCOLATE

NEW OPPORTUNITIES: Updates and changes don’t always come as a consequence to a negative event. Staying alert to the changes in your industry also means staying on top of marketing opportunities that could benefit your business.

Although jumping on trend trains and creating an account on every new platform won’t be the answer, be aware of new channels, potential partnerships and events where you could boost your business. Thorough knowledge of your market will allow you to make a decision and take advantage of these opportunities when the right time comes.

CHANGES IN CUSTOMERS’ NEEDS AND WANTS: As it is expected in most industries, if your target audience’s needs or preferences have evolved, you might want to check if your current marketing strategies meet these new client demands.

INTERNAL CHANGES: Are you moving? Are you opening up a second shop? Maybe you’re giving your brand identity an unexpected makeover. Big changes like these will impact your clients’ expectations and if they’re met or can be met. To stay on top of your game, all changes should be clearly communicated.

LEGAL OR REGULATORY UPDATES: Don’t be surprised if there are changes in legal or regulatory requirements that impact your marketing activities. These can range from social media platforms changing their algorithms and preventing you from reaching your usual number of online audiences, all the way to political or economic events that prevent you from delivering orders, accepting certain forms of payment or even receiving ingredients.

The only way to check all these boxes is by regularly reviewing your marketing plan to ensure it remains relevant, effective and aligned with your business goals and the changing factors that may impact your company.

Whether you are drafting a marketing plan from scratch or updating an existing one, recurrent performance checks are the key to your success. This isn’t only to make sure that your goals are met — recurrent checks make sure you stay relevant in a market where consumer behaviour is always changing, new trends are coming up and different seasons call for innovation.

DARIO SIRERO

CHAPTER 7

YOUR FINANCES: BUDGETING AND CASH FLOW

Enric Rovira plays with shapes and textures to give traditional chocolate formats (bonbons) a personal and differentiating twist

David Maenhout makes sure to set aside a budget for professional photography of his confections

One of the critical aspects of running a successful business, regardless of its scale, **IS HANDLING YOUR FINANCES EFFECTIVELY.** To do so, there are two essential tools that will provide your company the foundation for financial clarity, and eventually, market success. Detailed financial planning is not only used to keep track of your capital, it also represents an important aspect of your business plan (Chapter 3).

"You can always start with a burner, a table and a cooler. But it all depends on the level and scale and quality you want to achieve. We always update our machinery based on our needs. Our machines constantly change as we grow our business."

LAMA BASSAM AL-GHRAWI – BASSAM GHRAWI CONFECTIONERY

These tools will also help you understand and control your business' inflow of revenue and outflow of costs, and incoming and outgoing cash. By knowing how your finances work, you will be able to monitor your profitability, make informed decisions, learn from them and adapt. Combined, these tools are unmissable during the first months of setting up your business, and after, as you grow.

In this chapter, we will talk about two such tools: budgeting and cash flow planning. We'll explore what these are, why they should be in place and how you can make them work for your business and maintain its financial health.

Whether you're just getting started or continuing an existing artisanal chocolate business, strengthening the foundation of your financial knowledge will be critical in the short and longer term. So, let's dive in!

MONEY, MONEY, MONEY...
WHERE TO START?

Since you're starting your business, or already running one, you need to know what to expect financially, or at the very least, have clear objectives to guide your work. Access to a revenue forecast and a cashflow forecast will allow you to calculate initial investments, prepare for funding or financing, compare the forecast to the real progress of your business and find aid to make decisions to help you keep your business on track.

There are two key tools that can help you to manage your business from the day you're planning to start. Although many chocolatiers are not too fond of the financial theory and calculations behind their project, these will prove invaluable once you're making decisions regarding funds, sales objectives and business changes.

- **TOOL 1**: budget plan
- **TOOL 2**: cash flow projection

Both tools are essential for managing the profitability and the financial health of your business. With a budget plan, you'll be able to accurately plan and allocate resources over the specific period of time you've chosen. And your cash flow projection will forecast your financial needs, helping you make short-term decisions to meet them.

TOOL 1
BUDGET PLAN

A budget plan is a financial plan that outlines the estimated income and expenses over a specific period of time. Budget plans can be annual or monthly, and are used to plan and monitor estimated revenue, costs and investments, and make decisions accordingly.

Budget plans are usually set upon a 12-month time period. Your budget plan should include revenue estimates, costs of goods sold, operating expenses, and legal requirement costs (such as taxes).

A thorough budget plan will allow you to compare real-life results against budgeted amounts. In other words, you will be able to determine the net income your business needs to be profitable: the revenue after you've deducted all expenses, interests and taxes.

TOOL 1
CASH FLOW PROJECTION

A cash flow (projection) plan is a financial forecast statement that shows you exactly how your cash is flowing, in and out of your business over a period of time. Cashflows are usually designed to analyse your finances on a 12-month basis as well. By understanding and documenting your cash flow, you will be able to determine how much money your business needs to cover its expenses.

Cash flow projections take into account when money is expected to be received and paid out. The purpose of this tool is to help your business understand if it is possible to meet its financial obligations as they are due. And, as a business owner, it's a tool that will help you guide your decisions and make backup plans in case of a cash shortage or surplus.

Not a financial wizard?

Seeking professional assistance when it comes down to your business finances is, in fact, one of the most recommended things by chocolatiers from all around the world. KIRSTEN TIBBALLS is one of them:

"There's a lot of documentation and paperwork that goes along with running a business, from paying invoices and payroll for your staff, to contract negotiations for your staff and business maintenance. You can have an accountancy firm or a book-keeper to help you do that. I think that's essential. If you can afford it, it's always good to have somebody in that role, who has the ability to take that pressure off you so you can focus on what you're good at."

To summarise all chocolatiers' advice: having a professional set of eyes or bookkeeper with relevant experience will take a load off your shoulders and give you back time to invest in your craft.

Accountants can also help with creating a comprehensive budget plan and cash flow projection, and they will help you understand how your business finances work and what they're trying to tell you.

When looking for professional help in this regard, trust is a must! STEPHEN TRIGG's experience with his financial expert is that of a close friend, which paved for honest communication:

"My best friend and accountant turned to me and said, 'have you done a cash flow spreadsheet?'. I said, 'no, there's plenty of money in the bank, we'll be alright'. He said, 'you need to sit down with me and do it'. We sat down and did it... and it was minus 70.000 pounds. I said, 'what? What's happened?'. He said, 'it's because you have to pay for everything upfront'. So, if I could go back, the biggest thing I would change is I would run the company on a cash flow spreadsheet from the start. Today, I know all the margins, know they're profitable, I have a 12-month plan, a week-by-week one, know my forecasts and my actual flow. When the company is run completely on the spreadsheet, everything else falls into place."

Your accountant will be a crucial part of your team. You want to look for someone who is not only qualified, but who possesses the communication skills and attitude you look for in any of your other team members.

In addition to working with a professional in the field, you can make use of uncountable free planning digital tools or software to be found online. These (often automated) tools ask of you to input specific elements to make your financial calculations, and will most likely do the calculations for you.

To boost revenue and minimise business risk, Enric Rovira focuses on third-party sales, B2B commissions, event installations and bespoke creations, requiring less investment in retail space and front-of-house staff

Budget allocation often contemplates packaging and other elements that help with brand positioning

"A financial plan is always needed if you need money from the bank. At the bank, they have never asked us for a business plan, I just told them about it and that was it. However, they wanted to see the financial plan.

To make a financial plan, you know the costs you need, you ask for quotes, you look it up, but how do you really start? I took a chance with an accountant to get it done. It can cost you €1.500 or so, but you just give them all the input and they put it together. That's where I really just outsourced, because everything numerical was Latin for me. And you don't know in the long run, *'are we doing well or not?'*. In my first financial plan, there was a €30.000 loss, but the banks believed my story. Last year we had zero loss!"

JUSTINE LANNOO – GOÛT FOU

TOOL 1
BUDGET PLAN

You've seen why a budget plan is necessary to keep track of your finances by forecasting your revenue, expenses and profit.

If you have taken over an existing business or are continuing a family brand, access to past finances will be of help. These will help you estimate future sales volumes and product margins, and understand where your business calls for changes to meet your financial forecast.

However, it might also be you're starting a brand-new chocolate business, which usually entails not having previous financial information to guide your estimates. You'll have to estimate costs and earnings based on initial costs, and how much you think you'll produce and sell.

TIP!
Your previous market research (Chapter 3) can help you to get clarity to estimate sales prices.

Now, to create your first budget plan, you should consider its main elements:

1 — Sales Revenue

Sales revenue, also known as sales income, is the total amount of income your business expects to generate from the sales of your products during a specific period (a month, a quarter, or a year).

Your sales revenue will be the starting point of your budget plan, as it determines your business' projected income. In simpler terms: your sales revenue tells you how much money you expect your business to make.

To get an accurate sales revenue, start by breaking down your sales by product category and the way these are sold (units, weight, boxes). Then, calculate the revenue according to how much you sell. Your calculations will look something like this:

Sales Revenue
=
Sales Volume (Quantity) × Unit Price

For example, imagine you own a business like Lauden Chocolate, and you need to calculate your sales revenue according to each product category. If your products sell by the unit, then this is what your revenue will look like:

Sales Revenue
=
18 No Compromise Bar (dates and cashews) × £ 4.00

Sales Revenue = £ 73.00

Now, if you're like Mary's Brigadeiro, you might be selling your products in boxes. Mariane Oliveira sells small gift boxes of 4, 6 and 12 brigadeiros. However, she also offers bigger boxes that go from 38 to up to 60 brigadeiros per box. If that is the case of your business, each box will take the place of the "quantity" variable, and the retail price of the box will take the place of "unit price". It will look like this:

Sales Revenue = 5 Gift Boxes (12) × $ 36.00

Sales Revenue = $ 180

This model will help you to calculate revenue for all kinds of sales in different channels, including all your product range, your online sales and additional products or services (like wrapping gifts or add-ons if it's a customised order).

Accurate sales revenue projection is vital for your budget plan, as it serves as the foundation for other elements, like pricing, costs or profitability forecasts.

By carefully estimating your sales revenue and comparing it to your business' real performance, you can expect to manage your finances effectively, and to make informed decisions or implement changes to achieve your financial goals.

2 — Pricing

Pricing is critical when creating a budget plan. It's not only one of the elements needed to calculate your revenue, it is also a factor that impacts your business' profitability directly.

To set the right prices (and make enough money) for each of the products in your assortment, here are some of the aspects you should consider before writing down a price tag:

PRODUCTION COSTS
This includes the cost of ingredients, packaging, labour (your own and your employees'), utilities and expenses directly related to the production of your chocolates.

MARKET RESEARCH
The prices of similar businesses in the market will have come up during your market research. To find businesses that might be your competition, take into account product quality (ingredients), uniqueness, brand positioning and target audience. Prices set by companies with similar target audiences and brand positioning will help you tailor your own prices at the same, higher or lower level, depending on how your offer differs from theirs.

PROFIT MARGIN
Your desired profit margin is the amount of money you want to make from each sale. To set a profit margin that answers your business objectives, consider your financial targets (how much money you need to pay off your costs) and profitability goals (after paying off your costs and investments, how much money you want to make as a profit).

PRICING FLEXIBILITY
Some special occasions or strategies may call for prices that differ from the initial ones you set. It might be the case that you're looking to gain new clients by offering a free sample when they buy a product. Or it could be that you're looking to quickly sell short shelf life products before their ideal consumption cycle is over.

Whenever an occasion calls for pricing flexibility, determine the conditions of this new price (products, duration, new pricing) and calculate revenue for these products based on the new prices you've set.

You might find there are more elements to consider when setting a price tag, like your uniqueness and your business' added values. Combined, all the relevant factors will influence your pricing strategy. But, remember that nothing is set in stone — the economy, materials and tools' price fluctuations and market behaviour will also impact your costs and your selling prices.

The impact of the energy crisis and inflation in 2022 and 2023 are a perfect example of how costs of energy and ingredients increased rapidly and unexpectedly. Many artisans were forced to adjust their selling prices to remain profitable. Some artisans decided to make few and lighter price increases spread over time, choosing to sell at a lower margin in hopes that the market would go back to what it was. For you to eventually be able to make decisions like these, it's important to conduct regular checks on your pricing list, making sure your business stays profitable as time goes by.

3 — Sales volume

When we talk about sales volume, we talk about the estimated quantity of products you *expect* to sell during a given period. Projecting your sales volume as accurately as you can will have an impact on the final estimation of your revenue. In turn, you will be able to set more realistic financial costs for your business to meet.

Now that you've got the budget plan elements pinned down, it's time to estimate your sales volume for the first time. To keep you from guessing, here are some of the elements you should consider when ball-parking how many sales you expect:

PAST SALES DATA
If you're continuing a family legacy or taking over an existing business, you'll have previous sales data that you can put to good use. Analyse the sales volume of different products throughout different times of the year (seasonal changes, special occasions, holidays) and use it as a guide to estimate future sales. Although helpful, it's not necessary to have previous sales data to estimate your sales volume.

MARKET ANALYSIS
Take a look at your local artisan chocolate market to estimate your sales volumes every month. Traditionally, cooler months and seasonality will influence your sales volumes. Now try to pinpoint key elements that will help you see how much other businesses that are similar to yours are selling; some factors to consider include location, scale, target audience and product assortment.

SALES CHANNELS
Are you planning on setting up a brick-and-mortar store or will you start selling online? (Chapter 11). Maybe you'll do both! Whichever the case, make sure you consider your different sales channels — you may estimate different sales volumes for each of them. Simply remember to add them up to get a total sales volume for your entire chocolate business!

Because accurate sales volume projections are necessary for creating a budget plan (and will also impact your cash flow projection), estimating sales alone won't cut it. Make sure you monitor changes and adjust your estimated sales volume as time goes by — if you see your first month of sales proves to be significantly different from what you've estimated initially, adjust your budget plan. Yes! Even if you've created an annual one.

> **"You have to know the margin of your product. You have the cost of your product and at what price you'll have to sell it to others. And based on this, you have to know how much you want to increase prices year by year."**

RENATA ARASSIRO – RENATA ARASSIRO CHOCOLATES

4 — Types of costs

Considering the different types of costs a business has it's important for your overall financial management. Costs allow entrepreneurs like you to understand the structure of their business.

By calculating your costs, you will have a key element to estimate when you'll be profitable and even allocate resources to optimise your financial and profitability goals, which are making more money than you need to cover your expenses. There are three types of main costs you should consider.

FIXED COSTS

Fixed costs are expenses that remain constant or fixed regardless of how much your business produces or sells. Fixed costs don't shift as changes in production do. For example, if you start selling more bonbons and less chocolate bars, your fixed costs will remain the same.

This also means that fixed costs will be present even at times when you don't produce or don't sell anything at all. It's important to understand that fixed costs have to be paid, regardless of your business' ability to generate revenue.

Make sure you include the following expenses under your fixed costs:

» Rent
» Utilities
» Insurance(s)
» Accountant/Legal Services
» Salaries
» Equipment (in instalments)
» Depreciation of machinery and equipment
» Depreciation of shop furniture and online

If you're just getting started and you decide you need to make an initial investment on equipment, the way you pay for it will influence where you will have to place it in your budget plan.

Some chocolatiers save up money to buy their first piece of equipment in a single payment. Some others decide to buy machinery and pay for it in instalments. If you buy a machine and pay for it at once, then this machine will become one of your one-time costs. If you're paying for equipment (or any other tools and services) in instalments on a recurring basis, then it will become part of your fixed costs until it is fully paid for.

VARIABLE COSTS

Variable costs are expenses that change according to the level of your production or the volume of your sales. This makes these costs directly proportional to your entire production: variable costs increase or decrease as the production volume increases or decreases.

Make sure the following expenses are listed under your variable costs:

» Raw materials (ingredients)
» Packaging
» Shipping and delivery costs
» Sales commissions (if applicable)

Note that because these costs are directly connected to the size of your production, they can be reduced by producing fewer products, choosing less pricey packages (unless packaging is part of your core offer or brand identity) and even by negotiating better prices with suppliers.

As a general rule, artisan chocolatiers don't lower their variable costs by choosing to lower the quality of their ingredients. You'll see it's more often that they choose to produce things at home (and strike "rent" from their fixed costs list) than to lower the standards of the chocolate recipes they create.

Remember that production-related elements are not the only thing that influence variable costs. Inflation, change in suppliers, discontinuation of a product and price fluctuations can impact your variable costs. Just like all financial elements that make your budget plan, you should update your variable costs continuously.

“You have to be very careful with your choice of ingredients. You don’t want to overcharge. But if you charge high, then you have to explain why you charge that much because you use a certain type of, let’s say butter or special something.”

JANICE WONG – JANICE WONG PURE IMAGINATION | 2AM: DESSERTBAR | SOFTHAUS

ONE-TIME COSTS

These types of expenses happen once and are not expected to happen again in the near future. One-time costs are usually associated with a specific event, transaction or service.

These are some examples of expenses you could list as one-time costs:

- Shop design
- Packaging design
- Brand design (branding)
- Consultant fee(s)
- Business registration
- Required certifications

The more detailed you are with your fixed costs, variable costs, and one-time costs in your budget plan, the more comprehensive the outline you will have of your business performance.

MARKETING EXPENSES

Starting up a business, often requires investing in brand awareness to attract potential clients. Think of advertising online or social media, a PR plan or influencer activities to start spreading worth of mouth. The more people know about your brand, the more chances of you scoring trial sales. The more data you get from those early adopters, the better you can reach them after that first sale and earn income from repeated sales.

In Chapter 6, we have outlined the theory behind marketing strategy for the grand opening of your chocolate business, or the improvement of your existing one. For your budget planning, it is important to take marketing expenses and any costs related to it into account and budget them.

“It’s hard to give precise figures. But I would say that 20% – 40% of the total cost is ingredients. Exceptionally, 20% for packaging. The whole machinery is actually factored into the cost of chocolate and ingredients. Personnel costs should be counted at about 50% of the total costs here.”

DAVID MAENHOUT – CHOCOLATIER M

Calculate your budget plan

With all the elements in place, it's time to calculate your budget plan. To get started, decide the period for which you'll be calculating this budget. We recommend an annual budget, with detailed income and cost statements per month. It allows you to monitor every month's financial movements based on real data, and to adjust your business decisions as you go. Now, go back to your budget plan elements and place them in the budget plan template.

If you're calculating your budget plan monthly, you will have to fill out this template each month. In this case, the bottom line will indicate the profit or loss per month. On a longer term, it will also indicate the monthly growth you're achieving with your business, as revenue from sales is expected to increase. The other great thing about this tool is that it will give clear indications of how your different product categories are doing in real life, compared to your initial estimates.

Before we deep-dive into Tool 2 and its uses, don't forget that budget plans serve as a guide of where you'll need to end up financially, and where/when you'll need to incorporate changes. For example, if your budget plan seems not to add up at the beginning, it might be telling you your business needs to start with a smaller assortment, that your prices per units should go up (or down) or that you need to manage costs more efficiently.

PRICE PER SELLING UNIT			SALES VOLUME - PER PRODUCT	
Product	Selling unit	Price	Product	Sales volume

SALES REVENUE			
Product	Sales volume	Price	Amount
Total sales revenue:			

FIXED COSTS		VARIABLE COSTS		ONE-TIME COSTS	
Cost	Amount	Cost	Amount	Cost	Amount
Total:		Total:		Total:	

TOTAL COSTS	
Cost	Amount
Fixed	
Variable	
One-time	
Total costs:	

EXTRAS	
Cost	Amount
Depreciation (machinery/furniture)	
Taxes	
Total costs:	

TOTAL BUDGET	
Source	Amount
(+) Income (total sales revenue)	
(−) Total costs	
Total:	

"I listen more to my heart about what I want to do with my products. But if something is too expensive to make, we just can't make it. We're still a business, we have to be profitable. My bonbons are obviously different prices, all of them in relation to the cost of the goods. But we're charging the same thing for all coffee for example — we have a very cool sign that says espresso, but that could mean a macchiato, a cortado, a cappuccino or a latte. We're not penny and cent, we have one price for either a latte or a macchiato."

HÅKAN MÅRTENSSON – HÅKAN CHOCOLATIER

TOOL 2
CASH FLOW (PROJECTION) PLAN

The cash flow projection plan will mainly focus on the solvability of your business. In other words: it will show if you have sufficient cash balance to pay your bills and loans in time. Where the budget plan focuses on profitability, the cashflow projection focuses on money coming in from sales and going out to pay suppliers, staff, rent, etc.

Starting a business (or continuing one) means you'll already have quite some expenditures in place before you start selling. Your shop (online or offline) and production infrastructure, branding, packaging, equipment and other essentials will have to be paid out before you make your first sale — this is where your cash flow projection comes in.

A cash flow projection will help you understand the money that comes in and goes out of your business. It's used to keep track of this cash flow, to make informed decisions about your finances, and to make sure you have enough funds to meet your financial obligations (bills must be paid!). This tool will also help you adjust your budget plan as you go.

A cash flow (projection) plan involves estimating the inflows and outflows of cash over a specific period. Because your budget plan and cash flow projection will work together, it's best if you choose the same time frame for both. We recommend a cash flow projection plan over 12 months, but with a detailed breakdown for every month.

Just like with the first tool, a cash flow projection will be made of a series of key elements.

1 — Cash inflow

Cash inflow refers to all the possible sources where cash will come into your business. There are three main sources of cash inflow you should consider:

YOUR START-UP CAPITAL

Start-up capital refers to the initial funding that your new business requires to get started. This is the money that is needed to cover the expenses associated with launching a new venture, such as market research, product development, marketing, legal fees and office space.

Starting capital can come from a variety of sources, including personal savings, loans from friends and family, bank loans, crowdfunding campaigns, venture capital, angel investors or grants. The amount of starting capital that you'll need will depend on factors such as the industry, the size of the business and your business model.

Having sufficient starting capital is crucial to the success of your new or growing business, as it allows you to cover its expenses during the initial stages before it starts generating revenue. Without enough starting capital, your business may struggle to get off the ground or be forced to shut down prematurely.

In the cash projection plan, you should list all the types of funding you have access to. They will accumulate as your available start-up capital. And remember! Some funds such as loans need to be paid back, so you will also have to state this as ouflow cash.

SALES REVENUE
Once your business takes off, cash from sales revenue will determine your main source of incoming cash. To calculate your cash inflow, you will need the sales revenue you've calculated for the budget plan along with a clear estimate on *when* you will receive the payment for the products sold.

For instance:

- **Online/offline stores:** customers will pay immediately for any purchase, so your business will receive the cash immediately after the sale.
- **Most B2B-focused business:** customers such as hotels, retailers, restaurants may pay you according to the terms and conditions agreed upon. It's common that payments take place 30 or 60 days after the invoice has been sent. In this case, you'll be pre-financing the ingredients, labour and packaging. 30 to 60 days can go by until your customer has paid the total bill. This means your cashflow will be impacted. You will have paid production/delivery expenses for the delivered goods, but the cash from the sale will only be available later on.

OTHERS
If your business would also generate cash revenue from other activities, such as payments from sponsored deals, fees from events, franchises, product licenses and others, also estimate the moments when the payments of those services would come in. They will add up to your cash inflow the date the payment is received.

2 — Cash outflow

You can probably tell from its name. Cash outflows represent the payments you will need to make every month. And just like you may have put together, you can also guide your cash outflows by taking a look at the 3 types of costs you calculated when working on your budget plan.

Typical cash outflows include the costs of:

- Raw materials and ingredients
- Packaging materials
- Rent and utilities: such as electricity, gas and water bills (usually the most significant cash outflow)
- Labour costs: monthly salaries such as production staff, sales associates and administrative staff
- Equipment and machinery: chocolate tempering machines, moulds, packaging machines
- Marketing and advertising: promoting the business and your products through activities on social media, online advertising, print advertising, PR activities, events
- Taxes and licenses: you will need to pay various taxes such as income tax, sales tax, other fees, licenses and permits required by local authorities
- Insurance: liability insurance and property insurance, to protect your business against potential losses and damages
- Maintenance and repairs: always include a cash reserve for maintenance and repairs of equipment and machinery, keeping the (online) store or brick-and-mortar facility in good condition

3 — Cash flow timing

When is cash flowing in or out? Think about how sales change over time. You might have a peak number of clients during seasons where artisan chocolate is on high demand, and get bigger cash inflows out of them. And just like this, you might have fewer sales and less cash flowing in during other periods.

In a nutshell, cash inflow and outflow won't always align. This is why it's important to plan for the *exact* time the outflow or inflow happens.

Calculate your cash flow projection

With all needed elements in place, you're ready to calculate your projected cash flow by following the next steps:

1. **START WITH YOUR CURRENT CASH BALANCE**
How much cash do you have at the beginning of your journey? This is the amount of money you have, and that will be allocated to your business as you start working on your cash flow projection. This amount will be represented as "current cash balance".

2. **ADD YOUR PROJECTED CASH INFLOW**
Take the calculated cash inflow for the monthly or annual (or even weekly) period you'll be working on and add it to your starting cash balance.

3. **SUBTRACT YOUR PROJECTED CASH OUTFLOW**
You've added your current cash balance and your projected cash inflows. Now, you'll have to deduct all the projected cash outflow from that sum. To do this, consider the timing of each cash flow based on pay cycles, invoice times and immediate transactions.

4. **CALCULATE YOUR NET CASH FLOW**
The net cash flow represents your cash balance during the period you have previously selected. This metric projects the cash availability you'll have to meet your financial obligations, and that you'll analyse to define a negative or positive total cash flow.

To calculate your net cash flow, you can use this simple formula with elements you've already calculated:

Projected cash flow
=
Beginning cash balance + Net cash flow

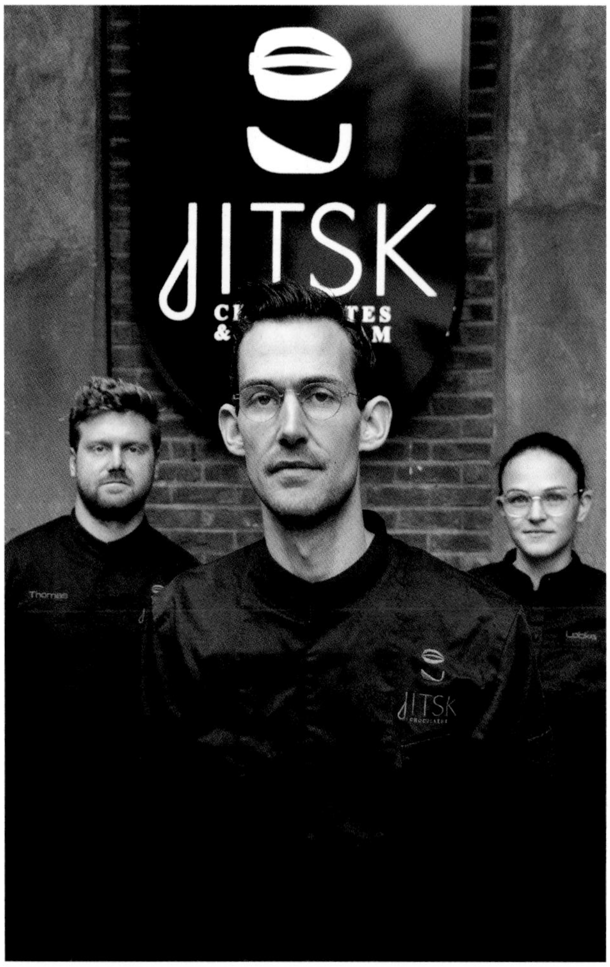

"After two years we had earnings and our loss was eliminated. So, it means we were making money after two years. In Belgium, when you start seeing a business model of food, that's just something you almost don't come across. Do you earn a lot then? No, you don't, but you run in the green."

JITSK HEYNINCK – JITSK CHOCOLATES

Let's see how this would apply to real-life. A positive net cash flow will tell a chocolatier they're making money after setting all their costs and debts.

POSITIVE NET CASH FLOW

Cash Inflows	**Cash Outflows**
Sales Revenue: $5,000	Cost of Goods Sold: $2,500
Loans: $2,000	Operating Expenses: $1,500
	Loan Repayment: $500

Net Cash Flow = (Cash Inflows – Cash Outflows)
Net Cash Flow = ($5,000 + $2,000) – ($2,500 + $1,500 + $500)
Net Cash Flow = $7,000 – $4,500
Net Cash Flow = **$2,500**

This chocolatier knows that, at the end of the month, he or she will have made profit to either reinvest or save for future financial decisions.

Now, this is what a negative cash flow would look like and the implications it may have.

NEGATIVE NET CASH FLOW

Cash Inflows	**Cash Outflows**
Sales Revenue: $3,000	Cost of Goods Sold: $1,800
Loans: $1,000	Operating Expenses: $1,500
	Loan Repayment: $800

Net Cash Flow = (Cash Inflows – Cash Outflows)
Net Cash Flow = ($3,000 + $1,000) – ($1,800 + $1,500 + $800)
Net Cash Flow = $4,000 – $4,100
Net Cash Flow = **–$100**

In this case, the business calls for changes since it's in a cash flow deficit — it's losing money. Financial adjustments can help turn the deficit into a break-even situation.

Money deficit sounds scary, but as a matter of fact, it's highly likely that your cash flow is negative in the earlier stages of your chocolate business, or that you're breaking even each month. Both scenarios are okay, as long as they are temporary.

As long as your projected calculations show that you will be able to go from a negative to a positive cash flow within an acceptable time frame, you don't need to call it quits.

BUT HOW LONG IS AN ACCEPTABLE TIME?

Unfortunately, there's not a single answer to say how long your business should take to be profitable, or how long you should wait before your cash flow turns positive.

In general, most of the artisans interviewed admitted it took them 6 to 12 months before their businesses started making enough money to become solvable. They pointed out that having sufficient funds to overcome those first months was crucial. They also pointed out that starting small and not over-investing in equipment and staff helped them to build profitability and solvability by the end of that challenging first year.

You're ready to put these financial tools to the test. As a good practice, you can make budget plan and cash flow projection mock-ups with different prices and products so you can get an idea of how small changes can have a big influence on your business' finances.

And bear in mind! Almost all businesses experience a cash drain during the first weeks (and even months). This doesn't mean your business isn't set up for success, it just means you should be prepared with a cash reserve to cushion this initial deficit, and to keep close track of your finances to understand where things could be improved. Cash reserves can include personal savings, donations or support from organisations that fund small businesses.

Besides the calculations these two tools offer, you should also calculate your personal living costs during the months you project your business won't be profitable yet.

AIM FOR THE TOP, PREPARE FOR THE DOWNHILL.

Even with the most thorough budget plan in place, unexpected situations happen all the time. As you embark on your chocolate shop journey, it's wise to save money for a couple of extra months of unprofitability after your calculations.

A clear forecast on your budget plan and your cash flow projection will offer a better overview of the type of funding and investments you need to get started. With this in place, it's time to take the next step in your chocolate business venture — *where* to look for these funds.

"I think, maybe at some point, being in a small town is probably beneficial to start. So, if you can be in a smaller town and you can be like the corner bakery, that's good... unless there's already 10 bakeries. And this is because small towns are interesting, the demographics are spreading out. People that were living in big cities, San Francisco, Los Angeles, have access to a computer, they can work remotely. What we're seeing is people moving out of these big cities, which were expensive, and coming to work remotely from the countryside. They're leaving a city where they had access to quality assortment, great restaurants, and then they go to a small town. So, I think that's where theopportunity is."

JULIAN ROSE – JULIAN ROSE CONSULTING

Don't be afraid to show off your products in a different way, like the Moreno brothers did in this creative photoshoot

CHAPTER 8

FUNDING OR SAVINGS?

THE MONEY TO GET STARTED

After you've gotten a clear forecast of what your finances may look like, as a chocolatier and future chocolate business owner, you have to consider THE BEST WAY TO FUND your venture. This often comes down to choosing between getting started with your own savings or seeking external funding.

Starting on your own savings means taking on all the financial risk yourself. Although it can mean that your starting scale will be smaller, it also means complete control over the business and freedom to make decisions without external influence. In the worst-case scenario, it means less risk in owing money to any organisation if things go south.

Now, in contrast to this option, external funding can provide you with the financial support you need to launch your business. However, it also means giving up some control and potentially having to answer to investors. If you think about the worst-case scenario once more, taking out a loan to kick-start your company could mean owing money regardless of the success of your investment.

Whichever the decision, it should be based on careful consideration of your business goals and personal circumstances. In this chapter, we will explore the pros and cons of these options and see how successful chocolatiers have managed their starting efforts in real life.

"I didn't start by calculating how much I wanted to earn. Ideally, it would be the right thing to do. But, when you're starting, the figures around suppliers and employees come first. If anything's left, then you can count on it as your own. Because, there are so many expenses at the beginning that you might just break even."

DAVIDE COMASCHI – DAVIDE COMASCHI

Davide Comaschi believes that the presentation of all his products must match the quality claims and positioning of one's brand

CALCULATE FUNDS AND INVESTMENTS

How much money do you need to start your business? Opinions differ. Depending on how luxurious, highly equipped or staffed your business will be. It is also related to brand choices: are your production and brand concept in need of a specific, exclusive appearance when it comes to shop design and furniture, packaging, tools and even a location from the very beginning?

If you're unsure of your production size and wish to estimate how much money a business of a specific scale would need to kick-start, you will need these elements to start estimating a start-up sum:

1 Total costs

In the previous chapter, you've calculated the different types of costs you'll have. These are forecasted expenses for your business to be fully operational, and they are one of the elements you'll need to consider to estimate your startup costs.

2 Contingencies

It's important to calculate a budget that serves as a financial safety net for your business. Look back to the previous chapter, where we talked about the time it takes a business to be profitable. You might have estimated that it will take your company a determined number of months to reach profitability (the ability to generate money after accounting for all expenses). To calculate the financial contingency you need, it's recommended you add "safety months" to this initial profitability calculation.

For example, if your initial calculations are telling you your business can be profitable in 4 months, calculate contingencies for 7 months. This way, you are planning your budget based on 7 months without profit. If your business becomes profitable before what's expected, then that's a win! Now, if profitability is delayed, this will allow you to be financially prepared to keep your business afloat as you adjust your finances to meet your financial goals.

Although contingency estimation will vary, a general rule of thumb is to set aside a 10% – 15% of the total of your start-up costs for contingencies.

3 Time frame

It's a good practice to take your profitability period to use as a general time frame for your initial funds calculation. Keeping to the previous example, if 4 months is your calculated profitability time, and you're calculating contingencies for a total of 7 months, then this will be the time frame that determines your final start-up cost.

"I'm thinking of 3 good tempering machines. The smallest would be around €30.000 to €35.000. And I think you quickly come to €80.000 – €100.000 to start in a decent way, purely focused on production. You need worktables, equipment, small supplies and packaging. I think these days you quickly get to €100.000 to start. I remember when I started, I was so cautious, because I didn't know what it all meant or what I was getting into. All I knew was that I needed good machines and the right equipment. For example, a good blender rather than a cheap alternative. Because if you buy cheap, it breaks down quickly. It's better to pay a little more for decent equipment that will last 20 years."

DAVID MAENHOUT – CHOCOLATIER M

4 Calculate total start-up cost

Once you know your initial costs and are comfortable with the time period of your financial contingency, you can use the following formula to calculate your total start-up costs:

Initial start-up cost
=
Total costs × Time frame

Total start-up cost
=
15% of Initial start-up cost
+ Initial start-up cost

Knowing your start-up cost is necessary to determine your initial investment, which will help you weigh your options based on your financial possibilities and needs.

More than a craftsman – Mirosław Pelczar also understands the cost-benefit relation of acquiring new equipment, which helps de-risk investments in new machinery for his production

When we asked artisan entrepreneurs about their experience, two main pieces of advice were highlighted by *all*:

One: set your own limits according to what you can handle.

Sometimes, it's easy to get carried away by the stories of others. However, every chocolatier we've talked to will tell you that the best approach is to look only at your own context when you're about to take your first financial step.

What they did? They imagined the worst possible outcome before they got started. This was the strategy of STEPHEN TRIGG to avoid an over-investment in case things didn't go according to plan:

"That's always been my strategy, *'what does my worst-case scenario look like? Can I live with it? Am I comfortable?'* If yes, then I move forward. No? Then I go back to the drawing board and rethink things."

Stephen took the time to run over his calculations until he was comfortable with losing all his initial investment. Comfortable doesn't mean lavish, but he made sure he and his wife's personal circumstances wouldn't take a direct hit from losing money if the business didn't succeed.

Whether you use your own savings, loans from the bank or investors' money, remember money comes from somewhere. Stephen's strategy didn't put his house or daily life at risk. And this is an approach that can help you avoid being neck-deep in debt.

"You need to have an idea of the calculated risk. Even though it is a risk, it needs to be calculated. You have to be able to say, 'I am ready to lose this amount of money every month'."

NIKKI THAKKER – ÉNTISI

Stephen's advice comes all the way from the UK. And it's interesting how close it is to the suggestion offered by the owner and creative mind behind FIDÉE in China. JAP JOY doesn't know Stephen, but he had the same train of thought when we asked about his start-up costs:

"I tried to start this business with the lowest cost. I didn't go to the bank for a loan but started with my own savings. That's also why I started pretty slow. And when it comes to chocolate, if you just produce a little bit, you only need one or two people to get started and one or two machines. And so, I started producing everything myself in a very small room."

As Jap Joy explains, you might not even need a kitchen or renting a shop to start producing and selling your creations. At the time, investing his savings in ingredients and a tempering machine was all he could afford. And so, he started with what *he* could afford without putting his life at financial risk.

The lower-risk option can be translated into following the inverse path to calculating funds. Instead of calculating your total start-up cost, look at the amount of money you can invest without putting yourself at financial risk. From there, create a budget that includes all elements we've seen in Chapter 7. Once you choose a starting route, the extent of your production will be limited by what your initial budget can buy.

Consider that this might mean slower growth rates, but it doesn't prevent growth at all. Think of how FIDÉE started at a home kitchen. Today, it's a 2-shop artisan chocolate business in China.

Starting up small allows you to grow at your own pace. With no debts to speed up your pace or investors rushing profitability, you will find more time and agility to correct and adapt your financial plans and your offering based on your business' needs and market changes.

Above all, setting your own financial limits will give you enough time to *learn*. As a chocolatier, but also as an entrepreneur, you will need to acquire experience as you go. DAVIDE COMASCHI, skilled chocolate crafter and experienced consultant takes the advice he gives. When getting started, he didn't hurry the process of growth:

"Along with my wife and partner, we put our efforts into creating this luxury brand. It took us 1,5 years of investment to bring our brand to life."

Davide invested steadily and slowly to create the brand he had imagined at the very beginning. This was possible because he gave himself enough time, but also because he knew where he wanted to go and what he needed to get there.

"One of the most important things I think you have to have in mind, right now, and it's difficult, is when to say no to business opportunities."

JACOBO & PABLO MORENO – MALLORCA

Located all the way across the Atlantic from Davide, RENATA ARASSIRO has similar advice for all chocolatiers who are just getting started:

"I started with my own money. What I have to say for the beginners is: start with your own money, step by step, with what you've got. You don't have to start with something that you don't have, because your business may be a huge success, but it also may not. I think it's better to start with your own money, your savings, and do it little by little."

The Mallorca production site emphasises manual labour and optimises every recipe to meet their high artisanal standard – the Moreno brothers only consider mechanical production if it enhances product quality and outcome

Two: Don't underestimate the power of contingencies.

Especially if you've secured external financial money, make sure your financial reserves cover the first 6 months of your entrepreneurial venture without relying (only) on fast incoming revenue.

As a well-known and successful freelance consultant, SEBASTIAN PETTERSSON understands not only the concept of being financially stable without a profit, but the idea behind an income that is constantly fluctuating:

"As a consultant, sometimes, jobs come to you for 2 months, and then you need to go and find hustle jobs for the next 8 months. It's very up and down. I think that's something you really need to look into."

You can use Seb's guiding concept and apply it to you as a starting chocolate business owner: income isn't a certain thing.

It might be the case that you start being profitable in record time! But, as an entrepreneur, you should be prepared for the more realistic option: it takes starting businesses some time to make money.

As we've said before, it's impossible to pin down a specific time frame that will answer to all chocolate businesses. When it comes to funding or savings, a 6-month period is the usual safe margin for you to calculate the initial financial reserves you need (apart from any investments) to cover all types of costs (Chapter 7) without generating a lot of income at the start.

With the two most important suggestions we collected from chocolatiers around the world, the tools to forecast your financial needs (Chapter 7) and your start-up costs calculated, it's time to investigate the most usual places where starting chocolatiers find the money for their venture.

"The first two years, we didn't make any money. We had money coming in but we weren't profitable. That is quite disheartening. If I'm honest, part of it was down to my commitment levels. Psychologically, I wasn't 100% there, I was 80% there. And you can't work like that. I had a look in the mirror and thought, 'I need to start stepping up'. And it wasn't the next day, it was a snowball that slowly grew. The more effort I put in, the more I started to get out of it."

STEPHEN TRIGG – LAUDEN CHOCOLATE

Just like David Maenhout, many use "behind the scenes" photography to advertise the artisanal and authentic character of their businesses

SAVINGS-BASED STARTING POINT

Starting a business only with your savings is a feasible option for aspiring chocolate entrepreneurs. While securing outside funding or taking out loans may be the norm for different start-ups, relying on personal savings is not only possible, but offers a lot of benefits too.

Take the words of ENRIC ROVIRA. Since he opened his chocolate business in Barcelona until today, he managed his venture without external funding. Looking back to his experience of starting only with his savings, he's happy with the freedom he's had over the years:

"We never had investors. The business started small and grew quite naturally. Looking back, I would've done things the same way, because maybe with an investor, I couldn't have made all the decisions I wanted."

Although you will be limited to what your savings can afford, starting off only with what you've got at hand enables you to maintain full control over your business, avoid debt and keep your expenses in check. When he and his wife started Lauden Chocolate in the UK, STEPHEN TRIGG didn't have any economical help from third parties either. Reminiscing about the financial decisions he made throughout the years and as the business grew, he highlights the freedom starting independently gave him:

"The biggest thing for me was the freedom to be accountable just to myself and my wife, not to turn around and say to the investor why you flew business class to Japan — I don't need to justify myself. This might mean I'm not going to be a 30-million-pound company. But I don't want to be. I want to build something that's mine and my wife's."

It is often the case that many chocolatiers wish to avoid entering contracts and high-risk arrangements. This might be to avoid unnecessary debt, or like Stephen, they don't aspire to create an enterprise out of their venture.

Regardless of the intention, not every chocolatier will start their entrepreneurial journey with enough savings. This is where many inspiring events happen. Some business owners we talked to found the financial support they needed close to home because of one life-changing decision: they shared their story.

Although known for her artistic self and successful event-planning track record, JANICE WONG's personal savings had a little help to jump-start her business:

"There was a budget because my family supported my business a lot, combined as well with my own savings. But also, I think it was important, of course, not to overspend. You don't have to have everything in at the start. You can always build it in stages."

"You really have to make sure to cut expenses and start building things up slowly. Then when you have to start, think what you can do to promote people to come in, what you can sell or sample. And at the beginning, I think it's very important to cut every single cost you can without losing your quality. It doesn't have to be cutting costs in ingredients, but think about if you really need that fan or that pen, that new iPad or that tape. Or, get offers from three four different companies before you buy something. Like this, believe it or not, after one month I was cash flow positive."

HÅKAN MÅRTENSSON – HÅKAN CHOCOLATIER

Despite having an initial budget, Janice followed the golden rule of not investing more than was available at the time. And just like her, highly skilled and family-oriented NIKKI THAKKER received support from her family when she jumped into the artisanal chocolate world:

"So, the initial round of investment was actually done by my family — my husband and my father-in-law invested in the business, and that was very encouraging. It was encouraging because when your family feels that you have the potential to do something, it gives you the confidence to do it."

Getting financial support from her loved ones was more than an economic aid. Nikki felt inspired to fight for her business and step up to the challenges she faced along the way.

If you're starting your business with your savings or with family or friends helping you out, it doesn't mean you won't need careful planning, resource management and budgeting (Chapter 7). Because these will still ensure you can turn your creative ideas into profitable and sustainable products and business concepts.

Tip for success!

When borrowing money from family or friends, creating contracts helps establish clear expectations, provides legal protection, maintains formality and adds legitimacy not only to the transaction, but to your business if you were to present a business or financial plan for loans or investing purposes. If opting to create a contract to pay the money back, it's advisable to consult with legal professionals to ensure that the contract is legally enforceable and meets the specific needs of the parties involved.

Nikki Thakker started éntisi with the financial support of her family and grew it into a premium multi-shop business

“The hardest thing for me was just getting started. Ultimately, starting a chocolatery like I have today is not cheap. The machines that I have standing I could only buy by having had my career in the sector and been supported by connections. And I was just not taken seriously for the first few years, many colleagues said, ‘the thing you want to do doesn’t go. Everyone wants to do that. It makes sense that you want to do it, but that business model is not right’.

And, financially, it’s always the same story. At the bank I was not taken seriously either. Eventually, I did have someone who was able to help me out, which also ensured the business. The only thing that I notice now is that by growing, you keep facing those same things to get to the next step, but it’s ten times harder.”

JITSK HEYNINCK – JITSK CHOCOLATES

Jitsk Heyninck creates everything from scratch using seasonal ingredients; automation equipment helps him maintain consistency and reduce manual labour

EXTERNAL FUNDING:
WHERE TO FIND THE FUNDS?

Based on your calculated startup cost, your budget plan and cash flow projection (Chapter 7), if you consider you'll need external funding to open your artisan chocolate business, it's time to look for where these funds can come from.

ALWAYS REMEMBER! A business plan, budget plan and cash flow projection will be documents required by all legal entities to grant any form of external funding.

Now that you've put together the documents you need to ask for funds, here are some channels you can start considering:

1 Bank loans

One of the most straightforward ways to finance your chocolate business is to get a loan from a bank. This can be done through your bank of preference.

Consider that banks offer different types of loans. If you're looking to start a business, ask for a "business loan" and not a personal one. A business loan is an agreement with a determined interest to be paid back over a specific period of time.

Business loans are offered to people for the specific reason to start or expand a business or invest in the equipment or tools to work on that business. These loans are usually offered as secured or unsecured, and the terms and conditions (as well as the interest rates) can vary from lender to lender. It's advisable to get a quotation from different banks or lenders before making a decision.

The types of business loans you can find will also differ in different countries, according to their laws and tax regulations. Make sure you disclose the reason behind the loan and banks will guide you through your best options.

2 Friends and family

As you've seen, this option is not uncommon for artisan chocolatiers starting their business. Although family members or friends are often willing to offer financial support, remember that having a legal document stating the lend or donation is always a good idea.

It can also happen that friends or relatives become a valuable source of business in the form of investors or business partners. This is the story of HÅKAN MÅRTENSSON. After years of working on his first venture with a partner, things didn't go as planned and the business had to be shut down. Being a foreigner in the United States, where a credit score and other requirements are musts to get a loan or for an investing company to back you up, his situation didn't seem to get less complex.

Håkan discovered, without intending to, that a conversation with a friend can turn into a business proposal at any given time:

"Fika, my previous business, had closed like one and a half years earlier. Being Swedish in the US, I have a green card, but I'm not a citizen. It makes it very hard to get loans and that kind of stuff to start a business. And to start a business, you don't need a lot of capital, but you need some money to invest.

I talked to a friend of mine. He ran the Meridian hotel chain for 30 years and had built numerous places around that. After he had left that, he did not want to retire. So, he said, '*what's your idea? What do you want to do?*'. I explained my vision about building my brand and store preferably upstate. I told him what I had in mind and what I'd been planning for the last 10 years. He said, '*okay, should we do it together?*'"

Although Håkan's chat with a friend turned into a unique concept store and a strong partnership, it's always recommended to be critical and realistic. Critical because you may put close ones and your own venture at risk if tough decisions aren't made, and because sometimes personal and business relations don't mix too well.

You should also be realistic by shedding clarity on how much and how fast you expect the business to grow, and the risks involved in the worst-case scenario. Even though personal relations might help you get the money you need, it doesn't guarantee the success of the business or the partnership.

In case your friends and family would need the investment or loan back, make sure you draft a contract. Writing down agreements related to your business may come handy in the future.

3 Foundations and grants

This will vary from country to country. But many places around the world offer access to foundations that organise contests for start-up concepts, where the prize is money to fund the venture. Some other organisations (politically or privately funded) also offer support in the form small sums of money that are meant to help small businesses get started. Research the status of the start-up market in your area and you might end up being positively surprised.

4 Crowdfunding

You can use crowdfunding platforms (such as Kickstarter or Indiegogo, depending on where you're located) to raise funds for your chocolate business. This involves creating a campaign and promoting it to potential supporters, who can contribute money towards your business in exchange for rewards.

5 Investors and venture capitalists

Angel investors and venture capitalists are individuals or firms that provide funding to start-ups in exchange for equity. You can pitch your chocolate business idea to them and potentially receive funding if they see potential in your business.

A good practice before pitching your ideas to potential investors or partners is understanding the implications this may have on your production, your business identity and the way you build your customer experience. An advocate to stay independent for as long as you want is Mary's Brigadeiro's MARIANE OLIVEIRA:

"In the early stages of the business, I had an investor. Less than a year after we started, our vision for the company had changed and we could not keep going forward together. Based on this experience, I may not want to have an investor again. Nowadays, there are other ways to get funds or even money from the government."

Example of the power of a clear differentiating concept: Ryan L. Foote's 3D-printed bonbons are appealing to clients but also to investors

Also sharing her wisdom in the chocolate world, we have the queen of chocolate. Although KIRSTEN TIBBALLS began her journey as a chocolate entrepreneur with her own savings, she is well aware of the funding opportunities that exist in the country where she operates:

"In Australia we do have a lot of businesses that have a financial backer that doesn't necessarily work in the business. Some artisans will be either approached or will approach someone and say, '*I've got a concept, I think it'll work really well. I don't have the funds to make it happen. Do you want to go into some sort of partnership or agreement?*'. That happens quite a bit."

BERNARD PROOT believes business growth is a combination of opportunities and luck. Regardless of the financial backing you're considering, he advises you to always stay alert:

"You can't say yes to everything. My recommendation is to go slow in these decisions. Follow your nature and be vigilant. Avoid flash-in-the-pan relationships that only yield short-term gains."

Whether you're leaning towards external funding or your own savings to start your venture, the road ahead can be challenging. Each option has its own set of requirements and risks, benefits and disadvantages — be sure to carefully consider each of the options. And regardless of which you choose, remember you will need a business plan, a budget plan and a cash flow projection (Chapter 7).

"Some people will borrow money to start a business, but what are the implications for that? Because there are things that we can't control, like interest rates. I think having a business is very rewarding, but if you are a business owner, it's no longer just about the product. You are now human resources, managing your own finances, managing product rotation and budgets."

KIRSTEN TIBBALLS – SAVOUR SCHOOL

CHAPTER 9

STAFF & HIRING: BUILD YOUR TEAM

For Bernard Proot, every team member is essential to achieving success: each newcomer at DelRey is welcomed by a coach who provides guidance for the first six months

Nibbo
Beanto bar chocolate

Your staff will not only help you with the operations of your shop. Just like you, they will be ADVOCATES FOR YOUR BRAND IDENTITY and story. And your relationship with your staff will determine their relationship with your clients. The team you build will help you grow and represent your brand and will have a direct impact on your business' success.

JACOBO AND PABLO MORENO live by this philosophy. With their family legacy as a business that keeps growing through the decades, Mallorca's administration is run by family members:

"Besides our shops in Madrid, we also have shops in Mexico and Japan. We separate the business into three branches: shops, production, and administration. There are two directors in each of the branches, and they're all part of the family — we are brothers, and the rest are our cousins.

That's part of the differentiation element. We look at it as if each of the areas of the company are separate companies in a way. And then we just work together to merge everything, to have one way of looking at things."

Family or not, the idea behind this business approach is that your team members should be people you can trust. Trust, even if you are a solo entrepreneur, is not to be taken for granted when putting together a team. Travelling the world to give demonstrations and consult in other chocolate, SEBASTIAN PETTERSSON knows the importance of teamwork. A team has been trained by him to run the production operations autonomously while he is focusing on other aspects of the business. This is the one thing that allows his ideas to come to life, even when Seb's away:

"My team knows exactly what they're supposed to do. I have people that I rely on, so I can be wherever I want as long as they keep in contact with me."

If you're growing your business or are taking over an existing one, it's probable that you already have a group of people who are part of that business. The question to recurrently ask yourself is how those people are accurately representing the spirit of your brand, and how you can help them do so.

However, if you're starting from scratch, there's another a key question to be answered — do you believe you need help to start selling?

"The biggest advantage of more employees is that we can produce more. But if you're a beginner and you want to start alone, you can! Focus on the flavours and quality of your chocolate, and on selling locally instead of internationally or around the country."

JAP JOY – FIDÉE

Because Nibbo is a bean-to-bar concept brand, beans are hand-picked by the team and roasted on-site

BY YOURSELF, OR AS A TEAM?

Starting on your own or do you have a team that has your back? There's no wrong or right answer. The answer, however, will impact your revenue and costs, production line schedules, the volume you can produce and the reach of your operations. And last but not least, by relying on a (small) team you will get the support you need during busy or difficult times (like illness or unexpected life events).

Most chocolatiers who've talked to us expressed their preference to work with someone who supports them. In a lot of cases, the first team member wasn't a hire, it was their partner.

This is the story of STEPHEN and SUN TRIGG. Although their roles shifted as Lauden Chocolate grew, they found the team they needed in their significant other:

"We've worked so well as a business. My wife and I, we're like a yin and yang, we complement each other. She's this whirlwind of energy and goes 100 miles an hour, whereas I'm sort of the opposite. I will pull back to keep it grounded and keep that risk management structure in place.

My wife is now just R&D, so she doesn't do any daily production. She does R&D while I run the company day-to-day."

This was also the case of MIROSLAW PELCZAR. When he began his journey to create M. Pelczar Chocolatier, his wife who is a pastry chef, was with him every step of the way to create something new for the Polish market:

"Exactly 12 years ago, together with my wife who is a pastry chef, we decided we wanted to do something different than classic pastry chef work in a classic pastry shop. We wanted to produce handmade chocolates which are high quality and different from all industrial ones available in Poland."

With these examples, you might see how working by yourself will place more responsibility on your hands. However, there are multiple owners of successful chocolate businesses who started their journey on their own. JAP JOY has had a similar experience. He created chocolates at home and eventually asked his sister to help with the production as the demand grew:

"At the beginning, I did everything myself. The gelatos, the chocolates, even some cakes and pastries. I started at home, not even in a studio or a shop, just at home. Then I asked my sister to help. We created the packaging, packed the chocolates and delivered them all over China."

"I think nowadays it's probably better to be a team, to delegate different aspects and maybe do what you do really well and bring that to the table, bring that to the business."

JULIAN ROSE – JULIAN ROSE CONSULTING

DelRey's founder Bernard Proot advises against rushing into equipment purchases — he recommends making gradual high-quality investments that pay off in the long term

Belgian chocolatier DAVID MAENHOUT also started by himself when he gave life to his company, Chocolatier M:

"My wife Isabelle had a full-time job. So, I did everything: produced, sold whenever a customer came in, ordered ingredients and developed recipes. We both agreed at the beginning that this was a great way to see where the business would take us, while she remained professionally active in another industry and had an income. When my wife came home from work, she would help out.

Quite frankly, if I could go back in time, I would hire team members in production and for the shop way faster. My days were stretching to sometimes 20 hours a day and it simply wasn't sustainable.

On top of this, I made the conscious choice to set the price level of my products below the price other artisans were charging. I believed, at that time, it was a good strategy to lower the barrier and have more people come in and discover us. But at a certain moment you're hitting your own limits. After gradually raising the prices and finally hiring the first team member, the need for a second and a third came in.

It all made me realise that this helped me to grow my business, focusing on specific aspects of it. In the end, I'm more involved now in product development and commercial relations, while I can rely on the force and talent of my team to play their part."

David Maenhout and Isabelle (wife) run Chocolatier M as family and business partners whose different skills complement each other

In contrast to those who have started the journey on their own, there are other artisan chocolatiers who would rather start with a team and make less profit. This was also the case for SEB PETTERSSON:

"I would say 100% go with a nice team. Even though you're not going to make a lot of money in the beginning, because you need to split it by three, four or five. If you find the right team, they are always going to have your back, and that's the most important thing. You can't rely on only one person doing everything."

If you begin your journey with a small team, it will cut down the work hours while making production faster and more efficient. However, if you're starting on your own (or with limited help), decision-making could be faster and simpler and you'll have more freedom to innovate.

"So, I'll put all the orders together for the week, print them, and put them on the board. There is a guy who does all of the logistics of the internet orders and all of the B2B orders, packing them and making sure they're dispatched.

We also have what I call a junior sous chef who does all of the ganaches. There's another guy who does all of the shells for the bonbons. The there's a lady, almost like a mother figure, who knows where everything is in the factory. The head chef is not really a head chef, but he runs all of that kind of production of the ganache. And finally, if it gets busy, we've got some part-timers who come in. If it's really busy, my wife will come in, but she's usually only R&D."

STEPHEN TRIGG – LAUDEN CHOCOLATE

Whether you're leaning towards starting this journey by yourself or with a team, it's not a final decision. The number of people and roles that surround you can (and will most likely) change as time goes by. And as KIRSTEN TIBBALLS puts it, you shouldn't go beyond what you can afford:

"I think it depends on your financial situation and the cash flow that you have. Once you start, you need to have an almost equal amount of money for running the business for the first 6 to 12 months without relying on any profit. So, hiring a team really depends on your circumstances. I think it's good if you can start yourself, with very little assistance. This way, you have a full understanding of all the jobs within the business and then it gives you a better understanding of who is going to be the best person for each and every role."

NIKKI THAKKER also recognises the importance of starting small and allowing herself to grow as her business called for it:

"It was just me and a chef who still is working with us. We would make all the chocolates ourselves. I would always come up with new ideas and recipes and we both would do them together. Now, we are a team of around 50 people. It's come to a point where, although I really wish I could be making chocolates all the time, I can't because I have some mails or calls or other things happening. So, I'm not able to be in the kitchen all the time, but I'm completely involved with the product development."

You might be ready to start flying solo, hire some staff or you might be looking to grow your already existing team. Either way, you should set standards and steps for your recruitment process — your staff is an extension of your business, and your hiring process determines the staff your business will end up with.

RECRUITMENT AND HIRING

Hiring the right people means finding those who are a right fit for your company, your way of working and your brand identity. After successfully taking over and rebranding COCO Chocolatier, CALUM HAGGERTY acknowledged the difficulties and the relevance of hiring the right staff:

"If anyone asks me what the hardest thing in business is, it's building a team. That's the hardest thing. But it will depend on other people's skillsets. Building a team was the hardest change for me, and it's the most important thing you can do if you want to continuously grow.

When Calum acquired the business he turned into COCO Chocolatier, a team came with it. But he found that as the brand evolved, he would have to replace part of the staff members. Nonetheless, the future of the business was completely dependent on the skillset of the chocolatiers, who remained as a core part of the current team. Calum made staff choices after deciding on the purpose of the business, the uniqueness he would build upon and the route to market he'd have to take:

"If people want to run a successful businesses in the industry, they need to understand that, even on an artisan level (so, at a smaller level), you do need a certain amount of volume to be able to sustain yourself. If you were selling 100.000 chocolate bars a month, you would still be artisanal if you look at the rest of the industry. But someone who's an artisan and literally makes everything themselves might think that's colossal.

Ultimately, you can't do everything yourself. You're going to remain very small if you try and do everything yourself. And, you can do interesting independent things in an artisan way, even when using a lot of machinery and automation. You can make something pretty extraordinary and also make it scalable, to be able to grow."

For Calum, you need the right staff to delegate tasks, as you can't do everything on your own, particularly as you grow. Like many other chocolatiers, he believes chocolate can keep its artisanship at scale, but just like it means needing more automated process, it also means you'll need more hands on board. And to get them, different chocolatiers have different strategies.

"Teamwork is key. Everyone that's in the kitchen collaborates in the daily briefings. And there is interaction between marketing and sales — conversation and open communication are important.

The beginning is always hard, and you have to be realistic by taking advantage of the skills that you already have. I started my business with my wife and my right-hand man. If you can afford it, I would advise to hire a team, because it's an important investment and it helps develop the company quickly. The advantage of having a team is the ability to have a wider vision and to cooperate.

With time, I also realised that it's not enough to be a good chocolatier. If you want to grow, it's important to be a leader. I feel this strongly. Being recognised as a leader has helped me put together the team I have today."

DAVIDE COMASCHI – DAVIDE COMASCHI

Although his business keeps on growing, Håkan Mårtensson decided he will always be a part of kitchen duties and recipe creation

JANICE WONG's chocolate business carries her name. As a representation of who she is as a professional, she makes sure she is part of interviews of potential employees and never hurries the hiring process:

"I'm usually quite careful... you don't want to grow too fast. I interview everybody personally. They go through rounds of interviews and then they will also do a trial. It's important to have trials as well."

Just like Janice, HÅKAN doesn't just hire anyone to be part of his company. He looks for people who can truly become a part of HÅKAN Chocolatier and embody his brand:

"We are not going to hire just anyone. We have to hire the right person for the brand, because no one is going to care about this place as much as I or my investment partners do. When you're working for someone else, you'll care about the place but never as much as the owner does. So, it has to be a good fit. Someone that has the personality. It's not about what they do, it is about who they are, what they go for."

NIKKI has a particular perspective on hiring people for new roles too. Although she looks for the usual skills, she goes beyond the scope of the chocolate world to hire new people:

"The people we hire for sales need to have some kind of prior sales experience. However, having said that, there are people who have sales experience, but they may not necessarily have it in the same field. Whenever we hire, we call every staff member to our factory, to our kitchen, and we try to show them the whole process of chocolate making. This way, they can get a feel of what goes behind making artisanal chocolates. They understand our choices, our story and what makes us unique. It's important for them to bring that story across to every (new) customer."

At éntisi, all staff members are made part of the chocolate journey. This is because Nikki believes in the power of understanding the business inside out, regardless of your role in the company.

Similar to Nikki, STEPHEN and SUN look for attitude first. They know skills can be taught, but other traits cannot. They also choose this route for pragmatic reasons — they want to avoid rotating staff as much as possible:

"This was really key in our strategy. We hire local people who want to work and who have a good attitude. And then we teach them the skills of making chocolate. We get lots of CVs of people who are chefs or pastry chefs or chocolatiers who want to work in the industry, but we know they will be gone within a few months."

Have you figured out which is your approach to building a team yet? Before jumping into any hiring process, outline the roles your business needs and the description of each role. After you've decided which roles you'll be hiring first, you're ready to draft a hiring process.

But, what is a hiring process and what does it look like? A hiring process is the series of steps an applicant will go through before becoming part of your team. If you're unsure of how to begin drafting yours, here is some inspiration:

Who	Potential employee	You + team members (optional)	You + team members (optional) + candidate	You + team members (optional)	You + team member (optional)
What	Application form	Pre-selection based on application form	1-on-1 interview with candidate	Final selection	Give your new employee the good news

"It's important to understand all aspects of the business, regardless of your skillset. Because if anything changes, or specific roles leave, I have to hire the right people, or take that role. I have to know how to overlook that it's correct, but I don't think I ever want to step out of the kitchen."

HÅKAN MÅRTENSSON — HÅKAN CHOCOLATIER

To get a process like this one started, you should kick it off with a solid application form and a benchmark of what you're looking for in your new employee. Ideally, these are the steps before a new vacancy and application form are shared with the world:

1 Choose the role your business needs next

Are you in need of more hands in the kitchen? Maybe your online following has grown so you need someone to take care of your digital assets for you, or maybe it's time for new products and you're ready to hire Research & Development staff.

When hiring for the first time, most chocolatiers look to the needs of their chocolate production as well as the demand for customer-facing roles. However, the answer to who you need to hire next will be found in the needs of your business. No matter the scale, look at your company and ask yourself where your brand needs an extra pair of hands. This is also how you will define the role you'll be hiring for.

2 Build a role profile

Now that you know which role you're looking for, it's time to outline the tasks of that role. Write down all the main tasks that the new employee will be in charge of and what each task entails. Once you've created a role profile, ask yourself how much time you want to invest in training that person.

Although coaching a new team member is always necessary, you'll require more experience in some roles than in others. With 9 shops in Spain, and 2 international ones, it might come as a surprise how JACOBO and PABLO MORENO handle their family business' hiring process:

"We invest a lot of time in training. We don't really look for high-level employees, because we like people inside our company to grow. Normally, we don't care if the people we hire have background experience. Actually, we prefer someone that has nothing to do with pastry or with chocolate and hasn't even touched the product in their life, but who wants to work and really has a passion for learning something new. We do all the training, we've never hired anyone with more than two years of experience, for example. This gives us the chance to really train everyone the way we want."

You might have a particular technique when it comes to producing chocolates. If you have the time and you want your new kitchen assistant to adapt to your methodology, you might be able to hire someone with less experience. However, if you need a pair of very experienced hands as your business demands to grow, and you don't have a lot of time to coach new people, you might want someone with more experience.

For every task the role requires, repeat this process. Soon enough, you will know what skillset you require for each role and what is the minimum (or maximum) skill level you wish a candidate to possess.

This is what will help you create the right questions and will also help you with assessing with the candidates, both, in their application forms, and during their 1-on-1 interviews.

At DelRey, every kitchen and customer-facing team member undergoes six months of on-site training to embody the business' identity: team members with special skills are encouraged to further develop them throughout their tenure

3 Assess candidates

Because you've previously outlined the profile and desired skillset of the best possible candidate, going through the application forms will be easier. Regardless of how many candidate forms have impressed you, you should still conduct a 1-on-1 interview. These kinds of interviews will let you know if the attitude of the candidate has the potential to be the right fit for your brand.

After you (maybe with the help of existing team members) have pre-selected the applicants that will move onto the interview stage of your process, you're ready to prepare your interview. Unsure of what to ask in an interview? Here are some general questions you can get started with:

» *What inspired you to pursue a career in the artisan chocolate space?*
» *What do you think sets artisanal chocolate apart from mass-produced chocolate, and how would you communicate this to customers?*
» *Why do you believe you would be a good fit for this role and a great addition to the brand?*
» *Before we get into more detailed question about the role you're applying for, can you share a previous experience where you've received negative feedback and your approach to that experience?*

Although some questions might seem generic, understanding what drives someone into the artisan chocolate world is crucial for chocolatiers like MIROSLAW PELCZAR:

"I am picky regarding my staff, if they don't feel the chocolate, the idea and the passion, they are not for me."

Remember to always look back at the questions you asked on your application form when looking to ask more specific or detailed questions. If some of the applicants' answers caught your attention, ask them to elaborate on the subject.

4 Think long-term

One of the most important investments of a business is its staff. So, when you're hiring for a new role, remember to think about the future. Would you like this person to work with you for a long time? Would you like them to become part of the brand, so your team eventually grows into working like a well-oiled machine?

If your answer is yes, then you should include this information in the application form. Don't forget to specify if you're hiring for a full-time and long-term position (there are cases where you might need help for a limited period or high-demand season, during which you can always hire freelance or temporary staff).

Thinking long-term isn't only about how well the security and comfort that comes from a team who's been working together for a long time. It's also about the evolution of these roles as your business grows.

For example, your production assistant might have the potential to eventually be promoted to head of production. This is often the case, as many starting chocolatiers end up shifting roles too.

NIKKI is an entrepreneur, but also the creative mind behind of recipes. She has set a performance standard for her staff, and part of her work is making sure they learn how to sustain this benchmark she has set for her business:

"You cannot teach people, leave them, and then expect them to do things the way you want them to turn out. You have to supervise and monitor what's happening until it comes to a point where they can manage independently."

"I have an in-house training system regarding the chocolate, especially since our shops are not just purely sales places, they are like galleries, museums and information centres in one. So, my staff needs to know what they are talking about."

MIROSLAW PELCZAR – M. PELCZAR CHOCOLATIER

"Our people have their own key and get a whole lot of independence and responsibility. The more freedom you give your people to do the things they like to do, the better. We think that bond is very important, so invest in people when you start and check if those people are feeling good. You notice that immediately. And that's just a conversation. So, just be human... that's not so difficult, is it?"

PATRICK MERTENS & INGE LIJNEN –
CHOCOLADEHUIS BOON

If you have an initial idea of what your hiring process could look like, you can start drafting your job descriptions and questions for the application form and interview process. Once all of it is in place, you'll be ready to start sharing the news about your vacancies and how to apply.

To make this process a little easier for you, we've put together a guide according to the key roles most artisan chocolatiers have hired as the first members of their team.

As founder of Nibbo, Fan Yu made the business choice to include his team in all production steps, from checking the beans to the making of the chocolates

Research & Development (R&D)

Attract a motivated chocolatier to develop new product concepts and stay up to date with the industry's latest trends and consumer patterns:

1 – Job title

Start with a clear and specific job title such as "Experienced Chocolatier" or "Chef/Pâtissier/Chocolatier R&D Specialist".

2 – Job description

Provide a detailed job description outlining the duties and responsibilities of the position, such as:

» You will be responsible for researching and developing new chocolate recipes that align with our brand's aesthetic and taste preferences. This includes working with different types of cocoa beans, experimenting with flavours and developing new techniques.
» Studying and optimising existing recipes. This could involve adjusting ratios, experimenting with different production techniques or conducting sensory testing.
» You will need to keep track of your progress, document your findings and work collaboratively with the rest of the team to develop new products and flavours.
» Maintaining a clean and organised work area, including cleaning and sanitising equipment.
» Participating in quality control activities to ensure products meet the company's standards.
» Maintaining accurate production records and documentation.

3 – Qualifications and requirements

List the qualifications and requirements for the position, such as:

» A minimum of [X] years of experience as a chocolatier or an R&D position in the HoReCa/chocolate/bakery space.
» Experience working with various types of chocolate and confectionery techniques.
» Strong attention to detail and quality control skills.
» Ability to work in a fast-paced environment and meet production deadlines.
» Strong communication and collaboration skills.
» Ability to work a flexible schedule, including weekends and holidays.
» Formal training in chocolate making or a related field is preferred but not required.

4 – Compensation and benefits

Indicate the compensation and benefits package that will be offered, including hourly wage or salary, health benefits, paid time off and any other benefits that the position may offer.

5 – How to apply

Provide instructions on how to apply for the position, including a link to the company's application portal or email address to send the resume and cover letter (optional).

Overall, make sure to create an application advert that clearly communicates the duties and requirements of the R&D position while highlighting the benefits of working for your company. This will attract the right candidates and help you find a motivated and experienced researcher and recipe/concept developer for your business.

Production

Attract a motivated chocolatier to assist in the day-to-day production of bonbons, chocolate bars and other confectionery products with an application advert with the following elements:

1 – Job title

Start with a clear and specific job title such as "Experienced Chocolatier" or "Chocolatier Assistant".

2 – Job description

Provide a detailed job description outlining the duties and responsibilities of the position, such as:

» Preparing and producing high-quality bonbons, chocolate bars and other confectionery products according to company standards and recipes.
» Collaborating with the team to develop new products and flavours.
» Maintaining a clean and organised work area, including cleaning and sanitising equipment.
» Monitoring inventory levels of ingredients and supplies, and alerting management when inventory is low.
» Participating in quality control activities to ensure products meet the company's standards.
» Maintaining accurate production records and documentation.

3 – Qualifications and requirements

List the qualifications and requirements for the position, such as:

» A minimum of [X] years of experience as a chocolatier.
» Thorough knowledge about types of chocolate and confectionery techniques.
» Strong attention to detail and quality control skills.
» Ability to work in a fast-paced environment and meet production deadlines.
» Strong communication and collaboration skills.
» Ability to work a flexible schedule, including weekends and holidays.
» Formal training in chocolate making or a related field is preferred but not required.

4 – Compensation and benefits

Indicate the compensation and benefits package that will be offered, including hourly wage or salary, health benefits, paid time off and any other benefits that the position may offer.

5 – How to apply

Provide instructions on how to apply for the position, including a link to the company's application portal or email address to send the resume and cover letter (optional).

Overall, make sure to create an application advert that clearly communicates the duties and requirements of the position while highlighting the benefits of working for your company. This will attract the right candidates and help you find a motivated and experienced chocolatier for your business.

Junior/Apprentice production staff

Attract a junior staff member or apprentice who doesn't have a lot of experience yet, but who's eager to learn:

1 – Job title

Start with a clear and specific job title such as "Junior Chocolatier" or "Chocolatier Apprentice".

2 – Job description

Provide a detailed job description outlining the duties and responsibilities of the position, such as:

» Assisting with the preparation and production of high-quality bonbons, chocolate bars and other confectionery products according to company standards and recipes.
» Collaborating with the team to learn and develop new products and flavours.
» Maintaining a clean and organised work area, including cleaning and sanitising equipment.
» Assisting with monitoring inventory levels of ingredients and supplies and alerting management when inventory is low.
» Participating in quality control activities to ensure products meet the company's standards.
» Assisting with maintaining accurate production records and documentation.
» Willingness to learn new techniques and methods related to chocolate making.

3 – Qualifications and requirements

List the qualifications and requirements for the position, such as:

» A strong interest in chocolate making and confectionery production.
» A willingness to learn and follow instructions.
» Strong attention to detail and quality control skills.
» Ability to work in a fast-paced environment and meet production deadlines.
» Strong communication and collaboration skills.
» Availability to work a flexible schedule, including weekends and holidays.
» Previous experience in a similar role is a plus but not required.

4 – Compensation and benefits

Indicate the compensation and benefits package that will be offered, including hourly wage or salary, health benefits, paid time off and any other benefits that the position may offer.

5 – How to apply

Provide instructions on how to apply for the position, including a link to the company's application portal or email address to send the resume and cover letter.

Overall, make sure to create an application advert that highlights the opportunity for a motivated individual to learn and grow in a hands-on environment. Emphasise the opportunity to gain valuable experience and skills, as well as any training or mentorship that will be provided. This will attract the right candidates and help you find a junior chocolatier-to-be who is ready to contribute to your business.

Sales

Attract a motivated customer-facing team member to welcome and service your customers:

"I don't have shop staff. Only during busy days, we have working students come in. Currently, my main role is seeing that there are raw materials, that orders are correct for the customers and having contact with the customers. Also, seeing that certain projects that are ongoing come to a good conclusion."

JITSK HEYNINCK – JITSK CHOCOLATES

1 – Job title

Start with a clear and specific job title such as "Sales Representative" or "Customer Service & Sales Person".

2 – Job description

Provide a detailed job description outlining the duties and responsibilities of the position, such as:

» Develop and maintain relationships with clients to ensure that they are satisfied with our products and services through sales calls, trade shows and events and overall customer service.
» Help us achieve monthly sales targets by identifying new business opportunities, upselling existing clients and maintaining a strong pipeline of prospects.
» Stay up to date with emerging trends, competitor activity and other factors that may impact our sales.
» Know our entire range of products inside-out to showcase our products and services and highlight their unique features and benefits.
» Collaborate closely with other team members to ensure our products and services meet the needs of our clients.

3 – Qualifications and requirements

List the qualifications and requirements for the position, such as:

» A minimum of [X] years of experience as a sales representative or in a similar position.
» A passion for the world of artisan chocolate and its craft.
» Strong attention to detail and quality control.
» Ability to work in a fast-paced environment and multi-task.
» Strong communication and collaboration skills.
» Ability to work a flexible schedule, including weekends and holidays.
» Previous experience in the chocolate industry or a related field is preferred but not required.

4 – Compensation and benefits

Indicate the compensation and benefits package that will be offered, including hourly wage or salary, health benefits, paid time off and any other benefits that the position may offer.

5 – How to apply

Provide instructions on how to apply for the position, including a link to the company's application portal or email address to send the resume and cover letter.

Overall, make sure to create an application advert that clearly communicates the duties and requirements of a sales representative while highlighting the benefits of working for your company. This will attract candidates that are motivated, and who have a can-do attitude to serve your clients.

Marketing

Attract a motivated chocolatier to develop new product concepts:

1 – Job title
Start with a clear and specific job title such as "Marketing Specialist" or "Social Media and Online Manager".

2 – Job description
Provide a detailed job description outlining the duties and responsibilities of the position, such as:

- Develop and implement marketing strategies that align with our brand identity and business goals.
- Manage social media accounts, creating and scheduling posts, responding to comments and messages and analysing metrics to improve performance.
- Create and distribute marketing materials, such as visual elements, sample products, brochures or newsletters.
- Collaborate with other teams to ensure that our marketing efforts are aligned with our product development and sales goals.
- Monitor and report on marketing performance through key metrics, such as website traffic, social media engagement and sales.

3 – Qualifications and requirements
List the qualifications and requirements for the position, such as:

- A minimum of [X] years of experience as a marketing specialist, community manager or similar role.
- Formal photography, video and digital design training is a plus.
- Strong attention to detail.
- Flawless spoken and written English (or your preferred language/s).
- Ability to work in a fast-paced environment and handle unexpected situations.
- Strong communication and collaboration skills.
- Ability to work a flexible schedule, including weekends and holidays.
- Experience in the food space is preferred but not required.

4 – Compensation and benefits
Indicate the compensation and benefits package that will be offered, including hourly wage or salary, health benefits, paid time off and any other benefits that the position may offer.

5 – How to apply
Provide instructions on how to apply for the position, including a link to the company's application portal or email address to send the resume and cover letter.

Overall, make sure to create an application advert that clearly communicates the duties and requirements of your next marketing manager. This will attract the candidates with the experience you seek, and help you find a motivated person that fits with the spirit of your business.

As you get started, you might not have many applicants for a role, and your process might be short and simple. However, it's a good practice to have a hiring process in place, nonetheless. As your business grows and more staff is needed, this process and these roles will become a solid foundation to grow your recruitment system.

Sometimes recruitment processes have a higher purpose as part of your business. When she began hiring roles for her business, Mariane Oliveira realised that the work she was generating meant more than a position in a chocolate company. For some, getting a job was getting a second chance:

"Maybe because I'm an immigrant, most of my team members, they are women and immigrants too. Because I want to support women in business. I pay them decent salaries and give them the opportunities that they want. This way, I can also grow to support them more."

At Mary's Brigadeiro, hiring people is a philosophy that also takes part in creating the brand identity and philosophy. And this could be the case for your chocolate shop too.

Your work philosophy, your operations and customer service all stem from a good recruitment process. But even the best recruitment processes should be followed up by staff training. Your new staff should be carefully coached to fulfil their tasks, as well as to represent the identity of your brand.

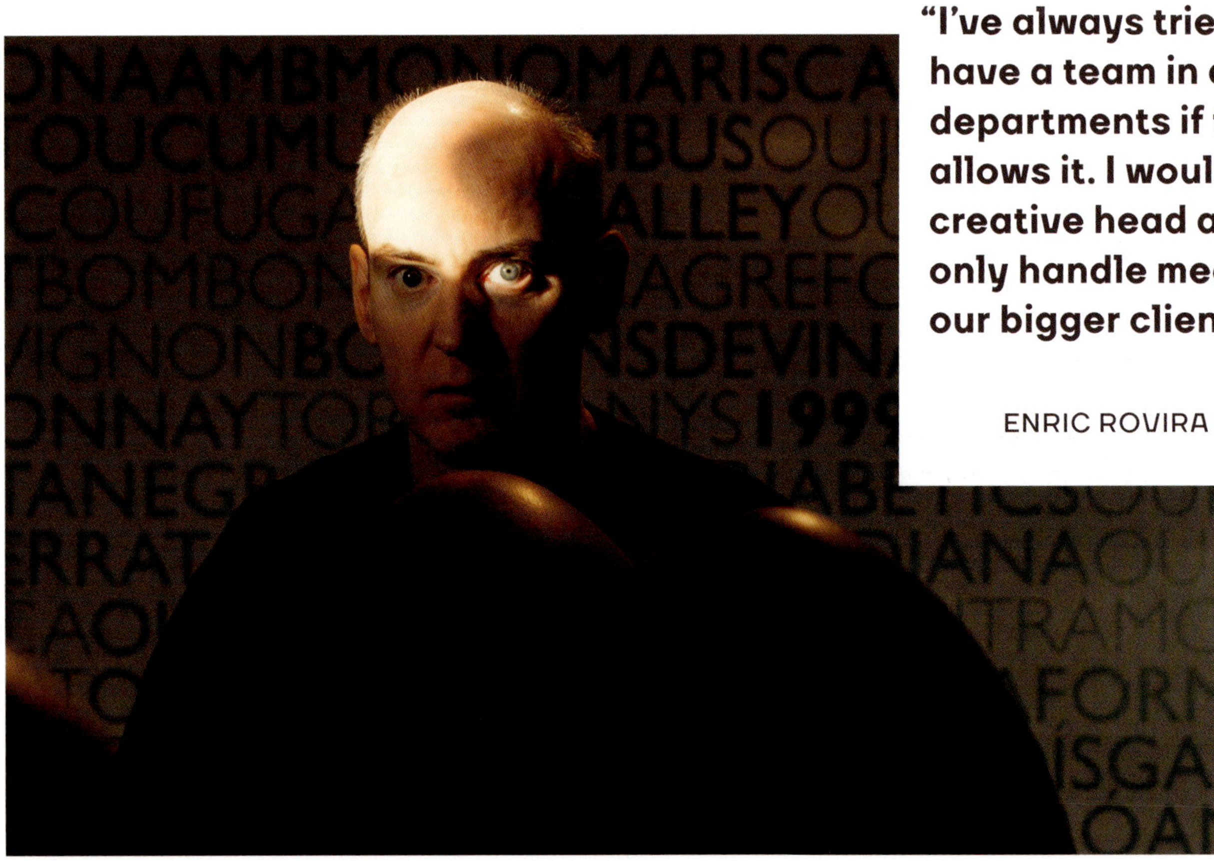

"I've always tried to have a team in different departments if the budget allows it. I would stay as the creative head and would only handle meetings with our bigger clients."

ENRIC ROVIRA – ENRIC ROVIRA

TRAINING AND COACHING

Manager and creator of Savour School, and chocolate and pastry instructor herself, Kirsten Tibballs has gained a lot of experience when it comes to training people. This includes her staff, because to her, a key to success is found in understanding when it's time to delegate tasks.

"I think behind most successful businesses is key personnel. I have my own TV show, I do collaborations with several companies where I'm creating content and I'm probably developing up to 20 recipes a week. So, you do need to look at how you can alleviate your time. It's sometimes better working on the business than in the business."

Recently hired or with you from the beginning — everyone needs training and coaching to improve performance in a specific role, even you! And besides role-specific training, remember all staff members should know the brand's identity inside-out.

To take your team from staff to real brand ambassadors, this is a list of topics that you can use to steer your coaching.

Training your kitchen team

Training and onboarding your new production team is crucial to ensure that they can run the operations in the kitchen effectively and efficiently. Recreating your chocolate recipes consistently is the key to maintaining the quality and reputation of your brand. We prepared some steps and strategies you can use to train your new kitchen team so they can help you make your recipes just the way you would do them yourself:

1 **PROVIDE DETAILED DIRECTIONS** and insights that cover the history of your chocolate business, its purpose, its uniqueness and unique selling points, the products you offer and the importance of quality control.

Just like many other chocolatiers, and although with a kitchen team bigger than himself, Mirosław Pelczar still takes it upon himself to train the new kitchen staff. And the training he starts in the kitchen doesn't end there. Mirosław makes sure his team interacts with consumers enough so that the business gets feedback for upcoming chocolate innovations too:

"I always oversee the production myself. If needed, I will employ more chocolatiers and train them myself as well. I listen intensively to my customers, and we train our staff in the shops to do so as well. It is very important to me from a few perspectives: I want their opinion on our current offer and their ideas on what they want, and what we can provide in the future."

2 **TRAIN THEM ON FOOD SAFETY AND HYGIENE** to ensure that your production team members understand these topics according to the regulations in place for food service companies. This includes coaching them on proper hand washing, personal hygiene and sanitation procedures in the kitchen.

3 **PROVIDE A DETAILED RECIPE BOOK** that includes all the necessary ingredients, measurements and instructions for each of your recipes. Make sure the book is easily accessible to your kitchen staff.

4 **DEMONSTRATE THE RECIPE** to your new team members, step-by-step, to ensure they understand how to make each product correctly.

5 **OFFER SHADOWING OPPORTUNITIES** to your new team members, allowing them to observe experienced staff members in action and get hands-on experience from the production process.

6 **PROVIDE VISUAL AIDS** such as videos, diagrams and photos that illustrate the production process and the final results. This can help your new team members better understand a recipe and the techniques required to make it correctly.

7 **OFFER ONGOING TRAINING** to your new kitchen team members to ensure they stay up to date on any changes or improvements to the recipes. This can include regular training sessions, product updates and refresher courses.

RENATA ARASSIRO has set up an interesting approach when hiring new staff, which not only helps her train the new hires, but create stronger bonds between team members:

"We have standard procedures, and new people have to become part of the team, learn to do what we do. So, when we hire a new person, they have to read these standard procedures, but they do it with another person who is already in that function. This makes it easier for them to get the vibe of the company."

8 **ENCOURAGE FEEDBACK** among team members, whether it's about the recipe book or the production process. This can help you identify areas where your recipes or training programme can be improved, and also gives your team members a sense of ownership in the entire process.

The secret behind successfully training any kitchen staff so they can craft your chocolate recipes is to provide them with the knowledge, skills and tools they need to produce high-quality products consistently.

By following these steps and strategies, you are more than ready to create a bespoke training program. One that your new team members can use to become more effective and efficient in reproducing your recipes.

With 9 shops in Naples alone, and more shops spread around Italy, remember the words of the MARCO INFANTE when it comes to training the people who bring his family business' recipes to life:

"We're leveraging a family experience of almost 80 years and actively collaborating with the store designer. Keep this in mind when I say that staff training represents 50% of our success."

"My case is special. I already lived in a fairly structured company with a one-century tradition in pastry and ice cream. It was a natural choice for me to look for specialised staff to shape the new chocolate unit.

Taking advantage of the experience gained in the management of my pastry and ice cream business, I dedicated an ad hoc department to chocolate, led by a skilled chef who also participated in the decision-making process. Then, together with the marketing person, we decided to create a specific brand that commercially identifies the line."

MARCO INFANTE – CASA INFANTE

“My wife and I work full time. We have a full-time salesperson who also works in the atelier, which is very convenient. She also has experience as a chocolatier. We work with flexi jobs, student jobs and then dual learning contracts too. So, in the whole business in total, we’re always between three to four people.”

OLIVIER WILLEMS – OLIVIER WILLEMS

Training your sales team

Training and onboarding your sales staff to become brand advocates and ambassadors is crucial to the success of your chocolate business. Remember that when customers are not previously acquainted with your business, many times, your sales team might be the first encounter with the brand. To make the right first impression, here are some steps and strategies you (and your team) can use to achieve this goal:

1 START WITH YOUR BRAND STORY

Before you can train your sales staff to become brand advocates, they need to know and understand your brand story. This includes your purpose and what sets your chocolate apart from the competition (Chapter 1). Make sure your brand story is clear, concise and compelling.

2 CREATE A TRAINING PROGRAM

As the chocolatiers we interviewed mentioned, it's crucial that your sales staff bring your brand experience to life. This is often found in the little things:

- The way you want your customers to be greeted when they enter and leave the store: "Smiles are for free!"
- Offering customers a sneak peek taste of a new product you're launching and asking for their feedback.
- Telling the story of how your products are made, the ingredients they contain and how that differs from peers in the same industry.
- Advice they may need when they're shopping for your products as a gift for someone else.
- Allergens: make sure your sales team is aware of any allergens used in each of the products in your range.
- Asking customers to be part of the mailing list for events, email activations, new products, seasonal offers and giveaways.
- Keep your customers updated on all services you find important, order and delivery updates, for instance
- Incentivise your customers with a small thank-you present for their first visit, and ask for ratings and reviews on trusted online platforms: Trustpilot, Google, Meta, TripAdvisor, Yelp!, among others.

As for your team, training on product knowledge, sales techniques, customer service and communication skills is the foundation of their performance. It starts with a good understanding of your product portfolio, the flavours, and ingredients and allergens. Not only knowledge is important — having your sales team taste your products to understand the flavour profiles should be a priority.

Make sure to provide plenty of opportunities for hands-on training. Sometimes, it helps to simulate sales scenarios so your team can train before facing real consumers. This training gives good insights on the interactions your customers can expect when doing business with your brand.

Olivier Willems balances full-time employees with on-demand roles filled in by flexible workers, student workers, and other temporary roles

3 **USE VISUAL AIDS**

Just like for your kitchen staff, videos, infographics, photos and product demos can be of help in your sales training program. Visual branded elements can help your sales staff better understand and share your brand, which ultimately leads to effectively selling products along with the story behind them.

4 **ENCOURAGE FEEDBACK**

Your sales staff may have rich feedback on your training process, so don't forget to ask for their opinion. This can help you identify improvement areas for your coaching methods as well as letting your client-facing employees know you value their input.

5 **PROVIDE ONGOING TRAINING**

Once your sales staff completes initial training, make sure you follow up on it to reinforce the concepts and skills they've learned. This can include regular meetings, updates on the product portfolio and coaching sessions.

6 **OFFER INCENTIVES**

Incentives, such as bonuses or commissions, can help to drive your sales staff to meet sales goals and get creative to achieve the desired performance. With the right motivation, your sales staff will not only become more effective, but more personally involved with the brand.

"There is someone 3 days a week now, but I want someone full-time and that's where it stops, because I don't want to have too big of a team. First, it's already hard to keep your team together because you have lots of different characters. And second, I want to be able to keep as much control as possible. I'd rather have things in my own hands and work a bit longer."

JUSTINE LANNOO – GOÛT FOU

At Bassam Ghrawi Confectionery, close attention to detail is mandatory in each production step, even when they are a large-scale international business

Staff meetings

Just like coaching and training, staff meetings should be a recurrent activity that is continuously updated and followed. This is regardless of how successful your business becomes. Besides being his own brand, SEBASTIAN PETTERSSON works in a restaurant as a lead chef, where staff meetings are a recurring event:

"In the restaurant we're working in, we have meetings on a weekly basis. We go through guest satisfaction and see how we're making our customers happy. If I bring in another mentor or coach, I need to be open-minded and really listen to what they're saying."

How often and how in-depth you train your staff will depend on your business activities, customer behaviour and, of course, on how fast your business grows. But, because there will always be some basics to cover, here's how you can arrange your first staff meetings without the stress:

Ask your team to stay for 20 minutes after a shift. Let them know about the meetings' goals and actively communicate that meetings are not in place to judge their work, but to facilitate it and improve the business performance and the team's efforts.

But remember that your meeting time should be limited, as is your staff's work schedule. Choose a specific topic you'd like to discuss in each meeting and prepare questions accordingly. These are some ideas that can get you started:

» What challenges did you face this week, and how did you overcome them?
» Did you receive positive customer feedback this week, and how did you respond to it?
» Did you receive negative customer feedback this week, and how did you handle the situation?
» Were there products that sold particularly well or poorly this week, why do you think that was the case?
» Did you notice areas where we could improve our operations, such as packaging, presentation or customer service?
» What new ideas do you have for creating unique and exciting chocolate products that we can offer to our customers?

Asking for feedback from your staff isn't the only good practice. It's also important to ask for constructive feedback about the internal dynamics of the company too, whether it's about communication and workflow with their peers or managers. This is the approach of the MORENO BROTHERS when they conduct their staff meetings:

"All the employees can give an evaluation to their peers, and they can also give points. They actually evaluate and assess us too. We want them to feel that Mallorca is not just a job, but it's something that they live with and are a real part of."

If you believe peer-to-peer feedback can be uncomfortable, encourage employees to talk to their colleagues one-on-one, but always from a constructive place.

Your business is planned, and your staff trained. But there will most likely be unexpected situations to deal with at all times — don't despair when things don't go according to plan! Negative feedback and bumps along the way aren't setbacks, but a way to learn more about your audience, the market and what you can do to become better.

Despite the number of roles your business starts with or grows towards, *always* make sure your hiring process and contract agreements comply with the labour law and tax requirements of your country or region.

WHEN IS IT TIME TO HIRE NEW ROLES?

Additional staff is also an investment in the success of your business, but it can be tricky to know when to begin a new hiring process. The key is to remember that the number of roles your business needs depends on your production volume, your market demand and each role's description.

If you're just getting started, you might need fewer helping hands, as the production amounts will be lower, and some roles might be in charge of multiple tasks. For example, it's not uncommon for shop owners to act as marketing managers or delivery staff during the early stages of their chocolate shops. As CALUM HAGGERTY says, it's okay to do everything when you get started, but it's important to know when it's time to delegate tasks:

"When you're small you have to do it all, but you're better off spending your time in a place where you add value, and there are places I just don't add value to."

"A business is basically all cogs put together. Take a cog out of that and things turn limp. We can't actually say which of those are the most important figures. Everyone has their job and role to play: we have a regular saleswoman; the sous chef, a very organised person who knows exactly what to go to each customer and what has to be made then; a full-time person who does invoicing and administration and a lady who used to work in factories for years on the belt."

PATRICK MERTENS – CHOCOLADEHUIS BOON

If you've been running your chocolate shop for some time, like Calum, you'll have to start paying attention to the signs that tell you when it's time to hire new people or delegate assignments. These are some of the signs to look for:

1 YOU HAVE 3 JOB DESCRIPTIONS AND A SHOP TO RUN

Although it's expected of you to handle multiple tasks when your business is brand new, as it begins to grow, you have to prioritise your tasks and start delegating.

MIROSLAW PELCZAR noticed he needed help when it came to his digital presence. Since the main value driver for him was in the craft of the chocolatier, he didn't think too long before identifying which areas of his business could use the extra help:

"We did all the marketing by ourselves, but things had grown to such a size that we decided we needed some help. Now, all the marketing activities are much more structured than they were in the past. Very soon I will be employing a person dedicated only to social media and e-commerce."

As you see, when demand is growing or you're running short on time for multiple tasks, it's time to look for someone to do those tasks for you.

2 CUSTOMER SERVICE NEEDS A BOOST

Negative feedback will happen, but is it happening more than it should? It might be a sign that you and your staff are spread thin. Use your staff meeting to assess the situation and, if needed, start thinking about reinforcing your customer service team or changing the approach of your sale tactics.

3 OVERWHELMED EMPLOYEES HANDLE YOUR BUSINESS

How many times have you been overworked but never said a word? It can happen that your staff members are overwhelmed with tasks they don't have the time to complete. Growing pains are good! But they are there to learn from them. Try to jump on one-on-one conversations with your team members about their workload and performance. Maybe this is the time to hire more people.

4 NEW BUSINESS OPPORTUNITIES ARE AROUND THE CORNER!

If new B2B contracts are pending or additional outlets are on the way, don't wait until the last minute to start recruiting. It might be that you will have to shuffle old and new staff members around so that the new hires can learn, but it goes without saying that new business opportunities call for more dedicated follow-up and a bigger team.

5 YOU'RE LOOKING FOR A PLACE TO INVEST THAT EXTRA PROFIT

You've found your footing and your margins allow you to invest in something that matters. Whether it's a new pair of hands in the kitchen or that one social media manager that will expand your digital presence — hiring a new (temporary or permanent) role can be the investment that takes your business to the next level.

"My wife still had her job for 6 to 9 months during the week. She joined on weekends and every night after work, and then we worked there for several more hours. We were exhausted, and I must say that the night work soon had to be given up, because it was not sustainable.

As you grow, you need collaboration. It's a different structure that you slowly start to get used to. Your workflow also changes quite a lot. In the beginning, we did a bit of everything, mixed up, so to speak. It was a bit of a mess when everything was done interchangeably. Then, you automatically take on certain tasks. For example, Isabel does all the planning with all the job students, the payroll processing and HR — a tactical role. I'm more involved in production and my creative work. But I notice with a lot of colleagues that at a certain point you become less involved in production."

DAVID MAENHOUT — CHOCOLATIER M

Even in successful businesses like Chocolatier M, some owners decide to minimise their administrative participation and keep to their roles in recipe development and crafting

HIRING OR OUTSOURCING?

When your business grows, you don't necessarily have to hire someone for every job. There might be times when you're in need of certain roles because of high demand, but that doesn't mean the demand will be the same all year around. So, what to do when there are fluctuations when it comes to the roles you need?

NIKKI THAKKER gives us a perfect answer to this challenge by sharing what it's like to hire specific roles on-a-need-basis, instead of permanently:

"The most laborious work is packaging. So that is where we need the maximum number of people, because everything is hand-packed. If someone wants 500 boxes of bonbons, they want a ribbon on each box, and it has to be hand-tied. That is extremely time-consuming. So, we hire some temporary staff on some occasions when the demand is simply too high. Because even though we can make and store the products in advance, they need to be packed at the time of dispatch."

You can also gauge whether it's more profitable and less cost-incurring to outsource certain temporary jobs like Nikki does.

When unsure if either outsourcing or hiring is the best move for your business, here are some typical roles or disciplines that other chocolatiers often outsource:

1 Accounting and bookkeeping

A professional firm or an individual who can take care of your financial statements, invoicing, payroll and related tasks is, according to most chocolatiers, one of the best staff investments. Because it requires a lot of dedication and specialisation to do this right.

In the case of STEPHEN TRIGG, hiring an accountant gave him more than what he bargained for. He was looking for advice when he had just started his business as a hobby, but the advice he got, in part, accounts for the existence and success of his business today:

"My brother is a lawyer, and my best friend is an accountant. So, I have these good resources to join. My accountant said to me, you're gonna kill yourself if you keep this as a side business, you need to do it full time. I was scared about the money, but he was like, *'you'll be alright, you can push the business forward'*."

Another good thing to do when thinking about hiring someone to look over your finances is to consider whether you'd create more value doing these jobs, or something you're truly an expert at.

2 Marketing and branding

Outsourcing marketing and branding roles can help you reach a wider audience and strengthen your brand image. NIKKI THAKKER realised this when the business outgrew her multi-tasker and business woman self, and it was time to reach out for help:

"I managed our social media account myself for 4 years. Then it came to a point where I was not able to work on it myself because I was not able to post regularly, I was not able to make content evolve myself. So now we have a team who's working for us. A lot of the content is suggested by me, what I think we should and can do. And of course, there are ideas that they also suggest. Then, we try to work towards both to have content that is engaging."

Today, Nikki understands the power of having ideas from experts to help her create content for her thriving business.

You may want to consider outsourcing tasks such as social media management, content creation and email marketing. For many chocolatiers, it's important to keep their authentic voice on social media. However, with a good brand book and a content calendar, it's a task you could easily outsource to any company with expertise in the field.

3 Packaging and distribution of big volume and/or online orders

You could outsource the packaging and distribution of your chocolate products to a fulfilment centre, which could save you time and money in the long run.

"Since it's mostly consulting, it's always going to be just me. If I get an order of pralines because of my brand name, I will ask my pastry chef to help me out. So, I do have a small production team that can help me out with deliveries and stuff."

SEBASTIAN PETTERSSON – SEB PETTERSSON

The essence of confections designed by Ryan L. Foote is his personal artistic touch, leading him to never outsource workforce when it comes to the creative process

When assessing whether to outsource or hire, consider the following criteria:

COST
Outsourcing can be more cost-effective than hiring, especially for tasks that are not part of your core business.

EXPERTISE
Outsourcing allows you to tap into specialised expertise that you may not have (and not need) in-house.

CONTROL
In-house management gives you more control over the quality and direction of the work, while outsourcing can mean relinquishing some control and decision-making.

FLEXIBILITY
Outsourcing allows you to be more flexible and agile in responding to changes in demand or business needs, while in-house staffing can be more rigid or structured.

Ultimately, the decision to outsource or hire depends on your business needs, budget and goals. Consider all these factors carefully before making any final calls.

CHAPTER 10

PRODUCT RANGE:

YOUR PORTFOLIO

The main range of Ryan L. Foote's portfolio is 3D-printed bonbons inspired by large art installations, but made at scale as small edible art collections

Mallorca
PASTELERÍA

One of the key aspects of your chocolate business is your PRODUCT PORTFOLIO, this refers to the different creations you'll be offering to your customers. But your product range doesn't stop at the chocolates you make. It includes everything you offer, even services and products that are not your main focus but are complementary to your main chocolate offer (like beverages or pastries).

The business term for this product range is "portfolio". Your business portfolio holds not only the names of the products clients can purchase from you, but a detailed explanation about them: their ingredients, how they're made, their life cycle (shelf life) and benefits.

But, why would you want to list the products you sell? Your product portfolio is the reflection of your brand identity and uniqueness. With different types of chocolates, flavour profiles and techniques, your portfolio is the soul of your chocolate shop.

FIDÉE is a great example of where the timeless character of chocolate and a unique identity and concept come together. Inspired by the European approach to chocolate, JAP JOY decided to start "classic" and then incorporate traits to serve his business' target audience in China.

"We definitely have some flavours that are very popular among Chinese people, like chilli peppers and white chocolate. But we started with some very classical flavours, like coconut, dark chocolate and pistachio because they are very popular in western countries."

Besides the relevance of your products as part of who you are as a brand, there is also the practical aspect of things: you need to know what you make, how much it costs, the packaging you need for each creation and the success rate of each product.

Regardless of how good of a portfolio you can create, there's always room for improvement. Not only because people's buying behaviours and preferences change, but because there are some teachings that can only come from time and experience in the chocolate space. STEPHEN TRIGG offers a simple explanation:

"I have a balance in my collection, like a range of stuff that meets particular customers' needs. But that developed over the years, it wasn't an instant thing."

Having a product portfolio (and a tool to optimise it) in place will guide your decisions in the kitchen: which recipes work and which need a tweak, your customers' preferences or where to increase and decrease your assortment according to your clients' demands. You're here to start or to grow a company, so a business portfolio is a must.

"One of the biggest failure factors in our industry is the fact that maybe you don't have a clear vision on the product portfolio you want to offer and how you're going to create it. So that's the first thing. You must have clarity about what products you're going to offer and to whom you're going to sell them."

JACOBO & PABLO MORENO – MALLORCA

"Our chocolates have a shelf life of about three weeks, but that doesn't mean they are bad after that, it's just a term we attach to it. Because after that, they are still good too. I have calculated and balanced the recipes so that the pralines have a reasonably good shelf life, without having to use chemical additives. It has to do with proper water activity, ingredients and other factors. But besides those things, it's just important that the ingredients are fresh. You also have to consider the temperature, storage and refrigeration of the chocolates. A refrigerated counter is also important. And packaging too: there are blister packs, which are sealed and then stored. I know some people pack their chocolates in a cardboard box, but when you eat those, you just taste the cardboard. With us, everything is sealed and well taken care of. That also has to do with quality. It's not just about the sum of the ingredients and the finish, but also about aftercare."

PATRICK MERTENS – CHOCOLADEHUIS BOON

THINK **SHELF LIFE** FIRST

As a chocolatier, you know that shelf life is the amount of time your chocolate creation can be stored and remain suitable for consumption. Although better enjoyed when it's super fresh, a chocolate's shelf life can vary. Understanding its impact is important, as shelf life dictates for how long the creation will maintain its quality, taste, texture and appearance.

HÅKAN MÅRTENSSON from HÅKAN Chocolatier goes the extra mile when it comes to the matter. He optimises his range knowing that although a product might have a certain lifespan, he doesn't want to sell it at the end of it:

"When it comes to product lines outside the bonbons, I'm thinking shelf life. I ask myself about what we're able to put on someone's shelf that stays for at least three months? But, even if you have a shelf life and something is still good in six weeks, it's not going to taste the same as those first five days. People want something that doesn't have a long shelf life here — long shelf life, for a lot of people, means that something unnatural is going on."

It's interesting to understand that the life cycle of your products also impacts the way your consumers perceive them. MARIANE OLIVEIRA believes communication about the product is key, and that it impacts her business reputation directly. She is one of the chocolatiers who insists her customers enjoy her creations as soon as possible:

"The brigadeiro is maybe one of the trickiest chocolate confections. Freshness is really fundamental. They don't last forever, so we even encourage people to enjoy them right away. I knew that part of my business would not be franchising because that would mean having products that are not as fresh. If I go the less-fresh way, I'm sure I will lose part of the quality and the identity of my business."

This makes shelf life not only an important aspect your consumers should know about, but crucial to develop a product portfolio that makes the most out of your ingredients and production times, optimises your sales and reduces waste.

The shelf life of your products will vary depending on a series of recipe-related and unrelated factors. On one side of the picture, you'll see that the ingredients, their quality and recipe ratios will all impact your chocolate's shelf life.

On the other side, production processes and storage conditions will be crucial to maintain the product's life cycle — if a product has an estimated shelf life of 6 months, but the storage conditions (humidity levels, light, temperature, etc.) aren't the right ones, you'll see your product's life shortened.

Since the beginning, and up until today, whenever NIKKI THAKKER comes up with new ideas or product concepts for her portfolio, she has to take into account not only the conditions they need to preserve their shelf life, but the conditions of her local environment. Just like a recipe will be affected by the climate, so will machinery and logistics (packaging, delivery methods). For instance, a cooling unit or a temperature-regulated display shelf will never work the same in a dry and cold country compared to one with higher temperatures:

"I saw different kinds of creations that could be made and how we could make these same products in India. But whatever we eat in Europe, the environment, the temperature and the humidity are all very different from India, especially in Mumbai, where humidity goes up to 99% This makes it extremely difficult for chocolatiers to work. The same recipe would not turn out to be the same because of environmental factors and other things, even using the same ingredients. The initial, I would say, one and a half years, pretty much went into understanding how to devise recipes in terms of having the right kind of consistency, texture and stability of the product. We also wanted to ensure it had enough shelf life for it to survive in the market. That's how we really started."

All successful chocolatiers acknowledge the importance of knowing and managing the shelf life of their chocolates to ensure that they are at their peak quality when they reach customers. To follow their footsteps, there are two key elements you should always watch out to maintain the shelf life of your product portfolio.

Like some of Bernard Proot's creations for DelRey, many artisanal chocolatiers use edible stamps on their bonbons to offer branded confections that also serve as a small advertisement campaign

Temperature and humidity: what to watch out for

Temperature management is particularly important when storing your chocolates. The main consequence of sudden temperature shifts is known as "fat blooming".

Fat blooming breaks down the stability of chocolate crystals. Your chocolate will still be edible, but it will lose the perfect balance between flavours and aromas, it will be less snappy when it breaks and won't have its sought-after finishing gloss. Needless to say, it will impact your consumers' perception of the quality of your products.

Fat blooming is reversible by re-processing the chocolate. However, this is an extra investment that is probably not accounted for in your production schedule.

Parallel to temperature changes, a result of uncontrolled humidity is the recrystallisation of the sugar within the chocolate. Unlike fat blooming, this process isn't reversible.

When chocolate is stored in a high-humidity space for too long, sugar lumps appear inside the chocolate.

To avoid these situations, you'll have to keep in mind what different storage conditions look like:

» **Negative temperature storage:** – 20°C (to store frozen products such as fruit pulp)
» **Positive temperature storage:** 0°C – 4°C (to store dairy products, fresh fruit, eggs)
» **Controlled room temperature storage:** 16°C – 18°C (to store chocolate, sugar, flour and other dry ingredients)

And when it comes to storing your finished chocolate products, categorise them according to their shelf life. All artisan chocolate products can be divided into three categories:

» **Short shelf life**
To be consumed from 0 – 14 days
» **Medium shelf life**
Can be stored from 14 – 60 days
» **Long shelf life**
Can be stored from 60 days – 6 months

Short shelf life

Fresh chocolate products that need to be sold within a few days fall under this category. They are usually known as "gourmet" chocolates that contain fresh fruit or fresh fruit jellies.

When showcased, these products need to be kept in refrigerated displays. At the end of the day, the unsold batches of short shelf life chocolates should also be stored in a refrigerated area.

Medium shelf life

The higher content of sugar and special cooking processes that these chocolates go through extend their shelf life (up to 2 months).

Some chocolatiers around the world, like JANICE WONG, choose a single type of shelf life to reign over their entire product range:

"We do everything with a shorter shelf life. We're not doing chocolate that has a one-year shelf life, but chocolate that has a two-month shelf life maximum. For us, this kind of shelf life is better and fresher."

When showcased, the display area of chocolates with a medium shelf life should remain at 16°C. These can be stored in their display space, as long as they are covered with panels so that the temperature remains the same and they are protected from elements in the air.

Long shelf life

These products contain even higher quantities of sugars and glucose syrups. They might also include dried fruit, specifically for chocolate making, and fruit pulp powders. The guidelines for medium shelf life products mostly apply to these products as well.

What we found out is that many chocolatiers reinforce their short and medium life offer with chocolate formats that have a longer shelf life. In other words, they make products like chocolate bars and dragées as secondary products next to their fresher, main offer.

One of the reasons behind STEPHEN TRIGG and his wife, SUN, choosing longer-life products is to adapt to their different sales channels:

"We need stuff that supports longer shelf life because bonbons are great for only some markets. We were too focused on that sales channel, but then we needed to have two or three sales channels. So, we looked at products, longer shelf life products, like dragées, to support those channels as well."

KIRSTEN TIBBALLS, always advices chocolatiers about the benefits of chocolate formats with a longer shelf life as a key part of a business' assortment:

"The advantage of doing tablets is they have a longer shelf life. You are ensuring that you've got a full counter without the pressure of making the product more frequently, because you've got longer life products."

As you might have put together, shelf life isn't only important to store your production the right way. You should actively communicate the lifespan of your products to your customers, to ensure their experience of your brand is the best possible one.

When you communicate a product's shelf life to your clients, you're not only managing their expectations, but you're also making sure that they are aware of the best time to enjoy your chocolates as they know the chocolate experience is affected by the shelf life.

As a type of ongoing marketing campaign for Savour School, Kirsten Tibballs uses longer shelf life chocolates as gifting options in a premium branded packaging that makes her business a top-of-mind option

“Shelf life is quite challenging, because we want to increase the shelf life of the products but without adding any preservatives. That, of course, requires multiple trials. Every time we develop a new product, it first goes to the lab for stability testing. Once we get the report and speak with the lab to understand what is required, we change our recipes, tweak them a little and then send it again to the lab. This is a very back-and-forth kind of process until we achieve the kind of stability that we want for the product.

But when we started, we only had three products. One was the bonbons in which we had about seven to eight flavours. And then we had four kinds of chocolate bars and four dragées. Over time, we have increased the number of products. Today, they have evolved to up to 80 different kinds of products.”

NIKKI THAKKER – ÉNTISI

At this éntisi shop, products are separated in categories according to shelf life and format, and are made easily accessible thanks to simple but clear store signs

THE IDEAL **PRODUCT RANGE**

There is no right or wrong answer when you choose the products you'll be selling. This will depend on your brand identity, how the products represent it and your initial production capacity.

For example, RENATA ARASSIRO makes sure that her portfolio represents the joyful spirit of Brazilian culture her brand stands for:

"First, we had to offer some products that people knew. And then, we gave samples, *'try this, this is new, this is a fruit that we have here in Brazil, nobody knows yet, but you can find it here'*. So, even if we started with the classics, my guiding light was always Brazilian fruits. I wanted to teach about these ingredients, offer more information to our clients — that in Brazil, we have fruits and that we want to appreciate that in our business."

There is no right direction to guide your recipes. There is, however, an ideal range of products to create a balanced assortment. As a general guideline, you can follow the 60/70 – 30/40 rule.

This means that 60–70% of your offer should be made of classic products, while you should dedicate 30-40% of your portfolio to edgier or more special creations. The reasoning is simple: classic chocolates tend to sell more and faster than special ones, this ratio is useful to create a balance between them both.

Although she only offered one format of products first, MARIANE OLIVEIRA learned this lesson the hard way when she created too many flavours based on her experience of a different market:

"In Brazil, people go above and beyond with the brigadeiro flavours. You can easily find, in one place, up to 40 or 50 different flavours! And it's easy to create different flavours of brigadeiros. You can change the topping and that's it, it's a different flavour. When I came to Canada, I had this mentality as well... such a mistake. I went crazy with so many flavours. Then, we had to scale this. It wasn't profitable and it wasn't time efficient. Today, we have basic core flavours and then some seasonal flavours."

Classic flavours might have a different meaning depending on where you are in the world. A traditional chocolate topping in the Middle East might be entirely different from a traditionally Belgian one. But despite these variations, there are certain types of chocolate you can consider to be universal classics.

DAVIDE COMASCHI is no stranger to the idea of how universal classics work, particularly when it comes to a place like Italy as your target market. Although he might have out-of-the-box ideas, he always recommends chocolatiers to let themselves be guided by their specific market:

"People here usually go for traditional and 'safe' flavours. I would advise chocolatiers not to make what they like, but what the majority of people like! This is how you get them to try new things, and it's where teaching clients about chocolate comes into play."

Davide knows that after you've gained consumers' trust by listening to their cravings and offering a good quality answer, you've got more chances to introduce new products:

"I learned that once the customer trusts you, they will follow your offer and let themselves be guided by you. When you become more experienced in the business, you can begin trying new concepts."

Before crafting fillings for his signature collection, Davide Comaschi engages with customers to discover their favourite flavours and ingredient pairings

If you want to see Davide's theory put into practice, just take a look at MIROSLAW PELCZAR. Although he started small, today, his product range and the wide variety of flavours he offers are impressive. His flavours and chocolate formats seem to expand with time, yet he still respects the "universal classics rule":

"Our core offer is the whole premium line of chocolate tablets. It consists of 18 different flavours. Some other of our core products in our range are truffles."

Another avid believer in the power of these classics is NIKKI THAKKER, and her beliefs are backed by how she handles her production. For éntisi, although the Indian market had to adapt to artisan chocolate as a new proposition, the classics still make up the core offer of the company:

"90% of the products are very classic, from Italian gianduja to caramel fillings and ganaches. We also do a bit of different quirky flavours, because there is also this audience who wants to try something new every time. So, we create things like lemon chilli, for example."

But, building the ideal product range isn't only about finding the balance between your market's preferences and your production line. It's also about making sure that your product range reflects your authenticity in a consistent way. Take JANICE WONG's experience as an example:

"We make some chocolate bonbons where you get all local flavours, like lemongrass, chilli and stuff like that. And we've been doing it consistently for years. Some of these flavours, they don't change at all because building a brand is all about consistency as well.

Although located on the other side of the world, MARIANE from Mary's Brigadeiro shares Janice's mindset when it comes to the relationship between how you create your product portfolio and how your business is perceived and experienced:

"I believe that when you do something really amazing, that becomes your signature, there's no need to change it. I also feel that, sometimes, the market is so saturated with new creations that it's really good when you go to a place and you try something for the 3rd or 4th time and the flavours are still the same, or sometimes even better. I decided to stick with a few flavours that we make really well, and then create different seasonal ones."

If like many chocolate business owners, you want to start your offer with some universal classics or choose a single product that is widely loved, make sure to include at least one of these in your assortment: enrobed pralines, moulded pralines, chocolate bars, truffles. These chocolate formats are not only popular around the world, above all, they are practical — they can be produced in bigger quantities and in less time.

CORE AND **SECONDARY** PRODUCTS

In the previous subtitle, we mentioned an ideal ratio of products to get started with. The 60/70 part of that ratio, also known as "classics", will be the one making up your core products. The remaining 40/30 section of your portfolio will be your secondary products.

While your core products should be consistent throughout time, your secondary range can change periodically according to seasons, trends, market demand and new products or services ideas.

Some decorative pieces by Chocoladehuis BOON are not part of the main range, but used as a representation of the brand's high-level positioning to gain attention from existing and new B2C/B2B clients

Core products

As you open your chocolate business, your core product or products will be the primary offerings that form the backbone of your portfolio — think of them as your signature creations, the chocolates that represent the identity of your brand. This means that your core offering should be easy to identify based on the consistency of flavours, designs and quality.

Although secondary products are also part of your offer, your core products are expected to always stay consistent regardless of seasonal changes and offers. Your brand perception and the expectations of your target audience will be built around these.

Core products are not only the way you represent your brand and position it in the market. These are also the connecting link between your clients and your business — they will be in charge of establishing customer loyalty.

Besides being advocates for your brand identity and a link to your audience, your core products have a financial function too.

A great example of this was shared by INGE LIJNEN from Chocoladehuis BOON, recognised by their original and art-like chocolate figures, yet profitable mainly for a more classic offer:

"We have bars, broken chocolate, truffles, nibbles and a type of product we call our 'cookies'. But, the absolute top selling point still remains chocolates. Many people come into our shop to look at the decorative pieces and creations too, but they end up buying chocolates. A decorative piece can have 2 or 3 different types of chocolate, but you are never going to have a whole pallet of flavours like with pralines. A decorative piece, you get it to admire it, so it is mainly bought by companies as corporate gifts or people who want to give a special gift during holidays; ornaments and special creations always peak during certain periods. I estimate that currently we are at about 40% ornaments or creations and 60% chocolates."

They provide you with a stable income base, leaving enough room to experiment with new recipes and product concept while making sure the sales don't drop.

Secondary products

As their name suggests, secondary products are additional or complementary products that enrich your assortment andare meant to be paired with your core offering. Secondary products can range from other formats of chocolates or beverages to non-edible products that are sold in your shop.

In this short section, we will focus on the chocolates that make up your secondary offer. These provide variety to your product portfolio and offer you creative space for you to innovate with recipes and ingredients, and to test products out. If a secondary product is successful enough, and the production logistics allow it, it can always become part of your core offer.

Think back to your core products for a second, these are the first step you take when putting together your portfolio. Secondary products will be step two. This is because these products are mostly developed based on your core products, to complement or enhance them.

Secondary products can be a series of shorter shelf life creations, seasonal or limited-edition chocolates, variations of your core products (flavours, textures, presentations) or completely new concepts. Although supporting your main offering, secondary products also play a crucial role to help you differentiate your business in the market.

RENATA ARASSIRO shared an example of how her secondary range of products helps attract new clients and keep existing ones coming back. When clients walk through the doors of RENATA ARASSIRO CHOCOLATES, they know unique bonbons are waiting for them — the seasonal creations that keep their excitement around the brand:

"I have many more different flavours compared to when I started. And we vary the flavours in different seasons. In wintertime, for example, we make some different kinds of flavours than in the summer. We have regular customers that come every day or every week and say, 'Oh, do you have something different today?' That's why we always have to keep pushing our creativity. So that every week we have a new kind of flavour for the clients."

With a clearer notion of what core and secondary products are, and what they can look like, it's time to start thinking about your own assortment.

You may have a lot of good and tasty recipes, and it might be tempting to have a big assortment as you start. However, not narrowing down your initial range makes production slower and investments in ingredients higher.

When getting started, sometimes it's better to aim for less waste and more efficiency. This is the case of HÅKAN MÅRTENSSON. Even though he's a renowned chocolatier, he prefers to be sold out than to let ingredients and hard work go to waste:

"If I see a product sells out much faster, I'll do that one again. If it doesn't, then I'll stop it. If we're selling, I don't know, five of these bonbons every Monday, why should I bake 20 now? I'll bake five and if I sell out, I sell out. I don't care if I lose a sale, but I don't want to have the waste."

As a way to cross-sell her core and secondary products, Renata Arassiro combines both and offers gift boxes as seasonal or limited-edition gifts

KIRSTEN TIBBALLS shares Håkan's concerns about waste. When asked about the ideal assortment balance, she shared some practical advice for new (and not so new) chocolate business owners. The queen of chocolate talked about two main elements to consider when outlining core and secondary products — shelf life and waste:

"I think if you're starting, it's really important to reduce wastage, to combine really long shelf life products and minimise your fresh products initially. This way, you can discover what consumers want without the waste. I would do a combination of tablets, snacking bars and individual bonbons, and see what people are looking for from there."

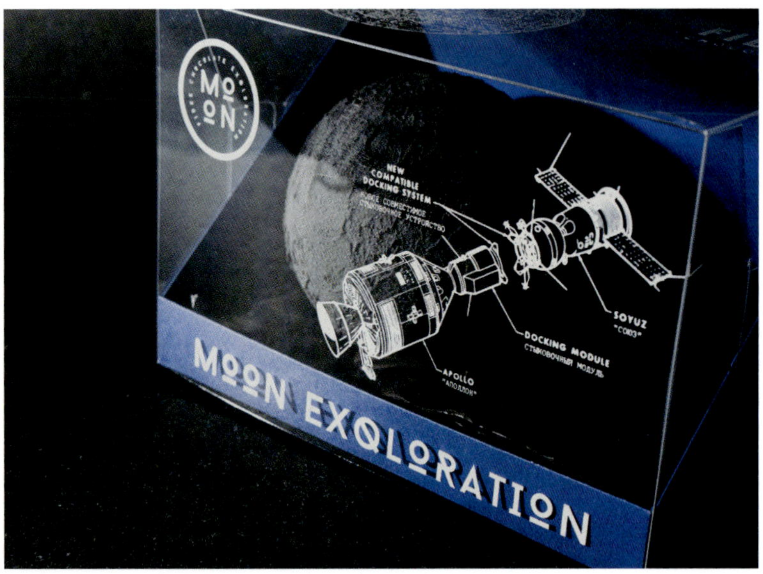

To match the expectations of his target audience in China, Jap Joy offers occasional creations with unique formats alongside his everyday classic bonbon assortment

"We're selling gelato and pastries as well. Because, if we only sell chocolates in a shop, it will close down very quickly in China. People will not come back, or maybe come back once or twice. Here, people always want something new, so we have to get new ideas all the time, keep innovating."

JAP JOY – FIDÉE

Although chocolate formats like bars are sometimes perceived as one of the less "special" or creative elements that are part of a chocolatier's arsenal, Kirsten believes in the power of these simple creations. Because these cannot be compared to bars of the industrial scale, and although a longer shelf life creation, these chocolates still possess the artisanal trait, and offer flexibility when it's time to sell them:

"I think tablets are more versatile in that they are often consumed by the purchaser, but they can also be given as a gift. I think individual chocolates are often given as a gift, but maybe not quite as likely to be consumed by the buyer."

An interesting example of product assortment is to be found in Shanghai. Even though the concept of artisanal chocolate is rather new there, the chocolate shop Nibbo thrives in this space with their core product alone. Does that mean there are no secondary products? No! Their secondary offer is simply comprised of special flavours. FAN's shop and concept focus exclusively on chocolate bars. And although the format of the product is always the same, the variety comes from the assortment of well-thought and unique flavours:

"We do flavour bars. We put together local ingredients and make a special edition of flavoured bars. We collect the ingredients from the regions we travel, for example white tea or oysters. And with them, we try to create something interesting based on our knowledge."

With this input on how different chocolatiers approach their core and secondary products, let's take some time to categorise them and think about how you can start creating your own product portfolio.

TYPICAL CHOCOLATE PRODUCTS

Feeling unsure of what products would be a better fit for your portfolio? This is a deep dive of the table we presented in Chapter 1. Here, you'll find the list of most common chocolate products along with detailed pros and cons of each of them:

Truffles

Truffles are a classic chocolate confection, popular with many customers. Truffles allow for a variety of chocolate colours and flavours, such as dark, milk, white, ruby and gold. The fillings can vary from fresh whipped creams, caramels and nut-based or fruit-infused fillings.

There are different techniques to create truffles, from hand-rolling to piping fillings into ready-made truffle shells to finish them afterwards.

Pros	Cons
Popularity: Truffles are a popular chocolate confection that many customers seek out. They are often associated with luxury and indulgence, and can easily become a top seller in a chocolate assortment. **Variety:** Because truffles can come in so many different flavours, including them in a chocolate assortment brings variety to a brand, and allows customers to experience different flavours and textures. **Versatility:** Truffles can be made in a variety of shapes and sizes. They can also be decorated or packaged in creative ways. These aspects allows artisan chocolate makers to showcase their creativity and unique style.	**Shelf life:** Truffles can have a shorter shelf life (compared to other chocolate confections), especially those filled with quickly perishable ingredients like creams or fruit. This can lead to waste if they are not sold in a timely manner. **Cost:** Truffles can be more expensive to produce compared to other chocolate confections due to the time-consuming processes involved. This can impact the cost of the chocolate assortment as well as the profit margins. **Temperature sensitivity:** Truffles are very sensitive to temperature and can melt easily if not stored properly. This can impact the appearance and texture of the truffles, which may lead to customer dissatisfaction.

Bars

Chocolate bars are another staple of any chocolate shop. Consider offering bars with flavours as well as different percentages of cocoa content. You could also incorporate unique and creative toppings such as sprinkles, sea salt, chilli, nuts, crispy cacao nibs, etc.

Pros	Cons
Popularity: As a staple of the overall chocolate industry, chocolate bars are one of the most popular confections. They are versatile and can be enjoyed on their own or used in recipes. **Variety:** Chocolate bars can come in 5 different colours of chocolate (dark/milk/white/gold/ruby), and may include fillings, crunchy toppings, shapes, etc. Including chocolate bars in your assortment adds variety to the range and allows customers to try different flavours and textures in a classic format. **Convenience:** Chocolate bars are easy to produce, package and store. They have a longer shelf life compared to other chocolate confections. This makes them a convenient and cost-effective option for all artisan chocolate makers.	**Competition:** Chocolate bars are widely available and can be found in many grocery stores and retail outlets. This means that artisan chocolate makers need to find creative ways to differentiate their bars from the rest. To do so, they may add artisan-made fillings, crunchy toppings or diverse shapes and designs to stand out. **Standardisation:** Chocolate bars can be seen as more standard options compared to other chocolate confections like truffles or bonbons. This may make it more difficult for artisan chocolate makers to showcase their creativity and unique style. **Ingredient quality:** Chocolate bars often contain fewer ingredients compared to other confections. The quality of the chocolate and other ingredients is even more important in these cases. This can impact the cost of production and the profit margins for the artisan chocolate maker.

Enrobed bonbons

Also known as chocolate-covered bonbons, these consist of a filling coated in chocolate. The filling can be made of various ingredients such as flavoured ganaches, caramel, nougat, nuts or fruit puree. The fillings typically have a more solid structure that melts in the mouth, yet allow the bonbon to be cut into small bite-sized pieces, then dipped or coated in chocolate.

Enrobing creates a thin, smooth, even chocolate layer around the filling. Together, the soft filling and snappy chocolate shell provide a satisfying texture contrast.

Enrobed bonbons are a popular and versatile type of chocolate confection. They are often sold as part of an assorted chocolate box or as a standalone item.

Enrobed bonbons can be made using traditional techniques or modern equipment, like a tempering/enrobing belt to ensure a consistent and high-quality chocolate coating.

Pros	Cons
Versatility: Enrobed bonbons can be made in a variety of flavours and fillings, providing customers with a wide range of choices. They can also be decorated with different toppings or designs, allowing artisan chocolatiers to explore and showcase their creativity and talent. **Aesthetics:** Enrobed bonbons have a smooth and polished appearance due to the chocolate coating, making them visually appealing and attractive to customers. **Packaging:** Enrobed bonbons of approximately the same size and shape are easy to package and transport. **Quality:** Enrobed bonbons require a high level of skill and precision to make, which can be a sign of quality and attention to detail, a positive image for every artisan chocolate maker. The process of enrobing also helps to seal in the freshness and flavours of the filling. **Production convenience:** Enrobed bonbons can be produced more efficiently than, for instance, moulded bonbons. This happens by creating larger slabs of the filling and cutting them using machine tools while an enrober helps make production more efficient, especially for larger amounts of quality output.	**Investment:** To produce enrobed bonbons in an efficient way and avoid hand-dipping each piece, investing in an enrobing belt may be required. Balancing out the need for investment over the forecasted sales volume may answer the question whether it is profitable for you to invest in automation at this point. **Quality:** The quality of enrobed bonbons is fully dependent on the perfect texture and flavour of the filling (even with simple ganaches) and the snappy layer of chocolate around it. Mastering this requires testing, fine-tuning and a higher level of skill. Multiple layers of fillings make the enrobed bonbons even more exciting, but finding the perfect balance in them makes the creation more complex. Every recipe needs to be balanced out thoroughly to make the product stand out. **Shelf life:** Enrobed bonbons may have a shorter shelf life (compared to other chocolate confections) especially those with quickly perishable fillings. This can lead to waste if they are not sold in a timely manner.

Moulded bonbons

Also known as moulded chocolates, these consist of a moulded chocolate shell filled with various types of flavoured ganaches, caramel, nut butter, fruit puree or other fillings. The process of making moulded bonbons begins with creating the chocolate shell. This is done by tempering chocolate, which involves heating and cooling the chocolate to specific temperatures to ensure a smooth and glossy appearance and a crisp texture. The tempered chocolate is then poured into a mould and spread evenly to create the chocolate shell. The mould is then cooled to set the chocolate shell.

Once the chocolate shell is set, it's filled. The filling is usually piped into the centre of the chocolate shell, leaving some space at the top. The top of the chocolate shell is then sealed with a layer of tempered chocolate to create a smooth and polished appearance.

Pros	Cons
Versatility: Moulded bonbons can be created in different shapes, sizes and flavours, providing customers with a wide range of choices. They can also be decorated with diverse toppings or designs, allowing you to let your imagination run free. Some chocolatiers prefer to order custom-made moulds, to create a unique and recognisable signature shape, others take advantage of the moulds to express the flavours inside. There is no right or wrong way to do this, but consider one or a few custom moulds — they can help you highlight your uniqueness. **Aesthetics:** Moulded bonbons allow for many creative possibilities. The use of colouring or (coloured) cocoa butter helps to standout, and to create a snappier shells, which make the moulded bonbons visually appealing, differentiating and attractive to clients. **Packaging:** When using a signature mould, moulded bonbons can be really easy to package and transport. **Quality:** Moulded bonbons require a high level of skill and precision, which can be seen as a sign of brand quality. The process of moulding also helps to seal in the freshness and flavours of the filling.	**Complexity:** The process of making moulded bonbons can be complex and requires specific equipment and techniques. This can turn into a barrier for some artisan chocolate makers. Partial automation is possible, but requires investing in tempering machines, a moulding belt and potentially a filling belt (in case of bigger volumes). Weighing off the investment cost versus manual labour cost is important when deciding for these bonbons, and it will be mainly driven by your sales forecast. Consider that many successful chocolatiers prefer a combination of manual labour and automation to safeguard the artisan status of their product. **Cost:** Moulded bonbons can be more expensive to produce compared to other chocolate confections due to the time-consuming processes involved. This can impact the cost of this chocolate's assortment and your profit margins. **Shelf life:** Moulded bonbons can have a shorter shelf life (compared to other confections) especially chocolates with perishable fillings. This can lead to waste if they are not sold in a timely manner.

Open bonbons

Open bonbons consist of a thin chocolate shell with an open top and a filling that is visible and exposed. For the shell, artisans can either design and order their custom moulds or buy ready-made shells such as mini chocolate cups.

The process of making open bonbons is similar to moulded bonbons, but without sealing the shell afterwards.

Pros	Cons
Visual appeal: Open bonbons have a unique and visually appealing appearance due to their exposed filling. This can make them stand out and catch the attention of your customers.	**Delicacy:** Open bonbons are more delicate and prone to breakage (compared to other bonbons) due to their open top. This can make it more difficult to package and transport them without any damage.
Variety: Open bonbons can be made in a variety of flavours and fillings, including ganaches, caramels, buttercreams, fruit purees and nut pastes. They are often decorated with additional toppings or designs to enhance their already striking appearance.	**Complexity:** Creating your own chocolate shells makes the open bonbons more complex and labour-intense. Yet, it may help to create unique shapes and textures, and charge a premium price for your creations.
Convenience: Using pre-moulded shells makes the production process slightly easier and more efficient, which can lead to manual labour cost reduction.	**Shelf life:** Open bonbons may have a shorter shelf life (compared to other chocolate confections) due to the exposed filling. This can lead to waste if they are not sold in a timely manner.
Different texture experience: Open bonbons typically have a softer and creamier filling compared to their chocolate shell, providing a different texture experience for customers.	

Chocolate mignardises

Chocolate mignardises are medium to small bite-sized chocolate confections, typically served as a sweet treat or *petit four*. The term "mignardise" comes from the French word "mignon," which means cute or adorable, and refers to the small size of the confection.

The word covers a whole array of confections: chocolate mendiants covered with dried or candied fruits, nuts, dipped biscuits with crispy sprinkles, enrobed nuts, filled cups, etc. Most chocolatiers mainly focus on mignardises that benefit from a longer shelf life and can be sold as snacks or "impulse products."

Pros	Cons
Visual appeal: Often, mignardises are pre-packed in transparent sachets or boxes, and are a great impulse item to boost sales. Playing with variations and textures creates visual excitement, which is a strong driver for these kinds of sales. **Variety:** Mignardises allow for lots of variations in the 5 colours of chocolate and in the finishings. Especially when using nougatine, biscuits or other toppings that add some crisp. This sensation offers a great taste experience. **Convenience:** Mignardises are often easier to produce in bigger volumes than bonbons. They don't require the same level of skill and technique, and can be a great add-on to enrich your assortment. **Shelf life:** For mignardises, most confectioners choose fewer perishable ingredients. Therefore, mignardises (when well stored and packed) often benefit from longer shelf life which makes them less dependent from short selling cycles.	**Shelf space:** To present a good range of mignardises (and offer them as an impulse item), you need to have the right shelf space for your customers to see and pick their favourites. **Storage:** As they are often presented at room temperature (outside the cooled display counter) investing in good air conditioning may be needed, especially in hotter climates.

Chocolate dragées

Chocolate dragées are small confections that consist of a hard or semi-soft centre coated with a hard chocolate shell. They typically have a rounded or oval shape. The process of making chocolate dragées usually involves coating the centre (such as nuts, mini-biscuits, semi-soft jellies, etc.) with chocolate in a panning drum, and eventually adding a layer of cocoa or fruit powder. These are tumbled until the chocolate is equally spread. Playing with hot and cold temperatures allows the centre to be fully covered and finally develop a hard and snappy shell. Chocolate dragées can be made by combining different types of centres with the 5 colours of chocolate. They are often presented in tins or bags and can be given as gifts or enjoyed as a sweet snack. Chocolate dragées are popular in many parts of the world. They can be a fun and playful addition to a chocolate assortment, providing a satisfying crunch and a burst of sweetness.

Pros	Cons
Variety: You can make chocolate dragées in a wide range of flavours and colours, providing customers with a diverse selection to choose from. **Shelf life:** Because of the hard candy-like chocolate shell that helps protect the centre from moisture and the air, chocolate dragées often have a longer shelf life compared to other confections. **Snackable:** Chocolate dragées are bite-sized confections, easy to eat on-the-go, making them a convenient but special snack option.	**Investment:** Even though producing dragées is less labour-intense, it requires investing in the right equipment: panning drums. There are quite some options available on the market. So, you should evaluate the volumes you want to produce and the drum's capacity before investing. Consider that panning is a time-consuming process. It takes several hours to produce one batch of dragées. If these become a core product in your portfolio, you may need several drums to serve the demand. **Competition:** Make sure to formulate unique and exciting dragée recipes to match your target audience's expectations. While efficient ways to produce them are necessary to sell them at a profitable price, this category may still be perceived by customers as "lower value" compared to bonbons, and may face competition from other popular snacks or candies.

Small seasonal pieces

Many chocolatiers build excitement around seasonal or festive moments of the year, such as Christmas, New Year, Diwali (India), Valentine's day, White Day (Japan), Eid (Muslim community), Chinese New Year and many others. For those occasions, small edible pieces inspired by the seasonal theme are on high demand. Think of chocolate eggs crafted around Easter — they're often a way for chocolatiers to gain press and bloggers' attention, sharpening their artisanal business' image. It's also a unique occasion for chocolatiers to show their creative skill and build a hype around their craft.

At Chocoladehuis BOON, seasonal offers can range from new flavour combinations to one-of-a-kind sculptures, either sold on-demand or crafted as a small limited-edition collection

Pros	Cons
Focus: Creating a limited series or even one specific creation can help you to create buzz around your product as a marketing tactic. Work on the idea behind the product, the way it is made and how it is finished to craft seasonal pieces perceived as high-value: something you can only find at a specific artisan's shop. **Value:** Because of the unique and limited character of these creations, the perception of value among potential customers is very high. As an example, at the end of 2022, Harrods chocolatiers created a mini-Harrods replica in chocolate with functional mini-drawers filled with chocolate delights. The price? £15.000 per piece. On average, most of the seasonal gifts would sell at a price range between €25 and €50, but the sky is the limit (depending on the audience you're targeting). Just take this as an example to always have in mind the idea of exclusivity that will drive the value and price customers are willing to pay.	**Skill:** It requires great creativity and mastery to come up with original ideas and ways to execute them. Yet, a stock of standard moulds, stencils and your imagination will help you create unique and good-looking seasonal pieces. **Cost:** Very often, the production and assembly of these pieces requires a lot of manual labour. Think of efficient ways to produce them in bigger batches to gain time, making the production more affordable, and allowing you to increase the profit margins.

"I have a wide assortment because I find that customers are hugely triggered by the variety they can choose from. And I think that's still a big selling point with us, the choices we offer. We also keep track of when chocolates are made and how long they last in the shop. If something stays on the shelf too long, we take it out fairly quickly. And if something keeps running well, we keep it that way. That's already a very strong foundation.

For example, we had problems with the ultra-soft ganache fillings. We had to change the recipes, because we noticed that we were running into problems with those. So after four to six weeks of seeing this, we had to make adjustments.

In the beginning, our focus was mainly on chocolates... we had a few small things, a few tablets, but not much. And pralines were the main thing. That was basically it. And then the assortment grew with cookies and more, you wouldn't even imagine what was in my store back then — it evolved! I started with an assortment of about thirty chocolates, but it has since become much more. We also started playing with the seasons and so on. Your chocolates are important, but it is also important not to make the range too small and to offer other products as well. Everything in an aligned way."

DAVID MAENHOUT – CHOCOLATIER M

"We have to consider the timing of certain projects. The Christmas collection has to be made in time because it has to be photographed for publication. Some stores start planning their Christmas activities as early as September, it's really amazing how early they start. You have the big disadvantage that chocolate is seasonal. We work six months in advance, so we have St. Nicholas first, Christmas comes, and then you have New Year's and Valentine's Day. It's a succession of peak moments for over six months. But then, when summer comes, there is no hustle and bustle, it's just quiet."

PATRICK MERTENS & INGE LIJNEN –
CHOCOLADEHUIS BOON

Arranging your production on a weekly basis is a great starting point to learn and improve your production schedules as you go. Your product range won't change on a weekly basis, but as you get started, supply orders, special dates and sales will still impact your schedule. Take the time to adjust your workflow and the time spent on each task as you gain experience and as occasions to introduce new products arise.

If your business follows a B2B route to market or you've decided to go for a hybrid route, there's yet another element to consider. Besides production capacity, what will determine your schedule and work hours will be strict deadlines.

When working B2B or for special events, you'll note that orders placed will sometimes require extra work hours and specific inventory and storage requirements. With almost four decades of experience in the field, JULIAN ROSE reminds all chocolatiers that deadlines will have a significant influence on their workflow, and that these should not be taken lightly:

"You can't put things off when you have a wedding. I often take the example of when there's a wedding. If the wedding is on Saturday, you can't say, *'well, I'm too busy, I'll do it Sunday'*. You have to make the cake or chocolates for that day and for a precise hour. This is something that you inherently have in the food industry: deliverables on time. You can't put it off. I mean, if you do, it's a tragedy."

And it is not only a tragedy for the clients who rely on you. Your ability to schedule production and keep up with your deadlines will be crucial for building the reputation of your brand, and sooner or later, your business' success.

Bernard Proot agrees that people are the key to a successful business: his new team members are trained to meet production and service standards he set for DelRey

2 Stock management and purchases

Stock and space management can be one of the most challenging aspects of production scheduling. Placing orders and managing the space where you have to store ingredients and finished products will impact the volume of your production, and delimit how fast and how much you can grow.

As you get started, it's normal that your storage space (hence, your production capacity) is predetermined. This means that your space availability will dictate how much you can initially produce. In other words, it will tell you how many core and secondary products you can make.

Considering that storage impacts your production, and that there are strict requirements for storage spaces to properly preserve raw ingredients as well as finished products, an inventory based on your core and secondary products is a necessary tool.

Inventory

After you've run your recipe tests, and knowing how much space you have to store ingredients and finished products, you can get started with your inventory. A good way to make the most of it is to categorise raw ingredients according to how many recipes require them, and each finished product's life cycle or shelf life.

This happens because the shelf life of your ingredients will determine the frequency at which you'll place supply orders. The time it takes to place orders and pick them up should also be considered when creating your weekly schedule.

Just like your production plan, an inventory management process will help your production run smoothly. We'll continue with the previous scheduling example to show you how some key elements should be considered.

DAILY INVENTORY CHECKS
At the end of each production day, check your finished products to determine the quantities of bonbons, chocolate bars and cookies available for sale or storage. Record the quantities in a spreadsheet.

Daily checks might seem redundant when production is small and you conduct weekly checks. However, having a daily understanding of your inventory will help you prevent unexpectedly running out of an ingredient and make sure the conditions are optimal for the inventory preservation, it will also allow you to act swiftly if any ingredient or batch is spoiled for some reason.

WEEKLY RESTOCK
Based on the production schedule and inventory check, create a list of ingredients and packaging materials that need to be restocked for the following production week. Place orders with suppliers to ensure timely delivery and inventory replenishment.

END-OF-WEEK INVENTORY CHECK
At the end of the production week, conduct a comprehensive inventory check to compare the actual inventory levels (based on production and sales) with the expected or estimated levels. Record any discrepancies and investigate the reasons behind them, such as waste, spoilage (or even theft).

ADJUST REQUIRED INVENTORY
Based on the end-of-week inventory check, update your inventory requirements to meet the anticipated demand for the production week that follows. This may include product transfer between storage areas, adjusting production quantities or ordering more/less ingredients or packaging materials.

TIP! For general ingredients (eggs, flour, milk, etc.), try to keep the number of suppliers to a minimum for convenience. When it comes to strategic ingredients (the ones that make your recipes unique), deal with a single supplier, when possible, for consistency.

To better understand the shifts among your ingredients and products, it can be useful to use inventory control measures such as: First-In, First-Out (FIFO) or Just-In-Time (JIT) inventory management. These will also help you optimise your production and inventory schedules.

As you get started, this is how your product and ingredient inventory could look like:

Product inventory						
Date:				Week:		
Batch number	Date produced	Date stored	Best before	Quantity	Price	Next production date

ANALYSE INVENTORY DATA

Take one day a month to review and study what your inventory data is telling you. Try to identify trends, patterns and opportunities for improvement. This may include comparing slow and fast-moving products to optimise your range and modifying your order-placing schedules for packaging and ingredients.

Ingredient inventory						
Date:				Week:		
Ingredient	Quantity	Supplier	Price	Date ordered	Date delivered	Current quantity

"I'm of the opinion that a fresh product comes with shelf life diversity. And that means it changes very fast. Another opinion I have is that a fresh product, you have to eat fresh. We are doing that more and more now. We aim for a shelf life of within two months.

Now, we have customers that we do customised orders for. Back in the old days, we would make anything customised because money had to come in. Now, customised means we'll make something you like, but that also fits our line. I have to stand in a place where I'm able to say, 'we're making this product for you', but also, 'guys, this does go a step too far'."

JITSK HEYNINCK – JITSK CHOCOLATES

Optimise your production processes

You've already tested your recipes, you know how much time each production batch takes and you've put an inventory together based on your product range's initial needs.

With all this fundamental information in place, you can further simplify your production efforts by taking a look at the processes your different recipes have in common.

To see overlaps in processes, start by breaking down each of your recipes into single production steps, making sure you write down how long each step takes you. Here's an example of how broken-down production steps can look like:

- Base preparation (i.e. ganache or pralines)
- Mould preparation
- Chocolate pre-crystallisation
- Chocolate stabilisation
- Product finalisation
- Cooling
- Decoration

When her business kicked off, MARIANE OLIVEIRA started by producing a couple of brigadeiro batches at home. Today, with an incredibly successful multi-product business in Toronto, she values categorising her inventory and her production phases, and preparing for upcoming special occasions and dates with enough time:

"We separate the phases of our production in three parts. The first two parts are done by machines. This is because we are producing at scale, which also means part of the production is frozen. For example, my entire production for the winter holidays is in a freezer since July. These are some ways in which you can scale your business while keeping it artisanal."

Like Mary, after you've pinpointed which production phases or steps make up operations, you can categorise them based on when they're scheduled for, the time each takes and which products they are needed for:

Production process			
Date:		Week:	
Task	Product	Time	Date

You'll note some of your recipes might share the same production steps (these are the overlaps we mentioned earlier!). Identify them so that you can work on more than one recipe at the same time. By doing so, you're making your operations more efficient while freeing some schedule time to work on something else.

This also helps optimise your schedule based on what each step requires. For example, if some production steps need more resting time, you can schedule them for earlier in the week, as you carry out the tasks with less resting time afterwards.

Keep in mind your schedule shouldn't be reserved for production hours alone. Scheduled work hours should also include administrative tasks, inventory orders, product shipping and innovation.

OPTIMISE YOUR PRODUCT RANGE

Regardless of which core and secondary products you've started with, and independently of your storage space, you can always do an exercise to optimise your product range. Small or big scale, this will allow you to better provide for your target audience and will make scaling your business a more efficient process.

Take the example of the MALLORCA bakery. Although a family legacy with decades of experience, a thorough look at their existing portfolio and its performance let brothers Jacobo and Pablo Moreno know it was time for optimising their offer:

"For the past few years, to sell more, we were offering a wider variety. But we realised we were offering many products that were all the same in some way.

All of the bonbons were nice, but none of them stood out. They didn't have a unique character or anything that spoke about the product itself. So, we classified our past portfolio. And when we looked at the profiles of the bonbons, we realised that 80% of all our chocolate fell only under two categories. So, we decided to start again, only with eight bonbons and a couple of other complements. We wanted to give value to each bonbon instead of having a typical box with 32 flavours that are pretty similar and don't have an added value.

We wanted to make a portfolio that covered everything, that was super diverse, but at the same time, each product had to complement the other. Because if you are an artisan producer, you try to sell really good products, and this means you have to strip down your portfolio."

"In the beginning, I wanted to make a lot... a bit too much. And at the end of the day, you may have to throw them away because they are no longer tasty. So, I said, 'from now on we are going to make small quantities and 24 varieties'. Also, if you have 50 varieties in the shop, eventually you get choice stress. The advice I give is to have everything as fresh as possible and don't go too big. Because if you give consumers too many choices, there is more room for confusion. So, make it easy on yourself, do a basic range and then add something new sometimes. And communicate things — today, our chocolates have a shelf life of up to 7 months because of the ingredients we use, we tell consumers the shelf life is only 3 months just to be safe."

JUSTINE LANNOO – GOÛT FOU

Even though the Moreno family had the production capacity to create a wide range of bonbon flavours, optimising their chocolate portfolio meant fewer products with more distinct characteristics. And this could be the case for you too.

Remember RENATA ARASSIRO? She creates anticipation in her clients by making sure her secondary offer is always innovative. However, to make this idea sustainable, sometimes innovations are not changes in a recipe, but in what her bonbons look like.

Olivier Willems is an example of how variety and consistency coexist while remaining production-friendly: identical shapes offer consistency and efficiency, while variety comes from diverse bonbon flavours and colours

This way, she manages to meet client expectations and keeps rotating her products without heavily reshaping her inventory or her production schedules:

"Compared to when we started, we have many more different bonbons now, but the base materials usually stay the same. We create something new visually, different textures in the same product. There are twists that we make, but the process and the products remain the same."

Like Renata, your offer can be rotated based on looks, toppings or little tweaks to existing recipes. But regardless of how you choose to make your product range more efficient, keep in mind to always keep track of the rotation of different products according to their specific shelf lives and sales volume.

Besides understanding how to carefully craft a product range that's varied enough, but that still lets her keep the production efficient, Renata considers other elements to make changes to her range:

"Sometimes you produce something that is not selling very quickly. In these cases, we can see that there's a problem over there. Or sometimes, people are simply getting used to a product. So, we take the product out of the range and put another one there instead.

We analyse each product like this. Then, we decide the ones we'll have to keep producing and the ones we won't. This doesn't mean that a bonbon is not good, sometimes we get sick of the same thing, right? That's why you have to be innovative often, but making sure you know the products you have to keep because people like them."

To get started with optimising your range, the first step is to write down all the products that make up your entire assortment. Group them together according to the best-selling ones (high rotation) and the ones that sell less (low rotation).

After you've separated your low and high-rotation products, it's time to categorise them again. This time according to their selling prices. For example, if you've set selling prices at a 10% margin, but some products are set at 12%, the latter will be part of the higher-price category.

After you've separated products based on rotation and selling prices, you're ready to complete the following optimisation chart with each of your products.

	Low-rotation products	High-rotation products
Products selling at a higher price than average	**QUADRANT D** Products with a higher price point that sell less.	**QUADRANT A** Products with a higher price point that sell more.
Products selling at a lower price than average	**QUADRANT C** Products with a lower price point that sell less.	**QUADRANT B** Products with a lower price point that sell more.

Now that you understand what your products are doing for your business, you can follow these basic guidelines to start optimising your range:

FOR QUADRANT A

Keep going! These products are the ones that will guarantee your shop's success. If you see that your client's demand for these grows, slowly increase their production to meet that demand.

FOR QUADRANT B

These products are doing well, but you can't put a higher price tag on them overnight. Use your experimentation time to find out if you can recreate these products with a twist or a new ingredient. This way, you'll be recreating a well-performing product with a slight margin increase.

FOR QUADRANT C

Products that end up here need your help. Compare them to your most popular products (don't be afraid to ask consumers for their opinion) and discover why they're not your customers' first choice. Depending on the answer, you can choose to tweak the recipe or replace it with a new product.

FOR QUADRANT D

These are high-value products that sell, but that don't sell much. It might be that they're too adventurous for consumers; but there's also a chance they're simply not being marketed enough. Could they belong in Quadrant A with the right marketing strategy?

To find out where these truly belong, tailor your marketing and communication efforts to showcase the value of these products and analyse the outcome after another sales cycle.

The quadrant framework isn't a miracle one-time exercise. Whether your profits are skyrocketing or you're breaking even as you slowly go through your first sales cycle, thinking about your entire range in terms of rotation and pricing is a long-term strategy. To keep your business relevant in a very competitive industry, this should be practiced recurrently.

Even chocolate experts with the most experience, like DAVIDE COMASCHI, rely on optimisation charts like this one, not only to understand their market but also to make recipe-related decisions:

"We absolutely use a decision grid. We know the flavours that sell more and the ones that sell less, and compile all the sales data to analyse it. Based on this, we make changes to the flavours, assortment, etc. It also helps us remove the ones that don't do as well as the others."

The optimisation chart won't only help you navigate your market, it can also help you make decisions when the unexpected hits. Just like a sudden lack of ingredients or social/economic changes, there are multiple external factors that could influence production. By understanding the rotation of your products, you will be able to make the best decisions and know exactly how they'll impact your business in these scenarios.

Think back to when COVID hit, taking the entire world by surprise. To deal with the aftermath, NIKKI THAKKER was forced to customise the offer of éntisi based on what was available at the time:

"There came the time when we introduced new products or developed new products using certain raw material which was available to us for a year's time and, suddenly, that material just goes away. We heard customers saying *'why have you discontinued? This was one thing that we used to buy so often'*. It was quite sad to hear, but there was nothing that we could do."

Faced with the lack of some key ingredients, and knowing the impact that discontinuing a product could have, Nikki made a decision that seemed to have a short-term negative impact, but that had a positive impact in the longer term:

"It would have been easy for us to buy any other ingredient and replace the ones that were not available. But I did not want to compromise on the taste. When people are used to tasting a certain thing, if they taste it again and it tastes different, you've just lost them. So, I was okay to discontinue rather than change the flavour profile."

The success behind's Nikki story wasn't only that she chose the essence of her brand above immediate sales. It was that she communicated it effectively to her loyal clients.

Since Da Vittorio holds a premium-brand positioning, secondary and main products are both required to meet this high-level standard

"What was very clear to me is that in the retail shop, it was a fairly common thing to have a bar with a 12-month shelf life. And it was a very common thing that a lot of products would get thrown in the bin for being out of date. When I took over, the range was massive. So my job at the time was to shrink the range in size rather than grow it."

CALUM HAGGERTY – COCO CHOCOLATIER

This is where you begin to see how different elements that make up your brand come together. From branding decisions to ingredients used, to how many and which kind of chocolates are hosted by your portfolio. All aspects should come together to answer to who you are as a brand in the end.

PRO TIP

Not all successful chocolatiers make a big profit with every product.

Nikki decided to discontinue a popular product before lowering its quality. In contrast, you could note that not every chocolate might be offering you the highest margins.

After studying your optimisation chart, you may see many loyal customers might be choosing a product that doesn't fall under the most lucrative category. But if this product keeps making them choose your business, then this product is a driver, for customers to potentially discover other products that you offer.

Although this chart offers you sales-based data, make sure your decision to keep or cut a product is made with a holistic approach in place. Don't let go of that lower-margin chocolate if it keeps people walking in, and be prepared to let that idea that you loved (but didn't perform too well) go!

"We do not produce on a huge scale, and are very selective regarding the ingredients. We work together with a selection of suppliers, such as Callebaut, and we try not to change them — there are companies and ingredients which are with us from the very beginning. New ones appear when we do new projects which require something different, mainly when we have totally new ideas, often in line with new trends.

And when it comes to innovations, there were some surprises on the way. One of the examples is bacon in chocolate. We introduced it as an innovation and more of a curiosity product, but surprisingly, we sell all we manage to produce! We don't do it very often as the smell kind of mixes with our desired aromas in the workspace, but when we do, it disappears immediately."

MIROSLAW PELCZAR – M. PELCZAR CHOCOLATIER

When should I start optimising my offer?

A good understanding of your target audience is enough to analyse where your offer stands. If you're unsure whether your business calls for product optimisation, these are situations where some chocolatiers have decided to take a look at their portfolio to see what can be improved:

Changes in the market

If changes in the market (particularly in your target space) impact the demand for artisan chocolate products, such as consumer preferences, flavours, textures or packaging styles, it might be time to optimise your range. Aligning with trends isn't a must, but it's interesting to study if there's an opportunity to adhere to them. Remember that all changes should always be made while staying true to your brand identity.

HÅKAN MÅRTENSSON underwent a decision-making process like this one. Although he found there was room for growth, he chose to stay true to the essence of the business he had built:

"We were discussing whether we should put out one of those sandwich boards, which say, 'we now serve coffee'. But then we thought that adding 'we now do this; we now do that', it kind of diluted the whole brand."

When in doubt, follow Håkan's footsteps. Identify the market changes and compare them with your brand identity. This comparison can help you see if it's in your brand's best interest to hop on a trend by developing some new flavours, making small changes to existing products or upgrading your visual elements or packaging.

Competitive upgrades

If you see competition growing in your space, don't despair! First, ask yourself if the competitors share any of your business' traits or similar differentiating elements. After you've assessed the competition, take a look at your offer and see if there are improvements or updates to be made to your product range.

Seasonal or event-based opportunities

Opportunities to optimise your offer are to be found in holidays, seasons, special occasions or special local dates. For example, limited-edition or themed products for Valentine's Day, Easter or Christmas are not only used to drive sales, but usually highly anticipated by all consumers.

Remember these events are also chances to think outside the box. This was the case of STEPHEN and SUN TRIGG. When faced with lockdown, they found a niche target audience that came directly from the unforeseen circumstances of the moment:

"There was, during lockdown, a guy who trains professional athletes. And, he said, *'they don't have enough healthy snacks'*. These were not a big Premier League football team, but they were usually on protein bars and stuff found in the supermarket. They needed something that had great macronutrients, but that also tasted nice, and they were sick of the supermarket options.

So, we did what we call Clean Snacking Bars, and created the No-compromise Bar. We put the best of everything we could into it. And then we gave it for a tasting. The athletes were blown away by it. It's just a simple recipe, but done really well."

As owner of Lauden Chocolate, Stephen Trigg is not only a recipe developer and chef, but a decision-maker in the logistics department

Production capacity

If your production capacity changes, or if the customer-based demand calls for it to change, it is also time to take a look at your current offer and how it can adapt accordingly.

Even when you have the production capacity of an enterprise behind you, the ability to produce something in the longer term should be contemplated. The MORENO BROTHERS understand that even if the market calls for a new product and you have the ability to make it happen, the production implications of such decision should be tested before making a final call:

"From our 90 years of background experience, we've learned that when you start a project, you have to study it on a small scale first. It may seem like it's really easy to scale something, 'just buy more ingredients'. But, it's much more complicated when you have to do it on a larger scale. You have to train people to produce it, scale the square meters, you have to actually be able to preserve and store your ingredients and your final products. Introducing a new product is about the logistics behind it, the distribution, everything."

Feedback and data

Along with regularly collected customer feedback, sales data and the information in the optimisation chart can dictate when it's time for some changes. A decrease in sales, less or more demand for a specific product and feedback and requests should all be analysed together to make decisions related to optimising your portfolio.

If you're unsure of how clients will react to a new product, you can always get feedback before you launch it as part of your offer. This is the case of MIROSLAW PELCZAR, who creates samples and small batches of his ideas before making important changes to his production line schedule:

"New products come mainly from my own ideas, but we, of course, listen to customers. We always check the feasibility of a new product and then make a decision, whether to introduce it or not. The process starts with a test, and we use our shops as a testing platform. We offer samples to our customers and collect feedback while closely observing the sales of new products."

If your chocolate shop is brand new, you'll have established your core and secondary products for the first time. Before you optimise your range, you'll want to wait until at least one sales cycle is over. After analysing the sales during that period, you'll be ready for your first optimisation round.

"The development of any product can be attributed to a customer's request or to studies and tests conducted on the product for its development. Before launching any new product in the marketplace, they are tested in our laboratories for sensorial analysis, and micro and physiochemical tests as well."

LAMA BASSAM AL-GHRAWI – BASSAM GHRAWI CONFECTIONERY

EXPANDING YOUR PRODUCT PORTFOLIO

Is your chocolate business a brick-and-mortar one or are you serving clients online? Maybe you're doing both. It's important to note that expanding your portfolio is also a type of optimisation.

Your existing sales model and the optimisation chart will serve as the first step if you're considering adding new products to your offer. Depending on the scale of your business, the type of product and your production capacities, the new product might be an addition or a replacement of an existing one.

For example, if you're looking to produce a chocolate format you haven't produced before, you might need a separate workspace, new equipment and tools, and some new ingredients and production phases. This is why, sometimes, expanding your portfolio also means a significant initial investment without guaranteed success.

Another scenario is creating a new product that doesn't require you to set up a new production line. It might be a new flavour or a different version of an existing product in your range. In this case, the changes needed will mostly impact inventory.

When it comes to completely new ideas and small changes, KIRSTEN TIBBALLS recommends prioritising the balance between innovation and production capacity:

"I do think you need to have a certain percentage of product of your business that evolves and rotates because you may have created the next big thing that becomes the most popular product in your shop. You need to keep changing and evolving to find that. I think you need to evolve 5% as a minimum, it's not viable to evolve more than that, to be honest. If you're in business, in production, which is hard work, if you aim to evolve 5%, that gives you the opportunity to change things within the business without putting too much strain on your production."

If you're unsure about the impact that a new product could have on your entire business, you can always take the inventory and product templates, the production template and the optimisation chart for a mock-up exercise of how your business would look like if you added a new product to your assortment.

And remember —expanding your portfolio can go beyond a new chocolate format. You may add new products that complement your chocolates, like different types of beverages or add related products (like branded items or baked goods).

Either way, contemplate that the ratio of core and secondary products doesn't change dramatically. Bear in mind the observations of the MALLORCA FAMILY: new assortments can lead to under-serving the demand for your highest rotating products, and even losing your identity in the process:

"Eventually if you overgrow yourself, you start getting weaker in the base. And I think that's something really dangerous right now, especially with the crazy economy changes we have right now."

It's also good to note that new products are best introduced once at a time. Remember they will require you to factor in new supply orders, cooking processes and storage space. Each new product will represent a significant change in your logistics.

Once you've selected your portfolio's newest addition, make sure you let your clients know it's there! Communication is how you push the sales of a new product and how you keep track of customers' responses to it.

INNOVATION: PILOT NEW IDEAS

Today's world moves faster than ever. Customers are more curious and have easier access to in-depth information about what they consume. This translates into a demanding audience that is in constant search of new things.

As DAVIDE COMASCHI tells his clients, innovation never stops, and it can be found not only in new products and recipes, but in all the elements that make up your business:

"Innovation is a daily thing. We always want to find something new. For example, we have a division that only works on research and development (R&D). They work on new techniques, machinery, ingredients, etc. Later on, we work together with the R&D department to understand how to incorporate these into a production line."

Unlike Davide, the innovations that make it to the final offer of the FIDÉE shops in China don't stem from an entire R&D department, but from inspiration that doesn't need a budget to be found:

"I get inspiration online. But also, I find inspiration in my daily life. And for the creation process, I first try out the recipe and then taste it with the staff. I will listen to everyone's input, and after I'll make the final decision.

An example of this is when I was online once, and saw a picture of a pastry chef from Europe who made a moon cake. After I saw that picture, I decided to make a chocolate moon. It was like a Kinder chocolate egg. The chocolate shell was shaped like a moon, and you had to break it. Inside, you would find toys, truffle chocolates and different candies for kids."

In contrast to those who find inspiration everywhere, some chocolatiers, like STEPHEN TRIGG, find the inspiration they seek within themselves. As a matter of fact, they advise others to follow only what they think can work and what their clients want to taste:

"We get driven by our customers as well as things that happen in-house. What other people are doing? We don't focus too much on it. We tend to do things that we want to do and like to do, or answer to someone that turns up with a requirement. We just aim to do these things, and do them really well."

"We adapt many products based on customers' feedback. And it requires a lot of innovation in product, packaging and design in order to stay up to date while satisfying their needs. At the end of the day, what we want to hear is, 'we love Ghrawi because they customise the designs we need'."

LAMA BASSAM AL-GHRAWI – BASSAM GHRAWI CONFECTIONERY

Unlike Stephen, who lets his clients partially guide his innovations, CALUM HAGGERTY and his team let their own knowledge of their business set the bar for what products can make it to the final offer of COCO Chocolatier:

"We don't really ask consumers what they want. We have a simple decision-making process: we make things that we like, things we think look cool or flavours that we personally like. And, we accept that it might not be for everyone. We're just a close-knit team that goes with their gut. If we like it, we think other people will like it."

Although there might be as many approaches to innovation as chocolatiers out there, most of them like to be part of the ideation and creation of the recipes. And just like them, most go to people they trust for feedback on these innovations (whether it's clients, team members or friends). RENATA ARASSIRO isn't an exception to this rule:

"The first thing is your feeling; do you feel it's gonna be good? If I make something that I really like, I then share it with my team and they taste it. I also share it with my sisters, they are very critical and very successful in their own businesses, and my husband too. If they say they agree or disagree I always take into account what I have to change."

When it comes to trying innovations out, NIKKI from éntisi has a fun and detailed way to go around it. With her, testing an innovation is an experience in itself:

"If there's a new kind of concept that we are launching, we do a blind tasting of the product, which is either with friends or family or maybe some people from our team. The thing is, when they're tasting it, they don't know how it's going to physically look. This is so that, in terms of the taste, they are able to tell us whether they like it or not."

"Some say, 'we need to increase that shelf life', but that is at the expense of the quality of the praline... I'm not completely in favour of adding certain products to do that. However, we are more used to working with less and new sugars. And well... that's also a bit of a trend. The more sugar there is, the longer your product will keep. But for us? From making it to bringing it to the counter, from the start process to the end of it, we're talking about 4 to 6 weeks."

OLIVIER WILLEMS – OLIVIER WILLEMS

Remember those hours for experimentation that you added to your schedule? This is where you put them to good use. Whether it's trying out new ingredients or taking your time to research market trends, these hours are part of your innovation process.

The process of innovating new chocolate ideas can be as simple as experimenting, testing ideas out, launching the product and getting feedback to track its performance. But a simple process can become complicated, as it's easy to get lost.

In order to make sure you innovate without losing who you are, remember the words of the queen of chocolate:

"Have your mission statement present. I think that's important so that you can keep referring back to that, as to what the core values of the business are and what you want to achieve as a business. Every time you make a decision, refer back to that."

CHAPTER 11

FROM BRAND TO WORKSPACE

Today, Lauden Chocolate is known internationally for its unique pairing propositions — a brand that started as a side gig by a husband a wife who simply loved chocolate

Understanding **THE KEY ELEMENTS** to take your business from a brand concept to an actual workspace, and eventually to create your (physical or virtual) chocolate shop, is a must.

There's simply no business if there's nothing (or nowhere) to sell. We will start this chapter by walking through the basic equipment to get your chocolate production going. Once you're ready to craft your first chocolates based on the product portfolio you've designed (Chapter 10), you'll be ready to sell them in your shop.

But, will you be selling your products on an online store? Are you opening a traditional brick-and-mortar one? Either way, we will tell you about the pros and cons that chocolatiers from around the world have shared with us from their own experience.

After taking a look at the production essentials and different options to sell your products, we will share some key elements that will help you put together an operations strategy: from countertop selling to delivery ideas.

"We have limited financial support, so we don't have really expensive machines. But, we are using good ingredients, like Cacao Barry and Callebaut, and that makes a difference. We also choose good local ingredients from China, like peppers andalmonds."

JAP JOY – FIDÉE

As a believer in slow but steady growth, Olivier Willems acquires machinery based on market demand translated into production requirements

THE **ESSENTIALS**

You don't need many square meters or even a chocolate shop to start producing and selling your products. As you will see in this chapter, all you need is your skillset and a whole lot of willpower.

Draw inspiration from the words of RENATA ARASSIRO, who started on her own, in a time and place where information wasn't available or easily accessible as it is today.

Nowadays, Renata is internationally acclaimed for her skill, and her chocolate business is a recurrent place for loyal customers:

"I started with nothing, just my hands. That's why I started making truffles. Because you don't need moulds, you don't need tools, nothing. And truffles were a very new product in Brazil, even though they were very popular in Europe. When I started to make them, I sold a lot. I waited until I had more customers before investing in my first pieces of equipment, which were a couple of melting trays.

The difficulty in Brazil at that moment was that we didn't have any kind of equipment. It was all from Europe, so the investment was higher because we had to bring the equipment here. It was so expensive."

As you read about the stories of chocolatiers that started with the bare minimum, you'll begin to note that the heart of your artisanal chocolate will be found in your ingredients, in your brand identity (Chapter 4) and in your craft.

You are the real starting point of your business. And to strengthen it, there's a series of elements that will help you to progress and grow.

"Equipment you must definitely have? An automatic tempering machine. The choice is if you want one or three. If you can budget to buy three, then do it. That has been my best investment ever, along with the enrobing belt. But for me, those are the 3 essential machines, one machine for each chocolate colour. So, if you have to start from scratch, the equipment you need would be: tempering machines, automatic because it's really easy, a little enrober and a melting cabinet."

OLIVIER WILLEMS – OLIVIER WILLEMS

Equipment

Initially, your chocolate skills are enough to get your foot in the door of the industry. Just like the example of Renata, there are many chocolatiers whose initial budgets don't allow for investment in machinery. This was also the case of MIROSLAW PELCZAR. Driven by his passion for chocolate, he didn't require more than a kitchen and basic tools to get his production running:

"From an equipment point of view, mine was very basic to start with. We even tempered chocolate manually. To get started, marble tops and some moulds were enough. And as the orders grew, we saw the need to buy tempering machines. Otherwise, we wouldn't have been able to fulfil the demand."

It might take you by surprise to learn that businesses like Mary's Brigadeiro, with thousands of online and offline fans, and sales soaring through the roof, started with no more than what could be found in the kitchen of its creator, MARIANE OLIVEIRA:

"In the beginning, I didn't have equipment at all. This is why I would say, start with what you have, don't wait.

And then the first chance you get, invest in a machine. The first thing I invested in was an automatic pot. The second investment was an extruder."

An example of slow but steady growth is BERNARD PROOT, who believes in being future-oriented:

"The business has to grow: you need to think ahead, not just about the 'now'. And when it comes to equipment, start with a base but don't over-invest! An enrober and a moulding machine are good equipment to start and scale up easily."

These chocolatiers started small while keeping an eye out for the right timing. They didn't hold back from investing in essential equipment as the demand grew. This kept the momentum of growth going and taught a valuable lesson: get started with the bare minimum and reinvest the first bits of profit on what your business needs to grow.

But... what exactly is the bare minimum your business needs to get started? And, most importantly, what is a wise first-time investment as you begin to make a profit? There are different takes on these answers, and we'll show you why.

Getting started

As you may have seen in the previous examples, the bare minimum will vary, since it is related to the type of chocolate creation you want to make.

Before you start listing random kitchen tools, take a look at your product portfolio (Chapter 10). Without considering equipment, write down all the elements that your kitchen can't do without, just like HÅKAN MÅRTENSSON did:

"It doesn't have to cost that much money to start. You need a marble bench, slab, spatula, bowls and pots. Of course, a good hand blender — you only need one if you clean it properly.

But before all this, you have to figure out how limited your space is, and what products you are doing. Because it could be you need machines right away. Also, if you're going to start producing a lot right away, you'll need one tempering machine."

If your list of kitchen essentials is way above your initial budget, consider doing what DAVIDE COMASCHI did when he got started. He rented a kitchen space with the right tools and storage requirements:

"When I started, I never invested in machines. I rented a kitchen that had all I needed to produce my inventory — I only had variable costs. After we grew, this wasn't enough anymore. We had to invest in creating a kitchen that fitted our production. So, before you invest, it's important to understand in what direction you want to go and to never invest beyond your capabilities."

For a long time, artisanship was tied to an only-by-hand notion. As times changed (and to be able to survive financially) the concept had to adapt. Today, the idea of artisan chocolates embraces the use of machinery, not as a replacement for human craft, but as an aid to the skills of the crafters.

Often, the artisanship standards are set by consistency in the textures and flavours of a recipe, and a chocolatier's ability to keep that consistency throughout their production. Based on this set of ideas, KIRSTEN TIBBALLS explained how artisanship and the use of automated equipment are connected:

"It's a combination of quality and consistency. If you think of hand-enrobing a product, that's sometimes not viable as a business. You could get an enrober that will reduce costs. And having some mechanical processes in place ensures consistency and continuity throughout your products. I think even if you are using an enrober, the chocolates can look very similar. How you finish and garnish the product is really what is going to set you apart from other chocolate shops."

Based on our conversations with chocolatiers about their approach to artisan chocolate production, we asked about the first pieces of equipment they had invested in when in their first days as chocolate entrepreneurs. Almost all the conversations resulted in the same elements being named:

Alongside the brand's colour palette, the moulds used to create the Fidée bonbons are one of the keys to consistent production and quality

WORKBENCH: A bench (or a surface that replaces it) is a key element for a chocolatier to work comfortably and in an organised way.

The main aspects to consider when choosing a workbench are its type and height. If you'll be using this bench exclusively for chocolate processing, it's recommended you choose a marble non-porous bench, with a minimum thickness of 3–4 cm.

Marble is expensive. However, this is the one material that allows heat to be conducted in a completely different way (for example when compared to steel). Steel holds the heat of the chocolate you've poured on the workbench, changing its temperature. Marble, however, expels absorbed heat. A marble workbench stays fresh, allowing you to work with your chocolate at the best possible temperature.

The bench's height is not a minor detail. When adjusted to the height of the chocolatier, it will allow working comfortably for longer. You will find there's a standard workbench size (90 cm), but you can find other sizes that suit you best.

Workbenches meant for chocolate-making are handy, since they're usually fitted with a (refrigerated) compartment below. This space is designed for professionals to have easy and quick access to tools, moulds or already finished items.

"The essential equipment I started with was automatic chocolate tempering machines. I started with two: one for milk and one for dark chocolate. The main supply was milk and dark, so the white chocolate was still tempered by hand. In January I bought one for the white because we started selling too much of it. Besides this, an enrober and machines for filling and vacuuming are also good to have."

JUSTINE LANNOO – GOÛT FOU

TEMPERING MACHINE: From small to large quantities of chocolate. A tempering machine is responsible for making chocolate stable and pre-crystallised for many hours.

This pre-crystallisation process is needed to allow the formation of the right number of "V crystals" in your chocolate. The process allows you to create premium quality products by activating three critical factors in your chocolate: getting perfect workable chocolate with a nice satin finish, enabling easy removal from moulds, achieving the right amount of gloss and crunchiness.

Time, movement, and temperature are the elements that influence these three critical factors found in premium chocolate. And this is where a tempering machine comes in to help.

Tempering machines offer the right descent speed of chocolate, which can be set manually. The movement of the chocolate is always consistent, which is enabled by the mechanical arm found in the tempering bowl. Finally, the tempering machine heats up the chocolate during the process to then cool it at the right time during the pre-crystallisation phase. The machines also allow the chocolate to remain liquid inside the bowl.

Although good pre-crystallisation is possible by hand, it is a time-consuming and high-effort process that requires the ultimate attention to detail. A tempering machine allows this process to be quick and consistent.

Because of this, you'll find that tempering machines are the first investment of most chocolate makers, regardless of where they are in the world. FAN YU, creator and owner of Nibbo, made sure a tempering machine wasn't missing from his business' initial stages:

"In my opinion there's a couple of things that are quite necessary when you want to start a business. One is chocolate melangers and the second one is a tempering machine, even if it's a small one. A tempering machine costs more, that's for sure. But if you don't have one, you have to temper by hand. You can do it, but you can find yourself grinding for days."

There are different types and sizes of tempering machines to choose from. This is the time to look at the size of your production along with the capacity of your kitchen.

Tempering machines usually range from 5 to 6 kg (workbench tempering machines) and go up to 100 kg (tempering machines with a high capacity per hour, suitable for bigger production of tempered chocolate).

Bigger tempering machines usually have a tank. This tank is a heated container that feeds the chocolate into the machine, to keep the tempering process a continuous task.

If you're a beginner, an ideal tempering machine will be one between 12 kg and 24 kg. This rule of thumb follows the advice of World Chocolate Master finalist and artisan chocolatier, STEPHEN TRIGG:

"For me, the number one investment should be a tempering machine. I think the 7 kg one. That kind of size, for me, would be a minimum."

Although the ideal scenario would be a tempering machine for each type of chocolate (dark, milk, white, vegan, gold, etc.), it's possible to use a single machine if it's thoroughly cleaned.

As the demand for your products grows, so will your production requirements. This is why different machines, such as the tempering one, are designed to be combined and work together. For example, you can invest in a melter that also pumps the melted chocolate directly into your tempering machine. This way, your production is never forced to take a break.

REFRIGERATORS & FREEZERS: Temperature and humidity control are crucial to achieve a consistent quality and avoid defects, such as sugar or fat blooming. Refrigeration plays a role even during the first production stages: it's a must to stock raw materials (between 2°C–6°C). Finished products require refrigeration too. Although different ones have different requirements, as a general rule they're usually stored at 16°C. Knowing all of this, the best refrigerators are those with controlled temperature and humidity (to guarantee stable temperatures and prevent humidity from contaminating stored goods). These two factors will be key to preserve ingredients as well as shelf life. Now, when it comes to storage of semi-finished or finished products, specific raw materials (i.e. fruit pulp) and anything that requires a negative temperature, airtight freezers will become a requirement. If you're about to buy your refrigeration unit, always remember: the only way to put a great refrigerator to good use is to know the temperatures needed for different ingredients and finished products. As your business grows, investing in separate refrigerators will become a must.

STEEL MOULDS AND FRAMES: Moulds and frames are essential to give shape to specific creations, and these also serve to enhance a chocolate's gloss. For some chocolatiers, moulds fall under the category of a generic tool, for some others like JANICE WONG, moulds are the soul of her creations, as these are the essential element that makes her offer unique:

"We designed a lot of our moulds ourselves. It's definitely important for us, they're our identity."

If, unlike Janice's chocolates, yours don't need a signature mould to be made, you will still need to pay attention to a mould's shape and material.

Polycarbonate moulds are the ones usually used to produce chocolates. However, you can also use thermoforming moulds or moulds made of rigid materials, as long as they have a smooth, non-porous surface. This allows cocoa butter crystals to reflect the sunlight and gives chocolate the right gloss.

There are companies who have entire catalogues on mould varieties, with different shapes and sizes, depending on what you wish to produce. Moulds are mainly used to make moulded pralines.

Next to moulds, you'll find that steel frames are very common when investing in product-specific tools. These are usually used for the production of enrobed pralines and truffles.

Alternatively, for bigger volume production, ganaches can be spread directly on the work-bench (on an acetate sheet) using stainless steel bands of the desired length. To use this technique, having a marble bench is a must, because of the heat dispersion mentioned earlier.

The bands can also be made of plexi-glass, but stainless steel is preferable for its durability, resistance to frequent washing and weight, guaranteeing a more stable spreading of the ganache.

GUITAR CUTTERS: These tools are used to make precise cuts, come in different sizes, and consist of a basic frame with inter-changeable ones that you can use according to the shape you want to give the chocolates. The most common guitar cutters are the manual and the electric ones.

A manual guitar cutter allows you to cut ganache squares or to make precise and thin cuts for chocolate decorations. Meanwhile, an electric guitar cutter is used to cut frozen items or products that contain dried fruit pieces (for example, things like cremini and gianduiotti), since it has more precision and cutting speed than the manual one.

INDUCTION PLATES: These plates are used to cook, heat up or boil milk and syrups and to produce caramel. They are an alternative to a gas cooker, with the advantage that plates heat up faster, helping you increase your productivity.

MICROWAVE: Never underestimate a good microwave. From melting, to heating up and defrosting. A reliable microwave is always an asset in your kitchen.

"While tempering machines are important, a small selection of moulds can also be compelling. It is good to have a direction so that the production person can make dosing easier. It always depends on how big you start. In any case, good air-conditioning and a good refrigeration unit are essential. That is the basis for getting started. If you have that, you can do anything."

DAVID MAENHOUT – CHOCOLATIER M

GENERAL TOOLS: Don't underrate the reach of good quality basics. Combined with your own skills, good whisks, spatulas, scrapers, sieves, filters, pots and knives will have a big impact on the final result.

Good tools allow you to work quickly and with precision, but also impact your finances. Although pricier than lesser-quality items, high-quality materials in your everyday tools reduce the number of times you'll need to replace them.

Like many artisanal chocolatiers, Jitsk Chocolates is a business that thrives on the right balance between the use of machinery and by-hand production

Extensive equipment

As your business grows, the time will come when demand for your products starts growing. This is an extensive list of machinery you can begin to invest in as your need to increase production capacity arises:

BLAST CHILLER (WITH CHOCOLATE-SPECIFIC PROGRAMMES): This is a device particularly suited for small productions. It's useful not only for chilling chocolate but also freezing small batches of chocolates.

For example, if you need to take your production to another site (or if your kitchen and point of sales are in different places); this ensures the products' shelf life is kept during transportation and up until the moment they are ready to be defrosted.

Among the programmes in a blast chiller, there are specific modes for freezing chocolates, and also for cooling and ventilating chocolate moulds. Chocolate-specific mode in a blast chiller will also help you achieve a flawless chocolate pre-crystallisation.

A blast chiller may have integrated programs to melt chocolate too. In these modes, the chamber of the blast chiller heats up to 40°C – 45°C for you to keep melted chocolate that is workable inside the tempering machine. This mode can also be useful when there's a need to produce more chocolate than the usual capacity allows (double or three times the quantity you would usually produce). The chamber of the blast chiller is used to continuously feed the tempering machine.

ENROBING MACHINE: This is used along with the tempering machine, allowing the quick and precise enrobing of chocolates, an operation that would otherwise be difficult and expensive if done by hand.

To make production more efficient, an enrobing belt can be combined with other tools, such as a tempering machine. When paired with accessories, you can also use the belt to craft special chocolate designs, for example half-enrobed products or striped decorations.

PANNING MACHINE: This is a machine typically (but not exclusively) used to make chocolate coatings when producing panned products (such as hazelnuts, almonds, round elements and fruits).

Panning machines are versatile. They have a fridge (allowing the use of hot and cold air during the process) and an automatic spray for chocolate as well as other coloured substances. Playing with the timing (frequency/duration) and temperature of the automatic spray can result in a series of varied and unique finishing effects (marbled, dotted, satin or matte finish).

AUTOMATIC MOULDING MACHINES: Regardless of what creations you're working on, loading moulds and inserting fillings are arduous tasks that require good timing, skill, and a lot of attention to detail. As your production increases, so does the need to repeat these tasks while maintaining precision. This is where automation comes in. Whether you are loading a mould for chocolate bars or shells, there are machines to take care of each task for you. There are also **ONE SHOT** machines that not only take care of moulding, but that insert multiple fillings simultaneously, so you can rest assured that your production line works faster and remains consistent. If you're crafting more complex shapes, like creations with hollowed bodies, there are appliances ready to take on the job.

Enrobing is one of the time-consuming tasks that is automated in the Jitsk Chocolates production site, allowing extra time to work on production stages that require more creative or manual labour

"What I realised during these years is that you shouldn't rely 100% on one storage. For example, I've had freezer breakdowns here. That means that all of it went bad in four hours, and I had to start from scratch.

Technology helps. Now we have alarms on our phones. If the temperature starts to drop, I get an alarm and jump in the car to save everything. That's something you might not be concerned about when opening a small shop, but those couple of euros per month can actually save your business."

SEBASTIAN PETTERSSON – SEB PETTERSSON

COOLING TUNNEL: This is a machine that can be used as an extension for an enrobing belt as well as independently. Once the chocolates are enrobed, they run through the cooling tunnel, which allows precise control over temperature and airflow in every segment.

For example, in the first part of the tunnel you could program a soft cooling and in the following segments, gradually reduce the temperature to the desired level in order to achieve a perfect crystallisation as the chocolates reach the end of the tunnel.

This is a more efficient process compared to that of a blast chiller. Once out of the tunnel, the chocolates are ready to be placed in their packaging, having been cooled down to perfect crystallisation and firmness.

As many essential machines for chocolatiers, cooling tunnels are available in different sizes — they can go from 5 to 50 metres. If you're thinking about getting one, take into account not only the needs of your production, but the size of your kitchen! And always bear in mind that the longer the tunnel, the better refrigeration the chocolates get and the easier it is to vary the temperature to achieve different results.

BALL MILL: This machine is used to refine home-made pralines or fillings under a certain level of micron. It works with small steel spheres that consistently rub the filling, guaranteeing a better refinement.

The result is a finished product that is smoother and more velvety, ideal to create nut creams or fresh-fruit creams, or to make pralines or spreadable creams according to your own recipes.

WATERJET CUTTING TOOL: This allows you to create any chocolate shape and design: from chocolate characters or objects to the most sophisticated and detailed decorations. Waterjet cutting is also great for inserting writing or logos in the products (your logo or customised orders). As well as working on chocolate, waterjet cutters can be used on ganaches.

Although a waterjet cutting machine is usually used in medium to big productions, it can be for anyone who wants to leverage design to stand out from the competition, as it allows for variety and complexity in finished products in a short time.

Another advantage is that waterjets can be controlled through a computer. This maximises a product's workable surface and helps reduce waste. Therefore, it looks after your finances.

EXTRUDER: In this machine, you can insert pre-crystallised and anhydrous (without water) mixes. It will quickly create an extruded product in the shape you want by using wire cutting, placed at the end of the extruder.

CHOCOLATE FOUNTAINS: There are machines that not only get things done in the kitchen, but that play a part in customer experience. Chocolate fountains are a good example. They are designed to fit in your shop in a seamless way. These allow you to prepare specialities in front of your customers, such as marocchinos, chocolate decorations for ice creams, hot chocolate bases, and much more.

Some examples of machinery

TEMPERING MACHINES

See p. 275, 276

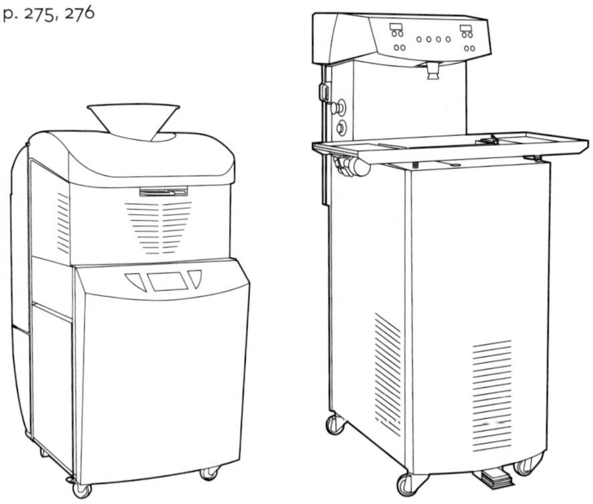

MELTING MACHINE

See p. 276

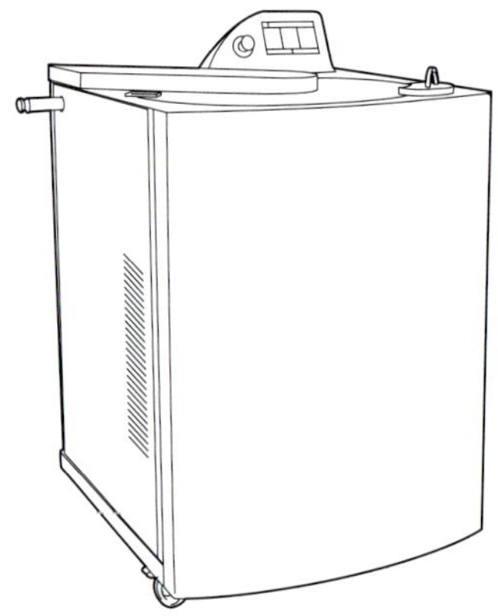

PANNING MACHINE

See p. 278

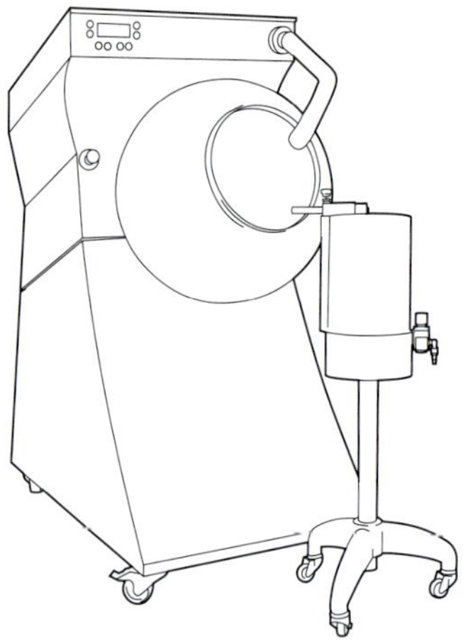

ENROBING BELT

See p. 278

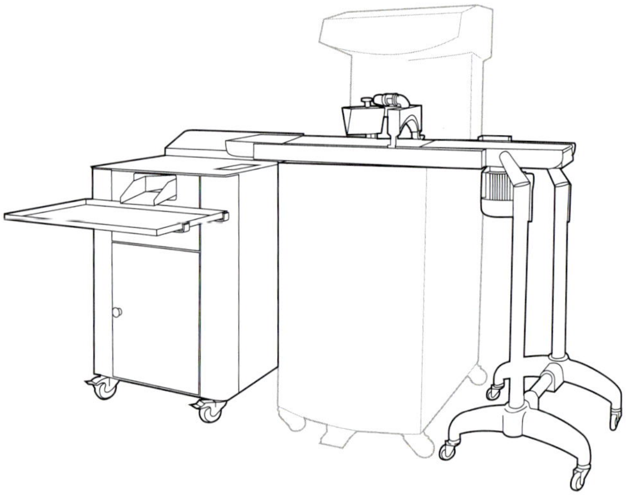

ENROBING BELT & TEMPERING MACHINE

See p. 278

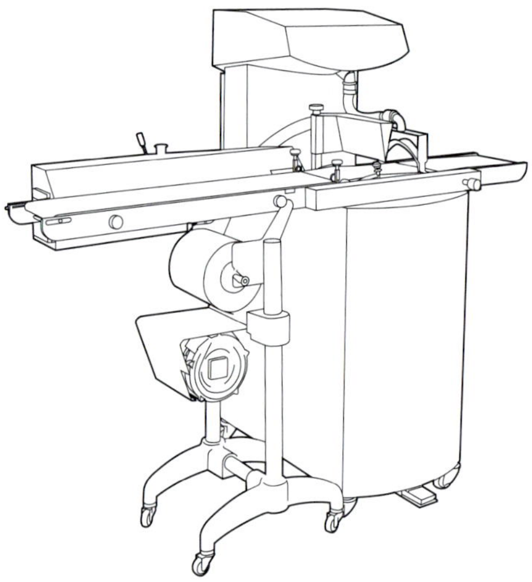

MOULD FOR HOLLOW CREATIONS

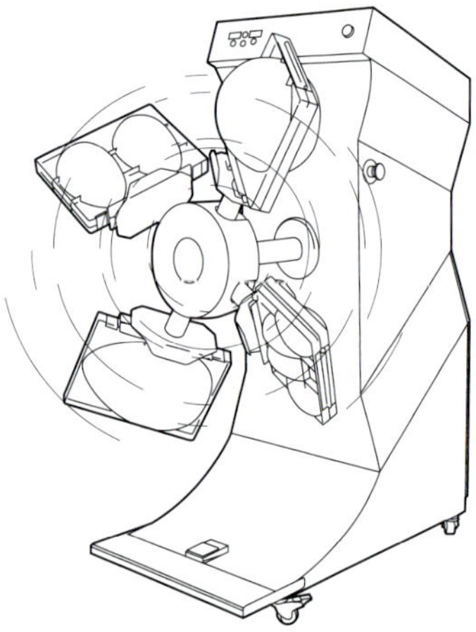

COOLING TUNNEL

See p. 279

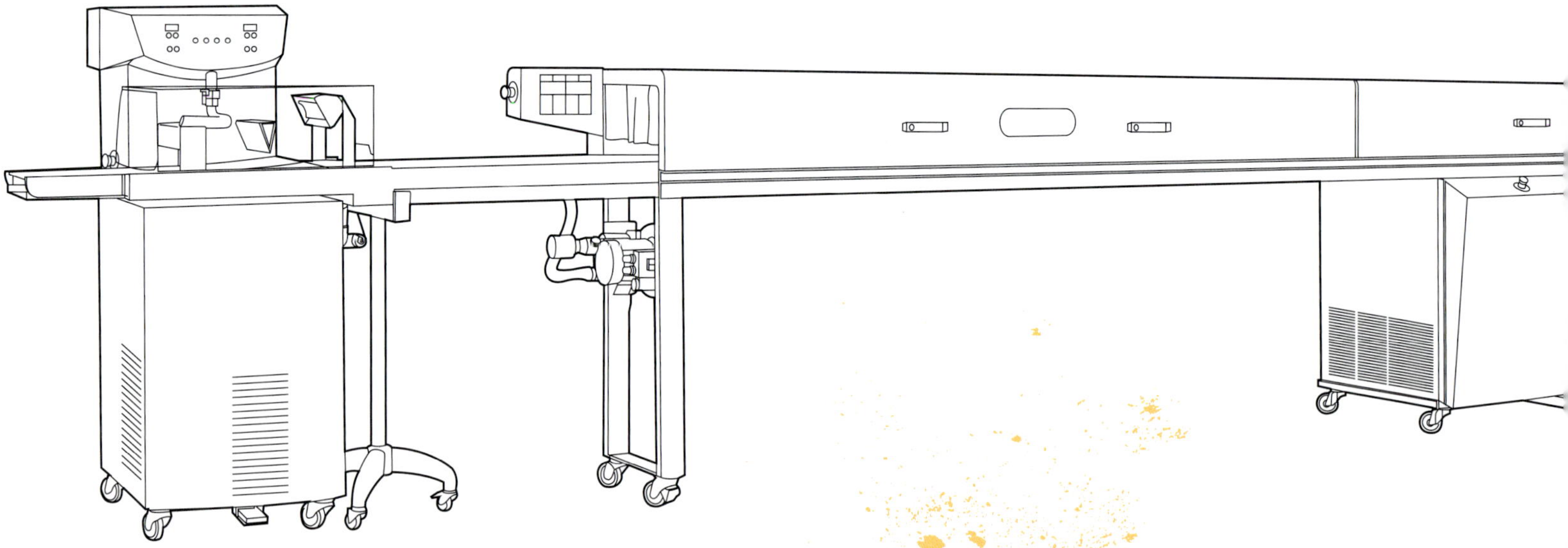

AUTOMATIC MOULD FILLING MACHINES

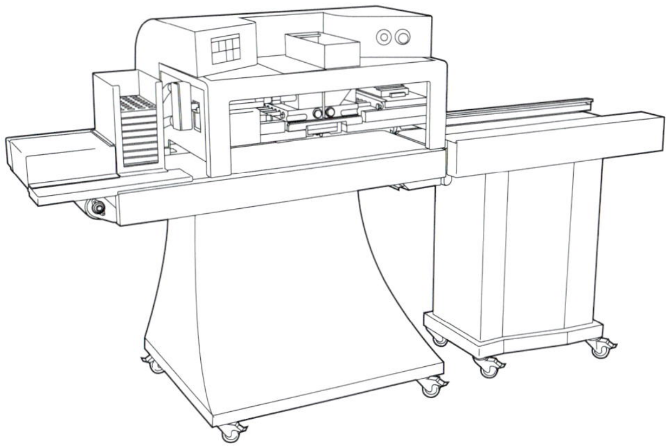

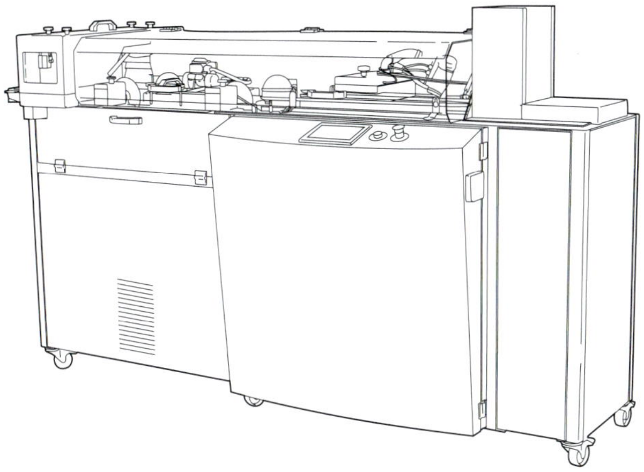

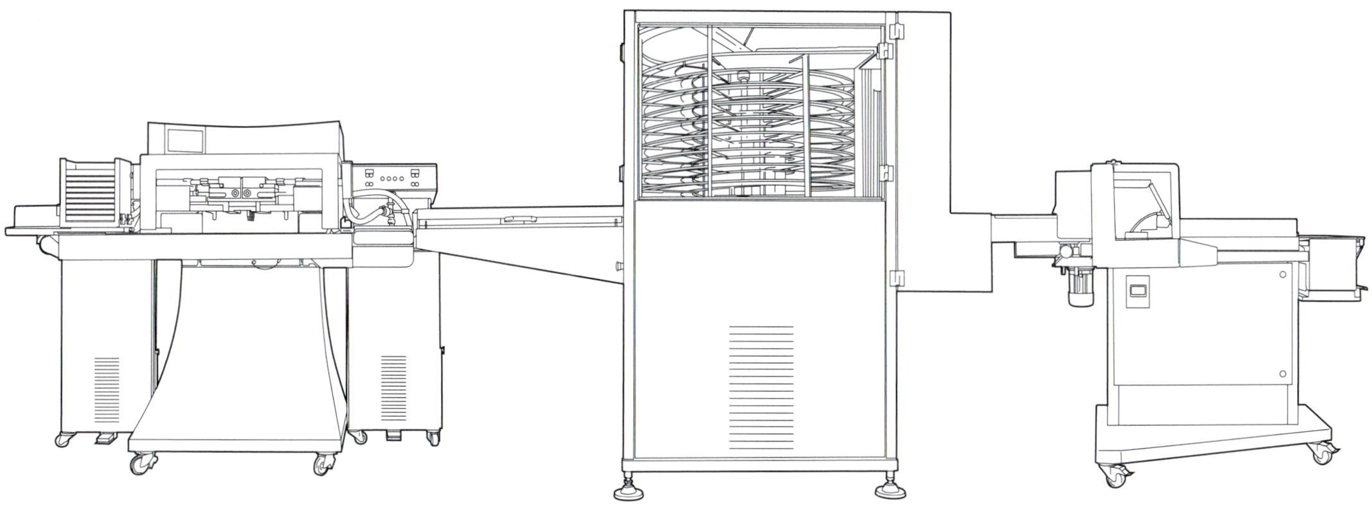

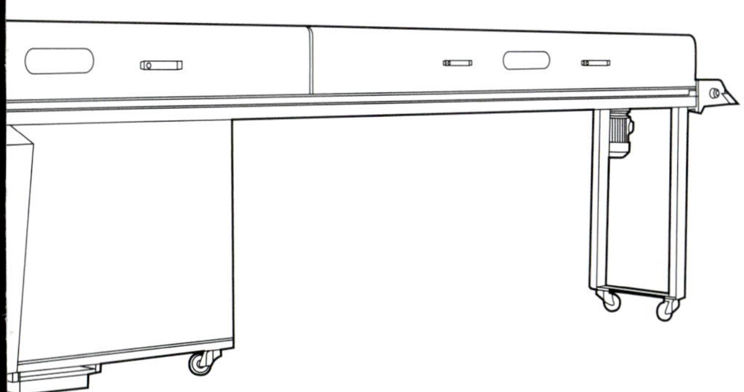

EXTRUDER

See p. 279

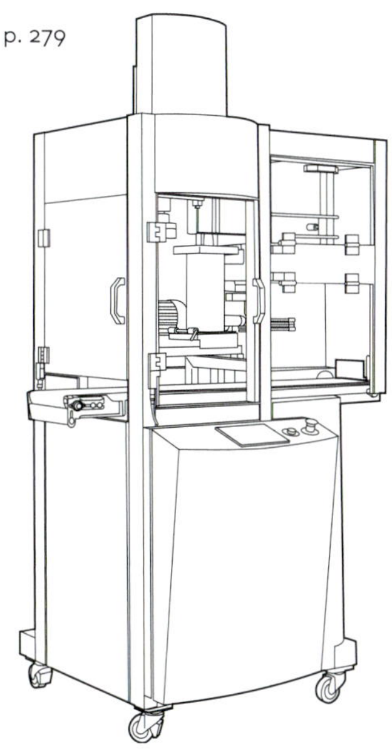

CHOCOLATE FOUNTAIN

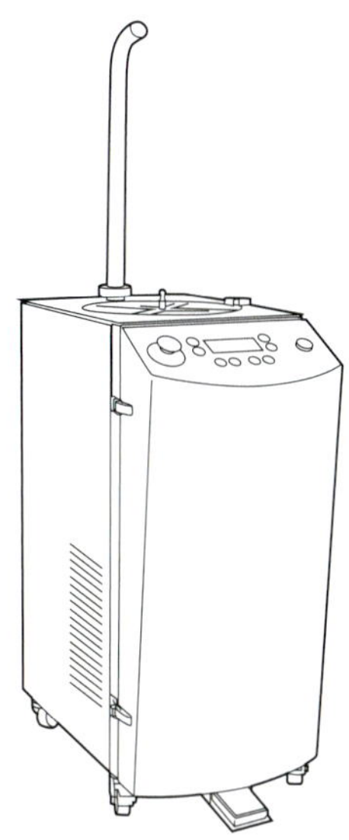

Machines and tools can be combined in different ways, adapting to the necessities of your production. For example, you could place an extruder at the end of a coating belt, attach a cooling tunnel after and finish your production line with a waterjet cutting machine for customised details.

When asked about how he approached investing in equipment, STEPHEN TRIGG told us about the second-hand machines he bought from a person whose business was closing down. Looking to get well-taken-care-of equipment, he wasn't surprised when the seller explained his reasoning behind selling his business' equipment:

"There was this guy, someone I bought some equipment from. When I saw him I asked, *'what happened to the business?'*. He said, *'I was young and naive. I put out all of this expenditure, got all this equipment, not knowing I actually didn't need it all upfront'*.

After that, I always tell people to get the minimum. You can always buy something else later. But you can't buy everything up front and then support it all if the business doesn't work out."

Like Stephen said, equipment should be tailored to your product portfolio (not the other way around). And this is a careful approach that even the biggest players in the market abide by.

To understand exactly which machine is need for a specific product and decide which parts of the process will be automated, the chefs at MALLORCA craft everything by hand first. Why? They want to understand exactly what parts of the product will be impacted by the use of machinery. Only after understanding the manual process of their recipes and comparing them to the process with machines, they decide on what type of equipment to get.

"We know there's machinery that can do it all, but we wanna do things ourselves from the beginning. We start by doing things by hand, seeing what each machine is going to take from the product.

You have two ways of seeing it. One way is, 'if I buy this machine and implement this way of production, I get so much more of production capacity. I can produce more for less money'. But, when you just look at it that way, you have to adapt your recipes and the product you make to what the machine can make.

So, a few years ago actually, we started doing it the other way around. It's like, 'I want to have this product and it has to be this way. What machines could we implement inside the chain of production to make life easier for our chefs?'"

Just like you will be customising your equipment to your portfolio, you should do the same with your financial decisions. In this regard, SEBASTIAN PETTERSSON always speaks of investment balance when it comes to acquiring new tools for your business and the things to take into account when looking to invest:

"You need to look at the way you store everything, the whole production line — when it's in its most fragile state. It's there where you want to focus. It's where we ask the right questions. Do we need a new fridge? A new blast? If that's needed, it can save us thousands of hours of work.

So, money should not go to fancy machines that are just nice to have. I see a lot of chocolatiers that make bonbons, snap them out and present them on some table or put them in a random fridge, but... is that fridge humidity-safe? For example."

Sebastian is not only cautious when it comes to choosing which pieces of equipment to invest in and at which time. He mentions a fundamental notion in the world of chocolate equipment: quality.

Investing in good-quality tools is like investing in good-quality ingredients. Both affect your products directly. NIKKI THAKKER shares Sebastian's perspective on quality equipment, even if it means increased expenses:

"I would say to not compromise on the equipment. Tools play a very, very crucial role in the production. I mean 99% of the machinery that we've got is from European countries. It's important because this is a very established market in Europe. There are many people there who manufacture chocolates, so there is machinery for it, naturally. So, you know, can't go wrong with it.

Even though it costs a lot more to buy and to import, I think it's been a great decision. Whether it's regarding the quality of the machine, the finishing or the output. I would also say it's great from a repairing and maintenance point of view."

Nikki makes a good point. The right equipment guarantees consistent results in automated tasks and makes the entire process more efficient.

This way, you (and your kitchen staff) have more time to dedicate to more pressing tasks while resting assured that the automated tasks will turn out just fine.

Bear in mind machines are not meant to replace your skills, but to give you the time to enhance them. In the world of artisan chocolate making, there will always be space for craftsmanship and made-by-hand production.

"Freezing and thawing chocolates correctly is even better than simply storing them for a few weeks. There are techniques available to do this the right way. And, every pastry chef who makes something of value keeps it all in the freezer, that's common. Making everything at the same time is impossible."

PATRICK MERTENS – CHOCOLADEHUIS BOON

Kitchen and storage space

Finding a kitchen and storage space to start from scratch is challenging. It's even possible that without external funding you won't be able to rent a kitchen, storage or shop space right away, or to fully equip your own. However, this shouldn't keep you from starting your chocolate business.

"Even though we want to scale, it's not easy to scale up when you're artisanal. For example, now we have more than maybe 70 to 80 products. If we want to scale this, we need to standardise some of our products and packaging."

NIKKI THAKKER – ÉNTISI

Today, it's an Italian family legacy, but Casa Infante wasn't born out of thin air. When talking to the MARCO INFANTE, he shared his thoughts on how to begin a chocolate business when space is limited:

"Space is important but not crucial. 30 square meters are really enough to do a good job. When we incorporated chocolates into our offer, we started by selling products online because opening a physical store was definitely more complicated."

Even owning an acclaimed family business, Marco took the less risky route to sell chocolates as the newest addition into his business' portfolio.

Because market demand requires faster production lines, Davide Comaschi also requires large-capacity storage equipment for his main and secondary ranges

"My wife asked to buy a chocolate cooling fridge in summer for £5000. And I was like, 'we just can't do it'. So, I thought outside the box, I bought an air conditioning unit for £200 and loads of plastic sheeting. I taped off the dining area of our home and opened the doors, put the aircon out and sealed it all up. We had a walk-in fridge for £300."

STEPHEN TRIGG – LAUDEN CHOCOLATE

When it comes down to the size of the kitchen and storage space, we asked MARIANE OLIVEIRA to share her experience too. She talked about how it influences more than just production:

"The kitchen and the storage size are both important. Right now, it's high season and we're stuck with the production. We already know how much we are able to make per year, but we can't grow it.

If I wanna grow, I need a second location to have a bigger production. For example, the shop where we are is big enough for a bigger production, but we can't put another freezer in here. If we buy thousands of boxes, we don't have space to store all of them either.

Here's another example, we have a second product: our cookies. We can't offer them as corporate orders because we don't have a stove that's big enough to bake them, or the space in the kitchen to introduce bigger equipment.

This is where you can see there are so many lines and layers when we talk about scale."

Like Mary said, having space to produce a certain number of products doesn't necessarily mean you'll have the space to store them, or to fit new equipment for the tasks at hand. For this reason, kitchen and storage spaces have to be looked at holistically — from every angle in your chocolate business.

There's yet another component to think of in terms of space. If your business is meant to be an online-only company, then this element won't impact your sales and decisions. However, this element is a must when you've decided to have a brick-and-mortar shop: space for sales. NIKKI THAKKER shares this idea in her own words:

"There are two things you need to think of. One is displaying the products on the shelf and how much space you need for that. And the second thing is that, as your sales volume increases, you also need to have enough stock within the shop for selling these products — you could run out of stock and gift boxes at any time, and these things take up a lot of space."

The storage not only of the products, but of the elements that accompany the selling of the products (such as boxes, wrappings and decorative assets) need a place to be stored too! Storage space for non-edible goods is a real necessity, such a relevant one that Nikki considered it a main driver to upgrade in size:

"The first shop we had was about 200 square feet, which was quite apt for the size and kind of offering we had. But we have so many new products in our portfolio that this cannot suffice.

We've increased our shop from 200 to 300 square feet now. That's more or less because we want to have enough space at the back end to store all the packaging material and goods. So, if there's someone who comes in for a big order and wants to buy it right away, we make sure it's available in the store."

TASTE MEETS SOUL
CHOCOLATE UNDERSTANDS
A LITTLE TOO MUCH IS
JUST ABOUT RIGHT
HAPPINESS YOU CAN EAT
QUETZALCOATL

Sales-specific equipment

Just like you've seen, space isn't limited to the kitchen. Important equipment pieces don't end within the kitchen walls either — there is a main piece of equipment you should own if you have a brick-and-mortar shop. We like to call it "the ideal display counter". This one falls under the category of storage and here's why:

An ideal counter for your shop is the presentation vessel of your creations. It's what consumers see when they walk in, and it is meant for so much more than to shine a spotlight on your chocolates. An ideal display counter needs to keep them cool and fresh.

The ideal showcase/display counters should be able to store your chocolates at a temperature between 12°C – 16°C, while also controlling the humidity around them.

Another relevant aspect when looking for your ideal display counter is the height. If you want clients to have the best possible view of your creations, then eye-level height is the perfect showcase for you. However, if the clients are selecting the products without assistance, you might want to go for a hand-level showcase height.

If your shop is home to more than one short shelf-life creation, your showcase temperature range should be wider, being able to be adjusted between 0°C – 8°C according to each product. Here's a little chart of how your fresh products should be kept:

Product	Shelf life	Storing temperature
With fresh fruit	4/5 days	0°C – 4°C
With fresh cream or butter-based	4/5 days	6°C – 8°C

You can use this chart as a guide to create your own. Make sure you list all the products in your portfolio, their shelf-life (Chapter 10) and what temperature they should be stored.

Consider that after investing in the best possible ingredients and the best equipment for your kitchen, you want to maintain your standards (and prevent the spoiling of the products). Then, you invest in the right sales-specific equipment as well.

Unlike many stores, Chocoladehuis BOON pushes impulse sales by displaying some secondary products right next to the short life main assortment

As you move forward, the logic is that the size of your kitchen and storage space should be proportionate to your production volume, your storage needs and business goals. But the overarching rule remains simple: the more you produce, the bigger the kitchen and storage you'll need.

Because the store deals with bespoke creations, Ryan L. Foote Chocolates requires chocolate boxes designed to fit the exact dimensions of his creations

Packaging

In the chocolate world, packaging can play many different roles. It will always be one of the essentials when opening your shop, but the importance it plays within your business will be ultimately up to brand identity and delivery-specific needs.

If the packaging isn't part of your key offer, then it will only play a pragmatic role: transporting your creations. This doesn't mean any box will cut it, but that the efforts and expenses regarding packaging can be brought down to an essential minimum.

A great example of a practical approach to packaging is that of éntisi. In the early stages, NIKKI wasn't looking for anything fancy, but a packaging that was functional. The functional aspect of it was so important that it even kept the diversity of the chocolates to a minimum assortment:

"Initially I wanted to start simple with the least possible inventory. So, we did not start with a lot of different shapes and sizes of moulds. I wanted to do the same shape and size because the packaging would become an issue otherwise."

> **"We struggled with packaging for quite a while. Nobody could offer us a project that fully satisfied our idea, so we designed them ourselves, and they are still in use today! It is the premium line of our chocolate tablets and those are our all-time bestsellers. This situation with packaging also represents our attitude towards our business: we can always do better."**
>
> MIROSLAW PELCZAR – M. PELCZAR CHOCOLATIER

For products offered as special editions, Enric Rovira allocates a higher budget to packaging so that it matches the creations' story and exclusive feel

It can also be that packaging is a fundamental piece of your business idea. In this case, investing in it will be crucial for your brand. This was exactly what CALUM HAGGERTY went through. Art in all its forms is the soul of COCO Chocolatier, so much so that packaging is almost as important as the chocolates inside:

"If we're going an art and design route, art and design and taste change in time. So, we're not going to be using the same wrappers in 2 years' time, let alone 10.

Through our packaging, we promote artists and designers while they promote us. Obviously, the brand, the flavour, they are important. But when it comes to packaging, on the front of every one of ours, now you have the name of the artist and the name of the artwork. I hadn't seen anyone else doing that at the time we started to do it."

For Calum and his team, packaging wasn't only a practical thing. It was their differentiating element and a cornerstone of their brand identity. Opposite to Calum, we have the packaging journey of HÅKAN. He paid the required attention to packaging at the beginning, but it wasn't until his business started to grow and get a bigger following that he saw the added value of really investing in it:

"We are in the gift business. You like to eat the chocolates, but we're still in the gift business. I'm changing my mind towards packaging because I realise that people are willing to pay for it. This means we are also making a little profit on the box too. The important part is, especially for a high-quality brand, to offer high-quality packaging. It's a representation of you when you're not there."

In the end, it might seem that even chocolatiers who don't have packaging as part of their offer still acknowledge the value it possesses on a business level.

In a nutshell, the main takeaway from the experiences of chocolatiers around the world is that, despite the particulars of your situation, packaging should always express your brand identity and be considered as an important element.

Invest as you go

We'd like to start the concept of investing as you go with a not-so-happy story. Before being the creative mind and owner of the renowned HÅKAN Chocolatier shop, HÅKAN was a partner in a previous business venture, also in the food industry. He invested almost a decade of his life in that business, only to see it fail in less than 2 weeks:

"We grew the place to up to 18 stores for a lot of different reasons. There were so many ups and downs, but eventually everything started to deteriorate. That sparked a big argument with the investors and they pulled out. The place burned down to the ground in 10 days."

As your business gets bigger, you'll have a better understanding of your production capacities. And as the demand for more products increases, so should your production. However, this shouldn't translate into going all-in too fast. Håkan experienced it first-hand and learned from it the hard way. Just like him, the CASA INFANTE family legacy stands by a steady and careful approach to expansion:

"Clearly, opening more sales points entails growing your volumes, although this does not imply higher margins. It's a matter of balance."

In contrast to businesses that grow too much and too fast for their own survival, there are also businesses that are successful so fast that it catches their owners off-guard. Mary's Brigadeiro didn't take long to become a lot of people's new favourite. Faced with unexpected demand and success, MARIANE OLIVEIRA confesses she would have liked to act before she did, and that she's learned her lesson for next time:

David Maenhout is a prime example of how packaging can be upgraded and updated to match the brand's evolution and positioning as it grows

Olivier Willems is one of the many chocolate chefs that acknowledges the importance of workspace dimensions, whether it comes down to kitchen space or essential equipment like a workbench

"If I changed something, I may not be where I am today. Everything's a lesson. But I will say that if I went back, I would try to make some choices faster.

In the past, the business had proved that it was ready to open a second and third location within a year of opening. Because I had received the return of my investment two months after opening the store. I took too long to make the decision, I was like, *'is this true?', 'what should I do now?'*. I was a little stuck because I didn't feel ready to grow, but the business was ready.

What I want to say is, try to understand what your business is asking of you. Your business will tell you exactly when it's the moment to grow, when it's time to wait a little, to take a risk or to analyse things."

Similar to Mary, STEPHEN and his wife realised their business was begging to be scaled as their life was, quite literally, submerged under chocolate:

"We worked in our apartment for about six months. It got to the point where we had four big Williams freezers in the apartment. We even had an area for deliveries in our home. We were living on takeaways in the bedroom so we wouldn't cross-contaminate the production."

RENATA ARASSIRO also took the careful approach. Whenever she would get her investments' return, she would reinvest the profit into her business, but never going beyond what was financially comfortable:

"When I opened the shop, I only had melting trays for each kind of chocolate and a lot of moulds. It was after getting money to invest in the shop that I started to buy things one by one. I didn't buy everything at the same time."

Just like these chocolatiers and entrepreneurs, learning to listen to all aspects of your business will guide you through your investment process. Remember to listen carefully, so that decisions are wisely made and that risk doesn't put your neck on the line. Or, in the words of Fan, from Nibbo:

"Start with what you've got and don't over-invest. Start small and invest something when it doesn't hurt you. For example, if I invest in something and fail completely, I want to be able to step back and live my normal life. That's where I draw my line."

BRICK-AND-MORTAR SHOP

When we talk brick-and-mortar, we refer to a physical store. A traditional shop where your chocolates are on display, where you welcome your consumers, whether they are individuals or organisations.

As with everything in life, there are different opinions surrounding the relevance of investing in a physical shop, particularly in digital times like these. During our conversations with chocolatiers from different places and who started at different times, we noticed that it all boiled down to different perspectives based on particular circumstances.

MARCO INFANTE, for example, believes that there is nothing in this world that can compare to the in-person experience:

"We absolutely recommend a physical store. The shopping experience is fundamental. For our recurring products, our online shop works very well (like Easter eggs for example), but the value of customer service and care cannot be provided through online tools."

In the eyes of MIROSLAW PELCZAR, a brick-and-mortar store was also important. In his case, the interaction with customers wasn't only an added value, it was part of the "chocolate museum" experience vision he had for his brand. He started with a small shop, and used it as a stepping stone to create what M. Pelczar Chocolatier looks like today:

"It was very important, from the very beginning, to set up a very small shop with one set of shelves where we could display and sell our chocolates. It was the way to start building our brand awareness in the local area, and the place was also our office, where we met with potential customers for bigger orders and B2B deals. It worked until we opened a much bigger Pijalnia Czekolady (Chocolate Drinking Bar). Our chocolate drinking bar is so much more than just a shop today."

"A consumer brick-and-mortar store in Edinburgh is not viable, it's financially not viable. So, it was obvious to me that we had to produce products and have other people retail them for us."

CALUM HAGGERTY – COCO CHOCOLATIER

Regardless of your feelings about a brick-and-mortar shop, it's important to consider it can serve more than a single sales model and route to market (Chapter 3). So make sure you take yours into account when you're making a decision.

If you're exclusively a B2B chocolate shop, you'll only be catering to other businesses and organisations. You won't need much besides a cooking station, storage and a space to welcome your clients and let them sample your products.

If your focus is B2C or a hybrid model, the shop will be more than a production and meeting space. It will be part of the brand experience. And, just like all other aspects of your business, this space should represent

The all-glass design of this Olivier Willems shop has the goal of inviting B2C consumers in by representing transparency in everything the brand offers

Renata Arassiro branches out from her main bonbon assortment to create a seasonal special for Easter while staying true to her brand's fun spirit

Savour School upsells longer-life products created by Kirsten Tibballs by positioning them next to the reception of the workshop space

your brand. NIKKI THAKKER was convinced of this idea when she redecorated her shop to fit her identity and business goals:

"In terms of the interiors, we wanted our products to be the hero in the shop. So, the interiors are quite clean instead of being very gaudy. Also, the kind of materials and finishes we've used are very premium. The main attraction in our shop is the display counter where the bonbons are kept, it plays a very crucial role. We were very particular about what kind of counter we wanted to place, what was going to be the size of it, how it was going to be lit from the inside, what the temperature and humidity had to be inside the counter. All of these things were super important."

You'll also have to decide if your shop will sell only chocolates, if you'll want to offer other products or even a café-type kind of service. If the latter, you'll need to account for extra space, customer service staff and a menu that includes beverages. LAMA BASSAM AL-GHRAWI, who runs a successful international business, shared how brick-and-mortar decisions are made based on their route to market:

"A physical shop was needed for our business because our purpose is to serve B2C and B2B customers. Our retail is considered a huge promotional door for our wholesale."

Once you've decided on your route to market and the way it'll shape your brick-and-mortar store, it's time to start looking for the right space for your new shop. Whether this is your first shop or you're branching out, choosing the location of your shop is a central decision in businesses of all kinds.

Where should I open my shop?

There is no single or simple answer when looking for the best area or neighbourhood for your shop. No matter where you are in the world, there will be neighbourhoods that are pricier, more popular or more exclusive than others.

Getting started can be overwhelming. And at first, investing in the best possible spot might seem like the only choice to get some traction. Although this can give you visibility, renting a space for your shop in a very popular area might also mean the competition is higher.

So, which way is the right way? The elements you've seen so far in this book will guide you through the often-complicated process of finding the ideal spot for your brick-and-mortar shop. One of these elements is your target audience (Chapter 3), the one RENATA ARASSIRO considered as a driver to find the ideal place for her shop:

"When I was choosing a neighbourhood here in Brazil, I thought about the public that I wanted to sell my products to.

That made me the pioneer here in the neighbourhood.

I think it's very important that you choose very well which public you want to sell to, because you have to know where that public is. Then you have to open your store close to them. But you also have to make some studies of the area. You don't want to open a shop in a place where there are two, three, or more places that sell the same product that you do."

Just like Renata, when planning to open the doors of Nibbo, FAN and his team in Shanghai went out of their way to make sure their shop was conveniently close to their ideal consumers:

"A good location is really hard to find in Shanghai. We spent three months to find a good place. We needed to be close to our customers, to our target group. Most of them are women between 20–35 years who like to try new stuff. So, we thought, 'where can we find this group?'"

When looking for the perfect spot for Mary's Brigadeiro, MARIANE also considered her target audience. But she paid special attention to that special something that an underrated (in someone else's eyes) neighbourhood had to offer:

"In Toronto, rents are crazy expensive in the popular places towards the West. So, we looked at the East. It was an area that was not developing as fast as the West, so the rents here were cheaper. And here, we saw there was a strong sense of community. One that supported businesses since these helped the development of the area.

At first, it looked like this place couldn't work out for reasons related to previous renters. But time passed, and it turned out the place was available after all, the price for the location was amazing, it was something the business could afford, there was a strong community and my target market was here as well.

It really all depends on the type of business and what the entrepreneur is looking for. We could not afford a place in downtown Toronto at the time, but even now, if I can afford it, I don't think I would open something there."

With two shops open today, JAP JOY, owner of FIDÉE, let himself be guided by the same principles and dared to choose different locations for different reasons. His first location evoked the essence of his brand's identity, the second one was driven mainly by commercial reasons:

"For the first shop, I really wanted to be surrounded by nature. Not too much traffic or people. I picked a place that's relatively quiet and beautiful. I wanted to avoid a shopping street that is full of shops. I wanted to be alone in one area that wasn't going to be affected by anyone else.

The second shop, we opened it in a really big shopping mall. It's the only shop on this floor, because I still don't want to be influenced by other shops. And this also makes our shop stand out."

As you have seen, the stories from different corners of the globe lead to a single conclusion — your brick-and-mortar shop is an extension of your brand identity. This means that the elements that make up your business should be the same elements that influence the location of your shop, as well as everything that happens inside it.

The interior of DelRey is designed with simple and wide shapes that don't overpower the shop's main focus: the presentation of chocolates in the glass display

ONLINE STORE

Regardless of your route to market, in today's world, selling online is an important aspect of any business — yes, also in the world of artisan chocolate brands!

An online shop consists of the same basic elements that an offline shop does. A menu that shows your products, limited-time offers for seasonal or special occasions and a check-out counter.

When selling online, you can choose to set up your own sales channel or to start selling under a third-party online platform. If you want to have your own sales channel, an option is creating a business website to start selling products exclusively through that channel. Either way, online sales as an option should not be overlooked.

Take JAP JOY as an example. He began his business online, only it had nothing to do with chocolate. After gaining a digital following, he ventured into the world of chocolate. FIDÉE was born as an online brand that evolved as the circumstances and market demand allowed it:

"I'm a designer and a photographer. Around 2007, I started selling on an online shop like Amazon, I sold boxes I designed, that were given as gifts. Then I noticed a lot of people liked to buy sugar and candies online, for weddings for example, to put inside these boxes.

In 2016, I met a friend who also made chocolate, and realised those chocolates could be used for weddings too. I thought I could sell bonbons inside my boxes because they also looked beautiful. I wanted to combine chocolates and packaging. So, I decided to begin making my own chocolate and start my own chocolate business. I started to sell chocolates inside my packaging around China, and in 2020 I decided I wanted to open a real shop, offline."

For Jap Joy, selling online was a conscious choice based on his existing packaging business.

Many chocolate businesses, such as DelRey, decide which products make it to their online shop based on their transportability and shelf life

For other chocolatiers like MARIANE OLIVEIRA, the decision was circumstantial, but with a positive outcome nonetheless:

"I had a crazy experience. We were actually ready to go for a physical store when the pandemic hit. So, before we opened the physical store, we had to launch the business through our online store. This was easy, because we were ready."

Although a successful opening, Mary still believes that the online store can never replicate the human connections that can be nurtured with clients when they visit your brick-and-mortar shop:

"The in-person experience is something that we tried to replicate online. But, it's still a challenge. I feel that the online shop, in the end, it's like a robot. We put images and videos, to create some emotion, but it will never replace an in-person experience. One will never replace the other."

Mary's last sentence summarises most of the perspectives of the chocolatiers. While some prefer online or offline selling for different reasons, these cannot be compared. Although many of them described the idea of online shops by comparing them to brick-and-mortar ones, we have DAVIDE COMASCHI offering a seemingly unbiased perspective on what online shops have to offer:

"An online shop is just like any other shop. And online shops will have more and more offerings in the future. They also extend the sales window to 24 hours — we often see online orders coming in outside the usual brick-and-mortar opening hours.

Now, for an online shop, appearance is key. When you land on it, everything needs to be clear: few clicks and user-friendly. Selling gets difficult as you're not able to speak with consumers in a shop. So, text and photos will be crucial.

It's true that online shops are a smaller investment. You don't have the need for the actual shop, the layout, and the furniture costs. You also don't invest as much in logistics, people who run the shop. With a brick-and-mortar store, the costs add up."

As Davide says, there are many elements that will define the success of your online store. From UX/UI design (user experience and user interface design) to the quality of the visual elements on it.

One of the chocolatiers who advocates the need for an online sales channel is CALUM HAGGERTY; not only because of the state of the global economy, but because digitalisation is a sign of the times:

"Today, our e-commerce is approaching 15% of our revenue, and that change has happened in less than 12 months! So, this is obviously the world that we live in now, you clearly need to have your own e-commerce channel. Because this is also where you get the biggest margins."

Because having an online store is also an investment (although a significantly smaller one than a physical one), testing the online market waters before investing in your own website is always an option. So, before investing in a website of your own, you can begin by selling your creations on third-party platforms like Amazon, Instagram or Facebook Marketplace, to name a few.

Note that depending on where you are in the world, you will have to adapt to the online selling options of your region. And delivering close to home is always a first rule to have in place as you start selling online. Don't try to hurry things — you'll have the chance to expand your geographical reach as your business and capabilities grow.

This is what MARIANE OLIVEIRA had to say about the subject when we asked if she would ever consider being an online-only shop:

"I could be an online business only, but then I would lose a portion of the people. There are still people who are refusing to shop online, they want to go to the store. So, it's a choice that has to be made based on what the business is asking and what the market is looking for. I started online, but the business was ready for a physical store."

So, virtual or physical — which comes first? The bottom line is that this decision will depend on your objectives, on your understanding of the unique benefits that both sales channels have to offer and, most importantly, which of these spaces can represent your brand best.

Remember that despite what has worked for other chocolatiers around the world, you've crafted your brand identity to be unique. And just like it, the different elements that conform your business will dictate if online or offline (or both) would work best for you. Let's take a look at these elements and how they can impact your online/offline presence:

BRAND AWARENESS

It might be the case that due to a previous business or personal following; people know your new brand already. If you are already known and potential clients know your new business, selling on social media platforms or your own website might be a good first step.

If you've decided to sell online, but getting those followers takes time, starting to sell under retailers or third-party online marketplaces is a great way to spread some brand awareness.

Calum Haggerty grows his business awareness on two fronts simultaneously: the culinary world (with high-quality chocolate) and the art scene (by working with artists who design the wrappers)

TARGET AUDIENCE BEHAVIOUR

If you've established your target audience as the modern and eclectic Gen Z'ers, you'll find them doing most of their shopping online.

Social media apps like Instagram and TikTok are not only good for growing these types of followers, but they're also great selling platforms. Investing small in ads on these platforms might be a good budget-friendly first move.

If you're crafting chocolates meant for Millennials, on the other hand, it's more likely you'll find them looking for the next big find on Amazon.

In smaller cities or towns, where word-of-mouth builds credibility, and where people still walk the streets to find the next new thing, opening up (regardless of how small) a brick-and-mortar shop might get you more sales than becoming a digital superstar.

LOCATION

Just like your audience targeting, where you are located in the world will impact the decision of going online or offline first. Do social media platforms support online sales in your region? Does Amazon ship in your country? Are there local alternatives to the most known international online marketplaces? What are your delivery options?

It's questions like these that will define what your selling strategy will look like, and if it should be digital or it should happen inside a shop first. And, in the end, it won't be about comparing one with the other, but about figuring out how to make them work together based on your business' needs.

At the helm of COCO Chocolatier, CALUM still believes in the power of brick-and-mortar stores, but properly combined with a digital sales channel. Putting his beliefs into practice, he called off any offline shop experience until he could build what he felt the business truly needed:

"About the brick-and-mortar stores we used to have... we had 4 locations: 3 stores and 1 space with a small team. Trying to manage this was kind of crazy. So, we made the decision to close them all and I said, *'the only time I'll open it back up is when I can have everything under one roof'*. Now that we're moving, I'm really looking forward to getting back into that, cause I think the one thing that you do miss about not having a brick-and-mortar shop is the instant feedback you get from a customer."

As part of the brand experience, Calum Haggerty welcomes clients with walls covered in unique art creations that they will later appreciate as wrappers for chocolate bars

Although passionate for an "old-school" approach with brick-and-mortar stores, Enric Rovira acknowledges the power of building a relevant online presence

SERVICE AND DELIVERY LOGISTICS

Whether you've started your online store, or you're getting ready to welcome your first clients into your brand-new shop, customer service and delivery options are a fundamental piece of your business. As DAVIDE COMASCHI explains, the logistics behind delivering your products are more than just about packing up your chocolates and putting a stamp on them:

"Shipping chocolate, with its constraints, it was very complicated. Studying boxes, optimising them along with pallets, using different shapes, thinking about how to make a chocolate travel: packaging, controlled temperature, unboxing, etc."

One of the benefits of a brick-and-mortar shop for a B2C clientele is that people walk in, select the products and walk out. But when your business sells online, shipping logistics are part of the equation. And when your route to market is a B2B one, larger orders and tight deadlines add up to the complexity.

Regardless of your route to market and the delivery options you offer, there is another series of factors and information basics that will always be in place, and that should be communicated to every client that places an order that requires to be shipped, picked up or delivered.

Business hours

Your business' opening hours refer to the moment your doors open until the moment you stop receiving customers in the shop.

Bear in mind that sometimes, if customers come right before closing time, they might stay for longer than the actual closing hour of the shop. Make sure you plan for this, especially if you're delivering orders after your shop's opening hours.

Regardless of how long you decide to remain open, you should be ready for customers to buy your creations and take them home immediately. For this to happen, having enough packaging and bags at your disposal is a must.

Customers might also come in simply to place orders. Whether they are placing a small one or ordering larger batches, you should be ready to walk them through your delivery options.

Delivery options

When clients walk into your shop to place an order, or they do it online, the best practice is to not only mention the delivery options you offer, but explain how they work in *detail*.

Pick-ups

Many chocolate orders are placed for special occasions, so you want to communicate clearly about when your shop is open for pick-ups: will pick-ups only be possible during work hours? Will you make exceptions for orders for special occasions or events?

The following is an example of a pick-up schedule for an artisanal chocolate shop. You can use it as a guide to create your own. If you have a brick-and-mortar shop, remind clients to take a look at it when placing their orders (and encourage them to ask questions if anything isn't clear). When selling online, remember to include this information on the checkout and on the shipping information:

Monday: Closed (No pickup available)
Tuesday: 10:00 AM - 2:00 PM (Pickup available)
Wednesday: 10:00 AM - 2:00 PM (Pickup available)
Thursday: 10:00 AM - 2:00 PM (Pickup available)
Friday: 10:00 AM - 2:00 PM (Pickup available)
Saturday: 10:00 AM - 2:00 PM (Pickup available)
Sunday: Closed (No pickup available)

Notes:

» The shop is closed on Mondays and Sundays, so no pickup is available on those days.
» Pickup is available from Tuesday to Saturday, from 10:00 AM to 2:00 PM.
» Pickup time slots may be limited based on the shop's production and staffing capacity.
» Customers may need to place their orders in advance to ensure availability for pickup.
» The shop may offer extended pickup hours or additional pickup days during peak seasons, such as holidays or special occasions.

The decisions you make regarding pick-up options should be contemplated based on the orders placed, the production time for that order and the shelf-life of the products ordered. Taking these elements into account, and considering the expected pick-up date, the operations might need to be adjusted to meet deadlines.

Delivery services

You should also take into account that clients might ask you to deliver the order. So, you should ask yourself, how far are you willing to deliver your orders? Will the delivery timings be the same as the business hours? Or, will you be delivering outside business hours and tailor your delivery schedule to your clients' needs?

Just like you did with pick-ups, you can create a visual guide so that consumers understand how far you can deliver your products:

» Monday: Closed (No delivery available)
» Tuesday: 10:00 AM - 5:00 PM (Delivery available within a 10-mile radius)
» Wednesday: 10:00 AM - 5:00 PM (Delivery available within a 10-mile radius)
» Thursday: 10:00 AM - 5:00 PM (Delivery available within a 10-mile radius)
» Friday: 10:00 AM - 5:00 PM (Delivery available within a 10-mile radius)
» Saturday: 10:00 AM - 3:00 PM (Delivery available within a 10-mile radius)
» Sunday: Closed (No delivery available)

Notes:

» The shop is closed on Mondays and Sundays, so no delivery is available on these days.
» Delivery is available from Tuesday to Saturday, with varying hours.
» Delivery is limited to a 10-mile radius from the chocolate shop's location.
» Delivery time slots may be subject to availability and may vary based on the shop's delivery capacity and staffing.
» Customers may need to place their orders in advance to ensure availability for delivery.
» The shop may have specific delivery fees, minimum order requirements, or delivery policies that customers need to be aware of.

Shipping details

When it comes to shipping details, this information is usually found at the checkout of online orders, or shared with clients before they place an order.

Although shipping is a form of delivery service, this might involve working with third parties and entails longer distances to be covered. Before committing to shipping your products, take into account the following criteria:

PACKAGING: Your packaging is one of the key elements that will ensure that the chocolates are protected during shipping and arrive in the best conditions. Appropriate packaging materials include insulated boxes, ice packs and cushioning to prevent melting, breakage or damage.

SHIPPING METHODS: Shipping methods (and companies) should be reliable and suitable for the type of products being shipped. It is always best to work with delivery agents that are experienced in the chocolate space.

Other things that should be factored in include speed, cost and tracking capabilities. Different carriers may offer different options, so request thorough information to find a company that meets your specific needs.

For the hot Hong Kong weather, Ryan L. Foote is developing new thermal delivery boxes with the same properties as polystyrene, but recyclable and more sustainable

RESTRICTIONS: Artisanal chocolates will have specific shipping requirements and restrictions due to their perishable nature or other factors, such as weather conditions, distance, costs and time.

If there are any shipping restrictions in your shipping policy, such as distance, limited shipping during extreme weather or delays because of peak seasons — it all should be clearly communicated to your clients in your online as well as your offline sales channels.

TIMELINE: The time it takes to process and ship online orders should be explained in detail. It's important to include cut-off times too.

FEES: If there are extra fees associated with the shipping of online orders, or the close-range delivery of orders made offline or online, these rates should also be clearly communicated before orders are placed and payments accepted.

RETURNS AND REFUNDS: Although it's unlikely returns are made or accepted in the chocolate space, policies regarding this (as well as refunds) should be clearly stated in your brick-and-mortar shop, as well as your online one.

Be thorough regarding refunds requested for shipped orders, including procedures for handling damaged or defective chocolates, lost shipments or other issues that may be caused by the packaging process, as well as third parties involved. These policies should be stated clearly in the shipping policy to set and manage your clients' expectations.

"It's not the same, delivering three blocks away from a shop than a thousand kilometres away — the challenges are different. We have to adapt the packaging of the product so that it can travel. And there are some products that we know are never going to be able to travel that much. As long as we have a shelf life of 5 hours, it's going to be impossible to deliver."

JACOBO & PABLO MORENO – MALLORCA

LEGAL AND COMPLIANCE CONSIDERATIONS: Before packing up your first order to be shipped, remember you are part of the food industry. Just like certain requirements are in place to set up a business that offers edible goods, there will be legal considerations regarding the shipping of these goods.

Food safety regulations will most likely apply on a national as well as an international scale. Inform yourself about the right procedure for shipping requirements before announcing your business is ready to start making deliveries!

COMMUNICATION: You might be tired of reading this by now, but communication is key in all stages of setting up a business. Although you've made sure to share the right information with your consumers through all your sales channels, establish easy-to-access lines of communication regarding questions, orders, confirmations, notifications and complaints.

Prompt your customers to read everything before placing an order, but also to give you feedback on how they've experienced your delivery options. It might seem like a hazy road to navigate, but with the basics in place, and by being willing to learn from your clients, you will have your delivery logistics pinned down in no time.

WEATHER: Depending on your location and its climate, weather conditions will largely influence your ability to ship orders. Consider factors such as temperature, humidity and seasonal conditions. And, take appropriate measures, like using insulated packaging, adjusting shipping methods or cancelling orders if it comes down to it.

TESTING AND MONITORING: Got any friends who live a bit further away? Try shipping them a sample of your products to test the playing field. Delivery test runs can help you monitor shipping processes and adapt your carrier choice and logistics based on the results.

The testing phase of shipping and delivery may include evaluations of packaging materials, carrier performance and customer feedback rounds.

PRO TIP!

Communicate to your clients about the shelf life of your products and how their orders are impacted by your inventory and stock. If the order is placed short-term and the production is in stock or frozen, you might not have to alter your operations schedule to meet the deadline.

If the orders placed require stopping your scheduled weekly production to create a specific number of products, you will have to schedule that separately. Remember that although these types of orders don't always sell at a higher price range, they might cost you more in terms of extra work hours, placing ingredient or packaging orders that haven't been accounted for in your schedule, utility prices going up, etc.

And never forget — transparency is not only the way to manage expectations, it is how you build and uphold the reputation of your brand. Your ability to communicate your choices and handle their consequences is what will make or break your business' logistics success!

CHAPTER 12

CHOCOLATE: A TIMELESS BUT SEASONAL INDUSTRY

Some sculptures by Chocoladehuis BOON are presented as in-store exclusive and limited purchases, while others make it to the webshop as an on-demand item

happy

CHOCOLATE CREATIONS ARE AGELESS, and they seem to always be in fashion. This is more than a result of chocolate being a food that dates back thousands of years.

Throughout history, chocolate has captivated the hearts and taste buds of people from all around the world. Transcending cultural and societal boundaries, its rich, indulgent flavours and texture, and its flexibility as an ingredient have made it a beloved treat for centuries. Since it was used by people, it was cherished as a luxurious indulgence, a superfood, and a symbol of celebration.

From ancient civilizations to modern confectionery creations, the appeal of chocolate has stood the test of time, making it a truly timeless concept. In this final chapter, we will explore how the timeless character of chocolate has taken on different forms without losing its essence, and how it could continue to evolve in the future.

"When something is artisanal, it's important to think about how close we can get to the essence or the base of the product, of the raw material. That's where it starts, having control over what we do and what we purchase. For example, for milk, I go to the farm twice a week, but we work with machines. For many people that means industrial, but we do it to have consistency. A natural raw material is very inconsistent, and if I were to use those and then also make everything by hand, then I wouldn't sell anything. So, it's challenging because people want artisanal products, but they also want consistency."

JITSK HEYNINCK – JITSK CHOCOLATES

Both, chocolate formats and seasonal offers can be timeless — Renata Arassiro always offers classic seasonal assortments without losing sight of her brand identity: Brazilian flavours and colourful presentations

REMEMBER **THE BASICS**

Chocolate keeps being a delight for the young and the old, for the ones with a humble palate, and those looking for exuberant indulgence. But as JULIAN ROSE would put it, chocolate basics will always be the thing we go back to:

"Some of the very well-known chefs in the eighties, they were trendsetters. They were innovating to change the scene, and people would be exposed to ingredients or the trend of bringing in culinary flavours into desserts. These things broke traditions. And before, trends would be five years. A trend now will last from 6 months to a year.

I think that in whatever you see today, I don't know if we can call it a mashup or international flavours, there's a little bit of everything. And now, you'll see people trying to come back to the basics: the source. I follow the trends myself, but also break them."

Chocolate was and still is considered a superfood, an ingredient that is paired with the sweet and the savoury, the element that seems to have it all: flavour and health. In turn, the (industrial) chocolate industry is a market that has seen consistent growth since its early days, expected to reach 220 billion dollars by 2025.

Since their international expansion, chocolate delights continue to be the heart of a lot of people's everyday life. Whether they are eating it as an after-meal treat or they are part of special occasions, chocolate creations are all around the world.

Particularly in artisanal shops, the timeless aspect of chocolate should not be forgotten when building and growing a business. Why? The specific traits of good quality cacao beans are what contribute to the unique character of chocolate craftmanship. We interviewed successful chocolatiers in different corners of the planet, and almost all shared the same definition of what crafting artisanal chocolate truly means.

For some, it is all about the use of their hands:

"The artisan soul is what characterizes my business. It has nothing to do with the number of employees or the size of production. It has, instead, everything to do with the use of hands. Almost all of our products are handmade, starting with our iconic product, the tarallo. My family has been making delicacies with their hands for eighty years and four generations."

For MARCO INFANTE, the use of hands while making Casa Infante's creations is what gives it its artisanal status. Although from completely different continents and cultures, Fan from Nibbo in Shanghai, also believes the soul of a chocolatier is to be found in their hands:

"When you use your hands, you put your heart and your soul on your products. This doesn't mean you can't use equipment. But it means that equipment is never going to replace craftsmanship."

"The artisan used to be the person that was working only by hand. There were no tempering machines, and they'd say that was not artisanal chocolate. But the world is changing. Now, it's about the knowledge, technology and the way one creates. And, the artisan still needs storytelling and craft to be different from industrial products. Differentiation is fundamental because, today, the world of chocolate is old. Something new is brewing now, but we're still not ahead compared to the worlds of wine and coffee, for example."

DAVIDE COMASCHI – DAVIDE COMASCHI

Casa Infante has retained their reputation as a family business by guaranteeing there will always be a handmade touch in each creation

RENATA ARASSIRO approaches this idea in a similar yet distinct way. When she thinks about artisan chocolate, she believes the differentiating aspect of the concept is the human being who's behind the creation:

"It's artisanal? Then there's a person behind the product. I am that person. You have to have a human behind your product. That, for me, is what artisanal means. And, of course you have to use equipment, you just don't have to do everything with it, just like you don't have to do it all by hand. Otherwise, it's impossible to grow."

We found it inspiring how the definitions of artisan chocolate were so similar although they came from chocolatiers from all over the world. What was even more astounding is that all of them shared inspirational perspectives about the essence of chocolate creations while understanding the practicalities of owning a business around it (and doing it while keeping up with the times).

STEPHEN TRIGG is a firm believer in machinery not changing the nature of the artisan chocolate craft. He is also convinced that artisanship comes from somewhere else:

"Artisanship, for me, it's the care. We have piping bags where we put stuff and pipe into a mould. But when we want to do big volumes, we have a filling machine. What's the difference? A machine that takes the strain off our arms is a tool, the other one's also a tool. There's no difference, but the public perceives it differently. But it's the exact same ingredients I'm using, and the care has gone in. So, for me, it comes down to the care of the products and ingredients you're using."

Stephen touches upon another subject that many other chocolatiers mentioned when asked about the artisan character of their creations. NIKKI THAKKER also puts the emphasis on the ingredients she selects to create her recipes, along with the attention to detail and made-by-hand as traits of artisanal work:

"It's about the selection of ingredients. Every ingredient is selected as per the recipe. So, every chocolate, every berry or every nut that goes into it has a reason behind it.

And everything is made, I would say, in small to mid-size batches because there is a time that is required to make something with attention to detail.

Also, there have to be things which are handcrafted, which can't be done in a large-scale machine. That is truly artisan, when something's handmade, hand-packed."

"One of the trends I've seen is that everything is made to look nice, to take pictures."

ENRIC ROVIRA – ENRIC ROVIRA

Before tasting the unique and elevated quality of the sweets offered by Mariene Oliveira, many clients are won over with products and packagings that stand out in different online channels

MARIANE OLIVEIRA chose multiple aspects to explain what she believes defines artisanal chocolate work. The elements she names touch upon all the aspects of a chocolate business that have been carved into this book. From brand identity to product crafting, to marketing a business' story:

"When we talk about artisanal chocolate, we go beyond making things by hand. It's about storytelling, the ingredients, the cultural background. It can be that somehow chocolate started being part of lives, stories, events and laughing together with friends."

As you can see, Mary's perception of artisanship also touches upon the place that chocolate has in the lives of its consumers. And this means that her idea of artisanship is open to evolving as long as consumers' behaviours change over time.

This idea that artisanship can change over time is one shared by multiple chocolatiers around the globe. One of them is consultant and chocolate expert, JULIAN ROSE:

"I think an artisan can quickly create something different and new. They're nimbler and their creativity is limitless. So, an artisan is, in other words, an artist."

JANICE WONG is another chocolatier who, like Julian, believes in the connection between artisanship and art:

"You can't be an artisan all your life because that also keeps changing. Just think about yourself as a paper maker, right? I mean, you are going to just be making paper, and then, one day everything goes digital. Are you going to continue to just be making the paper? I mean, for sure it's great to keep the story, but then it's less appreciated, right? You have come to terms with yourself and let go, do something else. Maybe you can keep the artisanal aspect, but this notion changes. And you have to adapt."

Having read about different chocolatiers' approach to artisanship and the timelessness of chocolate, it's time to reveal how the same chocolatiers navigate the constantly evolving changes of the industry.

DARE TO NAVIGATE THE TRENDS

The fast-evolving character of the world has a big impact on consumers and their habits. Trends seem to set overnight and, most times, being part of them can completely shift the future of your business.

Understanding trends is essential for starting or continuing an artisan chocolate business. It allows you to stay relevant and meet the evolving demands of the market, but also to keep your business afloat in an industry that's competitive.

Keeping a finger on trends means trying to stay on top of consumer preferences, flavour profiles, packaging trends and industry innovations. Although it isn't necessary for your business to adapt to all the novelties that hit the market overnight, knowing about them provides valuable information.

With a deep understanding of market trends and your brand identity as your guiding light, you will be able to identify and act upon the trends and innovations that can be a right fit for your business. The success rate of the chocolate shop owners who have managed to find this balance is higher than those who overlooked what trends have to offer, when to become a part of them and when to step aside.

To offer examples of how trends work in the world of artisan chocolate, we've compiled some of the trends have taken over the world in the past year — not only the artisan chocolate space, but over many other industries. You might recognise them as fleeting tendencies or see them as trends that showed up and that are here to stay as the new normal.

Product customisation

A trend that started as a reaction to mass production and industrial-scale sales. This trend was spotted by DAVIDE COMASCHI as one of the latest occurrences in the world of artisan chocolate:

"Gifting and personalisation of the product are trends we've seen. In these cases, the unboxing experience is very important, people are looking for that 'wow' effect."

Customers began paying attention to brands where customisation was part of the offer. From personalised clothes to tailor-made shampoos, customisation started to take over most industries, including the world of chocolate.

With customisation a growing trend, artisan chocolate stands to benefit from it in the next years. Offered at a higher price point than industrial chocolate by definition, artisan chocolate embodies the idea of a personalised product. Artisanal chocolate stands on the other side of the spectrum of sweet gifts one may find at mass-scale. This idea satisfies clients' needs for a personal touch in comparison to what industrial products can offer.

Not only this, but chocolate and the tools to craft it offer artisan chocolatiers to take this a step further. By offering on-demand creations and allowing customers to slightly tweak or personalise an offer, you can implement this trend in your business model without it affecting your production lines and over-investing.

"I assimilate specific trends as little as possible. When I started, this whole scene of 'everything should be sugar-free and vegan' began. That meant without butter and cream, and these are my soul. So, I'm very strict with keeping these ingredients."

SEBASTIAN PETTERSSON – SEB PETTERSSON

ANTICIPATE THE FUTURE

Customers' newfound curiosity and almost unlimited access to information will continue to shape their demands and expectations. Understanding your consumers' current wants and needs and staying up to date as they evolve is what will keep your business relevant, and your clients engaged.

KIRSTEN TIBBALLS spotted one of the possibilities that might be opening up in the space of chocolate.

Whether this becomes an upcoming trend or not, knowing that there are opportunities to be explored is always an exciting prospect for upcoming artisan businesses, and for existing ones looking to stay relevant:

"In the past three years, single-product production has become one of the fastest-growing areas for artisans. Focusing on a single range of products, such as a variety of snacking bars, in the same style but with multiple flavours and textures. This offers several advantages. It simplifies production, reduces equipment needs, minimises wastage, and lowers staffing and ingredient costs. Additionally, it creates a sense of scarcity and a fear of missing out (FOMO), as the limited selection can quickly sell out.

This approach generates higher demand, as consumers are eager to secure limited edition products and share their purchases on social media. People want to be the first to have something exclusive, often going to great lengths to obtain products that others cannot."

Do you believe single-product production will be a trend in the near future? Have you spotted any trends that will be taking over the artisanal space?

Acknowledging the challenges of the current market and the speed of consumption changes, the overall chocolate industry is anticipated to keep rising at a fast and steady pace. This opens the doors for new business owners and artisan chocolate innovators to take their first steps into the industry, to seize opportunities, and to explore what the future of chocolate may hold for you!

With the basics in place, the key to your chocolate shop's success will be at the crossroads where chocolate's long-lasting legacy, innovation and uniqueness meet.

“In 1974, I set foot in the DelRey shop as an apprentice. 10 years later, my wife and I took over the business. Gradually, we transformed it into what it is today: a high-end patisserie and chocolaterie with international renown and outlets in Belgium and Japan. After four decades of running the company together, it has now turned into a family business, with my son and daughter and the helm.”

BERNARD PROOT – DELREY

EPILOGUE

EPILOGUE

Well, this is it! You have the theory, and you also know how to put it into practice. Now, it's your time. So, dare to dream. Dare to get started.

You see, what began as a few timid yet careful questions from aspiring entrepreneurs to our academy chefs, soon blossomed into this pivotal project. One that lasted 3 years to complete: bundling and structuring key questions from starting entrepreneurs, interviewing contributors from all over the world to put together this book, bringing in business management and chocolate experts for detailed insights, and so much more that happened behind the scenes. We hope it's worth it. Better yet, we wish this book serves you endlessly. From starting, growing and building your business to making a significant impact with your brand.

Don't forget that this book isn't alone! *The Chocolatier's Shop* has somewhat of a 'practical' cousin. Alongside *The Chocolatier's Kitchen*, they form an unmissable dynamic duo. Together, these two books are a wonderful starting point for any chocolatier. *The Chocolatier's Kitchen* brings you 273 recipes for bonbons, bars, spreads and ice creams, with all recipes categorised in 3 different shelf lives (short / medium / long). These recipes were created by our chefs not only to inspire you, but to help you manage your chocolate sales and to control risks when exploring your market for the first time.

Oh! One last thing: by now, you know doing business is a serious thing. But building a chocolate business is probably the most fun and exciting one of them all. As a chocolate entrepreneur/chocolatier, you will be bringing joy to people. Without a doubt, that's a beautiful cause. It is a spark that lives in each of the contributors of this book, in their enthusiasm, stories, experiences and heartfelt advice. They showed us that there is probably no greater ingredient that can ignite so much love and excitement than chocolate.

We wish you tonnes of good luck in your entrepreneurial journey.

The Callebaut Team

Get practical!
Download all the practical overview sheets and completion forms via the QR code to the right and get started yourself.

For more information about Callebaut chocolate, please visit **www.callebaut.com**

www.lannoo.com
Register on our website and we will regularly send you a newsletter with information about our latest books as well as interesting, exclusive offers.

Photography
All images are the copyrighted property of the book's contributors.

Graphic Design
Steven Theunis, Armée de Verre Bookdesign

If you have any comments or questions, please contact our editorial office: redactielifestyle@lannoo.com.

First print run, 2024
Second print run, 2025

D/2024/45/389– NUR 440
ISBN 9789401487832